Anton Ehrenzweig, who was born in 1908, died in December
1966 shortly after completing *The Hidden Order of Art*. He
studied law, psychology and art in his native Vienna, and was
appointed a magistrate in 1936. He settled in England in 1938.
Until his death he was Lecturer in Art Education at
Goldsmith's College, University of London, and in 1956–7 he
was a Fellow of the Bollingen Foundation, under whose
auspices much of the research for *The Hidden Order of Art*
was undertaken. In 1953 he published *The Psychoanalysis of
Artistic Vision and Hearing*.

The

Anton Ehrenzweig

Hidden Order of Art

A Study in the Psychology of Artistic Imagination

Paladin

Granada Publishing Limited
Published 1970 by Paladin
Frogmore, St Albans, Herts AL2 2NF
Reprinted 1973

First published in Great Britain by Weidenfeld & Nicolson 1967
Copyright © Anton Ehrenzweig 1967
Made and printed in Great Britain by
Cox & Wyman Ltd., London, Reading and Fakenham
Set in Monotype Ehrhardt

To my wife

Contents

Publisher's Note to First Edition

At the time of his death, the author had passed for press the manuscript of his book, the illustrations and captions. He did not draft an acknowledgement, but had particularly wanted to thank the artists who have allowed their works to be reproduced in his book, and who supplied photographs and information about them:

Maurice Agis and Peter Jones, David Barton, Richard Hamilton, Peter Hobbs, Henry Moore, Eduardo Paolozzi, Bridget Riley, Feliks Topolski and Fritz Wotruba.

The publishers wish to acknowledge their indebtedness to Mrs Ehrenzweig, Miss Anna Kallin and Mrs Marion Milner, who read the proofs.

Plates

Line Drawings

Preface

The argument of this book ranges from highly theoretical speculations to highly topical problems of modern art and practical hints for the art teacher, and it is most unlikely that I can find a reader who will feel at home on every level of the argument. But fortunately this does not really matter. The principal ideas of the book can be understood even if the reader follows only one of the many lines of the discussion. The other aspects merely add stereoscopic depth to the argument, but not really new substance. May I, then, ask the reader not to be irritated by the obscurity of some of the material, to take out from the book what appeals to him and leave the rest unread? In a way this kind of reading needs what I will call a syncretistic approach. Children can listen breathlessly to a tale of which they understand only little. In the words of William James they take 'flying leaps' over long stretches that elude their understanding and fasten on the few points that appeal to them. They are still able to profit from this incomplete understanding. This ability of understanding – and it is an ability – may be due to their syncretistic capacity to comprehend a total structure rather than analysing single elements. Child art too goes for the total structure without bothering about analytic details. I myself seem to have preserved some of this ability. This enables me to read technical books with some profit even if I am not conversant with some of the technical terms. A reader who cannot take 'flying leaps' over portions of technical information which he cannot understand will become of necessity a rather narrow specialist. It is an advantage therefore to retain some of the child's syncretistic ability, in order to escape excessive specialization. This book is certainly not for the man who can digest his information only within a well-defined range of technical terms.

A publisher's reader once objected to my lack of focus. What he meant was that the argument had a tendency to jump from high psychological theory to highly practical recipes for art teaching and the like; scientific jargon mixed with mundane everyday language. This kind of treatment may well appear chaotic to an orderly mind. Yet I feel quite unrepentant. I realize that the apparently chaotic and scattered structure of my writing fits the subject matter of this book, which deals with the deceptive chaos in art's vast substructure. There is a 'hidden order' in this chaos which only a properly attuned reader or art lover can grasp. All artistic structure is essentially 'polyphonic'; it evolves not in a single line of thought, but in several superimposed strands at once. Hence creativity requires a diffuse, scattered kind of attention that contradicts our normal logical habits of thinking. Is it too high a claim to say that the polyphonic argument of my book must be read with this creative type of attention? I do not think that a reader who wants to proceed on a single track will understand the complexity of art and creativity in general anyway. So why bother about him? Even the most persuasive and logical argument cannot make up for his lack of sensitivity. On the other hand I have reason to hope that a reader who is attuned to the hidden substructure of art will find no difficulty in following the diffuse and scattered structure of my exposition.

There is of course an intrinsic order in the progress of the book. Like most thinking on depth-psychology it proceeds from the conscious surface to the deeper levels of the unconscious. The first chapters deal with familiar technical and professional problems of the artist. Gradually aspects move into view that defy this kind of rational analysis. For instance the plastic effects of painting (pictorial space) which are familiar to every artist and art lover turn out to be determined by deeply unconscious perceptions. They ultimately evade all conscious control. In this way a profound conflict between conscious and unconscious (spontaneous) control comes forward. The conflict proves to be akin to the conflict of single-track thought and 'polyphonic' scattered attention which I have described. Conscious thought is sharply focused and highly differentiated in its elements; the deeper we penetrate into low-level imagery and fantasy the more the single track divides and branches into unlimited directions so that in the end its structure appears chaotic. The creative thinker is capable of alternating between differentiated and undifferentiated modes of thinking, harnessing them together to give him service for solving very definite tasks. The uncreative psychotic succumbs to the tension between conscious (differentiated) and unconscious (undifferentiated) modes of mental functioning. As he cannot integrate their divergent functions, true chaos ensues. The unconscious functions overcome and fragment the conscious surface sensibilities and tear reason into shreds. Modern art displays this attack of unreason on reason quite openly. Yet owing to the powers of the creative mind real disaster is averted. Reason may seem to be cast aside for a moment. Modern art seems truly chaotic. But as time passes by the 'hidden order' in art's substructure (the work of unconscious form creation) rises to the surface. The modern artist may attack his own reason and single-track thought; but a new order is already in the making.

Up to a point any truly creative work involves casting aside sharply crystallized modes of rational thought and image making. To this extent creativity involves self-destruction. This self-destructive attack may explain why art is so often concerned with tragedy. In a tentative paper, published in the *International Journal of Psycho-analysis* [4] many years ago I first tried to grapple with the self-destructive imagery that characterizes so much creative work. Later, I followed a suggestion found in Marion Milner's book *An Experiment in Leisure* [21] and realized that the self-destructive imagery of the 'dying god' (Frazer) did not so much symbolize masochistic fantasy as the process of creating itself, that is to say the self-destructive attack of unconscious functions on the rational surface sensibilities. These tragic images are not symbolic in the usual way; they do not express archaic or infantile drives (id), but events within the creative personality (ego). When we fall asleep we may see scenes of falling into a bottomless abyss and the like. Such fantasies represent the act of falling asleep and are commonly called 'hypnagogic'. I have called the tragic images of creativity 'poemagogic' (see page 190) because they describe the act of creating. These poemagogic images have many levels. Paradoxically the deepest of all, which seems to lack any structure, is most easily extracted and I have treated it first. It is the 'oceanic' level where we feel our individual existence lost in mystic union with the universe. This level corresponds to Jung's image of the mandala and his archetype of the divine self-creating child. It is hardly familiar to the analyst. But, as I will maintain, the psycho-analysis of creative work may prove a better tool for tapping the deepest levels of creative ego functioning than the psycho-analyst's clinical experience in the consulting room. The higher levels of poemagogic imagery reach more familiar ground and can be associated with the oral, anal and genital levels of fantasy which clinical psycho-analysis has treated very fully. But again new structural aspects emerge which go beyond clinical ortho-doxy. In order to help the reader I have added an appendix, which will sum up technical psycho-analytic points and try to locate my findings within the framework of current clinical theory. Yet – to return to the point I have made in the beginning – it does not really matter if the reader has to skip over the more technical psycho-analytic theorizing that links my argument with the main body of psycho-analytic research. The book can stand on its own feet as an aesthetic analysis of art's deep substructure.

The gestation of the book took more than a dozen years. By and by the different aspects of art's undifferentiated substructure drew together. I could not have written this book in a shorter time. The Bollingen Foundation supported the research by a fellowship granted while the work was still in its initial stages. I feel most grateful to the Foundation's officers for their patience and forbearance.

Book One
Controlling the Work

Part One
Order in Chaos

1   The Child's Vision of the World

The classical concept of the primary process (which forms unconscious fantasy) denies it any structure. Unconscious fantasy does not distinguish between opposites, fails to articulate space and time as we know it, and allows all firm boundaries to melt in a free chaotic mingling of forms. Art, on the other hand, appears the embodiment of rigorous organization. So it has been assumed that art's structure is exclusively shaped by conscious and preconscious functions, the so-called secondary process. But this will not do. In her Freud-Centenary Lecture *Psycho-analysis and Art* [23], Marion Milner said that a revision of the concept of the primary process was in the air; the problems raised by the nature of art pressed towards this revision.

For once the 'applied' psycho-analysis of art may backfire and modify original clinical theory. Such a development would not be new in the history of science. The science of the human body also began as medicine, but soon branched out into allied non-clinical disciplines that owed little to research into pathological phenomena and could in turn modify existing medical theory. Psycho-analysis as the science of the human mind may now have reached this stage, where non-clinical branches of research may claim to be independent inquiries that need not take over clinical theory without criticism. Psycho-analytic ego psychology – the study of creative work belongs to this field of research – has largely been nursed by Freud's analysis of the dream, which was certainly non-clinical. After a period of long stagnation ego psychology has once again attracted attention. It may be that the analysis of art can continue where the analysis of the dream has left off.

Before Freud the dream was considered the chance product of

a half-paralysed mind. It was his achievement to have demonstrated its hidden meaning by referring it to a latent dream fantasy running on underneath the disconnected dream. While vindicating the dream's nonsensical content, Freud did not vindicate its seemingly chaotic structure. As I have said, he attributed it to a primary process lacking in the proper differentiation of opposites, of space and time, and indeed in any other firm structure. The formal analysis of art can make good this omission. The unconscious components of art demonstrate a deceptive chaos; for instance, the scribbles of artistic handwriting or background textures exhibit the same lack of precise structure. It has been my point in all my writings that their superficial appearance should not deceive us. They may be merely less differentiated, that is to say, they try to do too many things at once and cannot afford to distinguish (differentiate) between opposites and to articulate precise space and time. I will show that the complexity of a creative search, which has to explore many avenues, needs an advance on a broader front which keeps contradicting options open. In the solution of complex tasks the undifferentiation of unconscious vision turns into an instrument of rigorous precision and leads to results that are fully acceptable to conscious rationality. Of course, in mental illness undifferentiated material rises from the unconscious merely to disrupt the more narrowly focused modes of conscious discursive thinking; and the chaos and destruction which we are wont to associate with undifferentiated primary process fantasy overwhelm the patient's reason. In contrast to illness, creative work succeeds in coordinating the results of unconscious undifferentiation and conscious differentiation and so reveals the hidden order in the unconscious. Clinical work knows little about how creative sublimation works, because it is mainly concerned with interpreting and translating the contents of unconscious fantasy. Once the unconscious conflicts are resolved, it is left to the automatic action of the ego to sublimate the revealed unconscious drives into useful creative work. This procedure leaves the creative working of the ego obscure. The study of art's unconscious substructure and of the scanning processes in science offers the needed opportunity for observing the creative techniques of the ego and the way in which it makes use of the dispersed structure of unconscious perception. The chaos of the unconscious is as deceptive as the chaos of outer reality. In either case we need the less differentiated techniques of unconscious vision to become aware of their hidden order. The scientist has to face the fragmentation of physical facts with courage. He has to scan a multitude of possible links that could make sense out of apparent chaos. I would maintain that he needs the more dispersed (undifferentiated) structure of low-level vision in order to project the missing order into reality. At the same time – and this is the immense psychological gain – he will make a constructive use of his unconscious faculties and achieve the integration of his own ego. In creativity, outer and inner reality will always be organized together by the same indivisible process. The artist, too, has to face chaos in his work before unconscious scanning brings about the integration of his work as well as of his own personality. My point will be that unconscious scanning makes use of undifferentiated modes of vision that to normal awareness would seem chaotic. Hence comes the impression that the primary process merely produces chaotic fantasy material that has to be ordered and shaped by the ego's secondary processes. On the contrary, the primary process is a precision instrument for creative scanning that is far superior to discursive reason and logic.

The concept of undifferentiation as distinct from chaos is not easy to grasp. For the sake of a clearer exposition let me describe its character as it evolves during infancy. The undifferentiated structure of primary-process fantasy corresponds to the primitive still undifferentiated structure of the child's vision of the world. Piaget has given currency to the term 'syncretistic' vision as the distinctive quality of children's vision and of child art. Syncretism also involves the concept of undifferentiation. Around the eighth year of life a drastic change sets in in children's art, at least in Western civilization. While the infant experiments boldly with form and colour in representing all sorts of objects, the older child begins to analyse these shapes by matching them against the art of the adult which he finds in magazines, books and pictures. He usually finds his own work deficient. His work becomes duller in colour, more anxious in draughtsmanship. Much of the earlier vigour is lost. Art education seems helpless to stop this rot. What has happened is that the child's vision has ceased to be total and syncretistic and has become analytic instead. The child's more primitive syncretistic vision does not, as the adult's does, differentiate abstract details. The child does not break down the shape of some concrete object into smaller abstract elements and then match the elements of his drawings one by one. His vision is still global and takes in the entire whole which remains undifferentiated as to its component details. This gives the younger child artist the freedom to distort colour and shapes in the most imaginative and, to us, unrealistic manner. But to him – owing to his global, unanalytic view – his work is realistic. A scribble can represent a great number of objects that would look very different to the analytic spectator. However 'abstract' the infant's drawing may appear to the adult, to him himself it is a correct rendering of a concrete, individual object. His syncretistic vision allows him to disregard matching detail to detail.

I have said that the global syncretistic view is undifferentiated as to its elements. Their distortion and even complete change need not affect the identity of the object. The syncretistic neglect of detail in grasping a total object should not be dismissed as crude and primitive, or due to lack of self-critical faculties. We have to remember that the early work is better in its aesthetic achievement than the timid art of the older child. More important, syncretistic vision is never entirely destroyed and can be shown to be a potent tool in the hands of the adult artist.

E. H. Gombrich, in his already classic book *Art and Illusion* [12], has shown that realism in art does not simply copy the artist's subjective perceptions. Realism is only possible because conventional schemata for representing reality exist which have developed over the centuries. These the inventive artist can refine further and then match his new shapes against external reality. The initial 'making' (an intuitive act) of the schema has to be justified by 'matching' the tentative result against reality. What Gombrich implies, but never says explicitly, is that matching can be twofold; it can either be analytic or syncretistic. The matching of global shapes on the syncretistic level is freer and – wrongly – appears arbitrary to the analytic viewer. Gombrich matches usually, but not always, on the analytic level. Yet syncretism can be as precise if not more so, than the analytic matching of detail. Picasso's incredibly convincing portraits defeat all analytic matching by jumbling up and distorting all the details of a face. But we can judge the likeness of the portrait only if we have become attuned to this kind of representation. We then no longer judge the verisimilitude of the portrait by analysing single features, but intuitively grasp the portrait as an indivisible whole. Picasso's one-time secretary, the Spanish writer Sabartés, illustrated his book on the master with a series of portraits of him painted by Picasso, which range from youthful academic realism to the most arbitrary distortions. In a late

Figure 1. Episode from *Bristow* by Frank Dickens (from the London *Evening Standard*). Bristow represents an elderly unqualified clerk in a big business organization. His moods of apprehension, depression and high spirits are expressed by the various positions of his eyes. When his mood is happy the two eyes descend to one nostril, even in profile. The nose itself begins to smile. Such displacements would have been impossible without Picasso; but today they have become acceptable without causing a feeling of violence and fragmentation. The 'nose-eyes' can be read as a good likeness of reality.

portrait Picasso reversed the position of the sitter's spectacles so that they sit upside down on the ridge of the nose. Yet the whole holds together and makes this most arbitrary of portraits the most convincing and 'realistic' of all. Only superficially does this lack of proper differentiation and spatial coherence seem chaotic. The resemblance achieved by a syncretistic portrait relies on a subtle balance which is not amenable to conscious analysis. Yet we can judge the likeness with precision. Some hidden order must guide us (figure 1). The same reliability and precision is found in the young child's syncretistic grasp of reality. He may neglect abstract detail, yet his powers of recognition may be superior to the duller vision of the adult. Often some quite inconspicuous cue that escapes the more sophisticated adult may allow him to identify an object. A friend told me that his three-year-old boy could identify the make of some car which was almost totally hidden by relying on a single obscure feature in the car's bonnet. I will show that undifferentiated vision is altogether more acute in scanning complex structures. It treats all of them with equal impartiality, insignificant as they may look to normal vision. Normally our attention is drawn only to conspicuous features. These alone are then clearly differentiated. The others sink back to form an insignificant ground. Syncretistic vision is impartial because it does not differentiate figure and ground in this manner. Hence it also neglects what to analytic vision would seem important. But this neglect does not make it chaotic and still less unstructured.

In *Art and Illusion* Gombrich deals with the peculiarities of the caricature. Obviously the realism of the caricature is not based on matching analytically. The single distortions are certainly unrealistic and sometimes could not be recognized in isolation as parts of a human face. But they add up effortlessly to a global view which can bear a more striking resemblance to the sitter than a more conventional portrait (plate 9). We have no rational standard whatsoever for matching the likeness analytically. The spectator has to call up in himself the young child's syncretistic vision which did not differentiate the identity of a shape by matching its details one by one, but went straight for the whole. Syncretistic vision can override photographic correctitude in detail by focusing only on the total view. Syncretistic vision appears much more flexible than analytic vision. To this extent we could reverse the usual evaluation and consider analytic vision cruder and less sensitive than (syncretistically) undifferentiated modes of vision obtaining on primitive (infantile levels of awareness.

It is difficult, if not impossible, to describe the exact functioning of syncretism, which is so far removed from direct introspection. We can assume that complex unconscious scanning goes on. It balances one distortion against the other and extracts a common denominator or fulcrum from them that is somehow discounted. The subtle flowing distortions in Japanese art may be of this kind. The Japanese themselves are quite unaware of them. When I was a young boy I was asked by my father to guide a Japanese lawyer round the sights of my native Vienna. At that time, nearly half a century ago, the media of mass communication, books, periodicals, films, had not yet brought about the present diffusion of aesthetic sensibilities around the world. The Japanese gentleman, though highly educated, was quite unfamiliar with Western art. We soon became good friends, and I concluded that all traditional European art seemed highly stylized and decorative to him. I also showed him around a conventional show of contemporary post-Impressionistic art and this too impressed him as stylized. I was puzzled. It dawned on me that only Japanese art could be realistic to him, in spite – or rather because – of its conventional schema which somehow distorts every single line. Apparently once the Japanese spectator has become attuned to the secret regularity ruling the linear flow of this persistent distortion, he can discount it. He so arrives at a global (syncretistic) view that appears to him quite true to nature. It may well be possible to discover a mathematical formula that could average the distortion in Japanese draughtsmanship. But this would only deepen the problem how unconscious scanning could grasp the widely scattered deviations in a single immediate act of comprehension. Again it seems that the broadening of focus caused by undifferentiation brings about an enormous increase in the efficiency of scanning. I would maintain that the control which any artist must exert in building the complex structure of a work of art also needs this increased power of scanning.

If this view of syncretistic vision is correct we can no longer say that the child, in creating his fantastic equivalents of reality, lacks self-criticism. When the analytic faculty of the child awakens around the age of eight and he learns to compare abstract details, he certainly tends to disparage his older syncretistic ways as crude and ignorant. But is this not a failure of our teaching ? Is the awakening of self-criticism so self-destructive because we have failed to educate it earlier ? We always tend to underestimate the child's intelligence. Even monkeys may be capable of appreciating their aesthetic efforts. In our view we have to help the infant in appreciating his work on the proper syncretistic level. There are degrees of success and failure even in the invention of the freest and most fantastic equivalent. We have seen how we can judge Picasso's phantasmagorias or the wild colour distortions of the Fauves as right or wrong, though we have not any rational standard for judging them. If the child has been properly supported in his aesthetic standards on the syncretistic level, the later awakening of his analytic self-criticism will no longer be quite so harmful. It would be useless, and even wrong, to discourage the eight-year-old child from applying his new analytic faculties to his work. We have only to prevent him from destroying his earlier syncretistic powers which remain so important even for the adult artist. This might only be achieved by surrounding the child with an adult environment of works by highly spontaneous artists such as Picasso, Klee, Miró, Matisse etc. This environment can sustain his old syncretistic vision side by side with his new analytic awareness. Encouraging the old blind 'free self-expression' against the new faculties simply will not do. If his syncretistic vision had been aesthetically trained it might well survive the onslaught of the new analytic vision and infuse vigour into his tired pattern making.

I will have a great deal more to say about the scattering of focus inherent in syncretistic vision. But let us first consider the pattern of ordinary analytic perception. From the undifferentiated mosaic of the visual field we are compelled to select a 'figure' on which attention concentrates while the rest of visual data recedes and fuses into a vague background of indistinct texture. Gestalt psychology has investigated the principles that govern the selection and formation of one particular figure in preference to others. From a number of possible constellations into which the visual stimuli can be grouped, we will tend to select the most compact, simple and coherent pattern which is said to possess properties of 'good' gestalt. The goodness of the gestalt is judged by our habitual aesthetic tastes. This makes gestalt psychology dependent on aesthetics, not too firm a ground on which to build a reliable theory. A good gestalt approximates to simple geometric patterns such as are hardly ever found in nature. But this matters little. The gestalt principle not only governs the selection of the best pattern from within the visual field, but it will also actively improve it. Little gaps and imperfections in an otherwise perfect gestalt are filled in or smoothed away. This is why analytic gestalt vision tends to be generalized and ignores syncretistic individuality.

A portraitist once told me how the usual training in the life and portrait class counteracted the catching of a good likeness.

We are taught to analyse a face in terms of abstract almost geometric patterns that are equivalent to a good gestalt. Hence individual features and the almost imperceptible deviations from regularized pattern are ignored. The portraitist told me how he tried to re-invest the patterns in a face with a new individuality by transforming them into imaginary landscapes, 'a Red Indian riding in a canoe' and the like. That arbitrary reveries of this kind should make objects appear more individual sounds paradoxical. Nevertheless, the plastic reality of our external perceptions is directly related to the wealth of unconscious fantasy. Freud found that dreams looked particularly real not when the dream's imagery was precise and clear but when the dream was supported by a rich unconscious fantasy content. The same holds good of our waking perception. The schizophrenic, who is cut off from this anchorage, sees the world flat and unreal. Because syncretistic vision is anchored in the undifferentiated unconscious it is also more plastic and real (though less clearly defined) than the analytic vision of abstract pattern. Daydreaming of the lazy sort need not be plastic and real in this way. The portraitist who projects landscapes into a face is wide awake. It is the privilege of the artist to combine the ambiguity of dreaming with the tensions of being fully awake. In the moment of inspiration reality will appear to him super-real and intensely plastic.

If we want to observe fine differences in abstract form we must project fantastic meaning into it. It is well known that we can judge the relative position of three dots in a circle with astonishing accuracy if we interpret them as two eyes and a mouth set in a rotund face. The slightest shifting in their position will affect their physiognomic expression. A smiling face becomes sad or threatening and vice versa. A copyist will do better if he copies this total facial expression instead of attending to detailed geometric relationships. This again goes to prove the superior scanning power of a total syncretistic vision and its better recognition of individual features, though it seems oblivious of abstract detail. In this lies the paradox of order in chaos.

The analytic vision of the eight-year-old child represents the fully developed abstract gestalt principle. The child begins to focus his attention on abstract geometric details of his drawings and compare them one by one with elements of the objects around him. No longer can he scatter his attention to the total appearance without regard to detail. The current gestalt theory ignores syncretism. It proclaims that these comparatively late gestalt tendencies are innate from birth. The child opening his eyes to the world would at once be compelled to articulate the visual field into 'good' gestalt patterns standing out from a blurred ground. Fortunately, so the gestalt psychologists thought, biologically important objects also have good gestalt properties. For this reason the child would be led at once to perceiving those important objects. This was, of course, a theoretical assumption based on the gestalt compulsions tested only in the vision of the adult. But there are cases of people who were born blind – or lost sight at an early age – and acquired vision only much later through an operation. These people were of course conversant with the shapes of objects through their sense of touch and were aware of the simplicity of basic geometric patterns, like spheres and circles, cubes and squares, pyramids and triangles. Gestalt psychology predicted that on opening their formerly blind eyes to the world their attention would at once be attracted to forms displaying such basic patterns. What a unique opportunity for observing the gestalt principle at work in automatically organizing the visual field into a precise figure seen against an indistinct ground! None of these predictions came true! Case histories collected by von Senden [28] show the incredible difficulties encountered by patients as they were suddenly faced with the complexities of the visual world. Many of them (due to the lack of understanding of their difficulties on the part of their physicians) faltered in their purpose and could not muster the effort needed for organizing the buzzing chaos of coloured blotches. Some of them felt profound relief when blindness overcame them once again and allowed them to sink back into their familiar world of touch.

They showed neither great facility nor inclination for picking out basic geometric shapes. In order to distinguish, say, a triangle from a square, they had to 'count' the corners one by one as they had done by touching them when they were still blind. They often failed miserably. They had certainly no immediate easy awareness of a simple self-evident gestalt as the gestalt theorists had predicted. Simplicity of pattern played only a small part in their learning. The psycho-analyst will not be surprised to hear that a libidinous interest in reality rather than abstract form was the greatest incentive and the most efficient guide. A girl who was an animal lover identified her beloved dog first of all. A recent case showed that the face of the physician was the first shapeless blob picked out from the general blur of the visual field.

There is much scope for a better collaboration between clinical and perceptual psychologists in helping newly sighted patients in making proper use of their potential faculties. R. L. Gregory reported on the recent case I mentioned in his brilliant book *Eye and Brain* (World University Library, 1966) and rightly points out that the patient tended to use his new vision mainly for testing the old model of reality which he had formed by touch alone. He does not draw the rather obvious conclusion that this surprisingly limited use of vision may have been one of the main reasons for failure. It is indeed surprising that these patients do limit themselves in this way. Gregory's patient – I may call him this though Gregory attended the case only in the role of scientific investigator – was at first quite eager and ready to use his vision as an independent means of exploring reality, but soon lost interest. As in other such cases the visual world looked drab, confused, lifeless and flat to him, yet replete with irrational terrors. Apparently this withdrawal was directly due to his anxieties, which outweighed his initial curiosity and eagerness. Anxiety would have made him cling to the old model of tactile reality; he used vision merely to seek out the equivalent patterns. My main thesis will be of course that normal vision of reality is not based on the interpretation of pattern, but goes directly for the visual object with little interest in its abstract shape. As I will point out presently, we have to suppress our interest in pattern as such in order to make vision into an efficient instrument for scanning reality. The plastic quality of vision giving vividness to reality depends more on the suppression of form than on precise articulation. I have tried to show elsewhere [5] in some detail that both dreaming and waking vision acquires its plastic quality from its unconscious substructure. For instance, normally the shapes in peripheral vision are withdrawn from conscious attention. De-personalized vision tends to have a clearer peripheral field, but is also flatter and in a sense unreal. Clarity of detail is gained at the expense of plastic reality. I will also argue that the plastic quality of pictorial space in painting can be taken as a conscious signal of a vast unconscious substructure. Learning to see involves forming such an unconscious substructure of vision; suppressing irrelevant details produces an awareness of intensely plastic objects without definite outline. This blurred plasticity is more important for the efficiency of vision than making out precise shapes and patterns. Unfortunately the physicians and observers attending this patient seemed to have seduced him (as has happened in many cases before) to seek out precise patterns that he could relate to already existing tactile models of objects. This might well have hindered proper progress. The patient withdrew from a visual world cluttered up with irrelevant and terrifying details; after a few years he died in deep depression. In the past physicians erred grievously when, as often happened, they misused their patients in experiments where the patients had to identify abstract patterns that had no libidinous interest whatsoever for them. Great suffering and at best a painful delay in their learning to see was the consequence.

Recent research, partly based on experiments with young animals and babies, suggests that the young animal does not see abstract shapes but scans the total object for cues that are immediately connected with real objects. To some young birds the same wooden shape suggests, say, a goose with a long neck if it is moved in one direction, and a dangerous hawk if moved backwards with the long neck now turned into a long tail. Colour alone may serve as a cue for identifying friend, enemy, parents and the like objects. A young baby will smile at a terrifying crude mask if only it has certain minimum cues suggesting the mother's face, but will show signs of fear if the cues are missing. This recognition of objects from cues rather than from the analysis of abstract detail is the beginning of syncretistic vision. Analytic vision would only obstruct the recognition of objects. Every movement of an object can profoundly affect the abstract shape of its details. The human nose looks triangular in profile and a shapeless squiggle in a frontal view. The two views have nothing in common. Yet we easily recognize a face which we have first seen in profile when it is presented later in a frontal view (figure 2). If the gestalt theory had been correct and our first awareness of reality were analytic rather than syncretistic, the difficulty of identifying objects would become enormous. If we are able to discount the constant change and loss in abstract detail with such ease this must be due to the mysterious syncretistic grasp of the total shape which can be hypersensitive to individual features while ignoring meaningless abstract pattern. It is, therefore, wrong to speak of the child's primitive vision that is incapable of abstract form analysis; rather is it a superior faculty best suited to instant recognition of individual objects. When I once spoke in an assembly of artists about the dualism of syncretism and analytic abstract form, a painter working in simple abstract patterns felt indignant. Yet he readily came forward with a story which in all probability any of us could match. He had once gone for a walk on the beach at St Ives in Cornwall at dusk. He saw

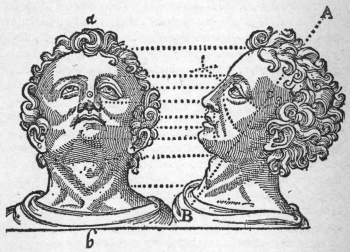

Figure 2. Turning from full face to profile causes every single feature of the face to change beyond recognition in terms of abstract form. But in the total likeness no change occurs. The recognition of real objects is not dependent on memorizing their many formal aspects. Understanding of reality comes before the appreciation of abstract form.

from far away the silhouette of a person whom he could hardly make out. Yet he instantly recognized, perhaps by an undefinable idiosyncrasy in his posture, an old acquaintance whom he had not seen for decades and whom he knew to be living in South Africa. Had he memorized the geometric shape of that man's characteristic posture? How could this vague outline in the dusk be characteristic enough to call up instantly an individual whom he could not remember in other ways? It hardly makes sense to assume that he memorized just this characteristic posture among a large number of other very different shapes. A more comprehensive memory other than the recall of specific details must have been at work. We do not know yet the full extent and structure of our (unconscious) scanning powers, but somehow we must search for undifferentiated low-level sensibilities not unlike syncretism for an explanation. I am posing a new problem without attempting an answer. The psychology of unconscious perception is still unwritten. (Perhaps only the close link of its development with a parallel evolution of the libido seems beyond reasonable doubt. I will revert to the parallel evolution of the id and the ego later on and maintain that the id's libidinous development guides the differentiation of the ego's perception.)

In this context I am content to establish that undifferentiation and syncretism, far from being chaotic, serves a vital purpose. As we have seen, the syncretistic faculty can abstract from differences in analytic details and so identify an object in its changing aspects. It also discounts the many malformations of abstract detail by which a good caricature distorts the 'correct' photographic projection. Undifferentiated unconscious scanning extracts from the many variable details a common denominator or fulcrum which serves as the 'cue'. Art teaching, instead of concentrating on abstract analysis of form, could train this precious syncretistic faculty and clear the way for the emergence of a new realism. It could exploit the still untapped resources of caricature. Without a trace of aggressiveness or ridicule, it could simply aim at a true likeness of reality without attention to detail. Giacometti had to squash the human figure in order to produce a more truly striking likeness. Unconsciously he might mount a destructive attack on the human body. But his initial destructiveness was linked with syncretism and so led to the rebirth of the inviolate individual.

It is extremely difficult to accept that thing recognition should be syncretistic and thus independent of the perception of well-defined analytic details. Bertrand Russell, almost as a matter of course, defines things as bundles of definite qualities. We have first to learn to memorize single abstract qualities such as redness, roundness, etc., and to associate them into coherent and concrete 'bundles' that tend to occur together in space-time. What a naïve view for so sceptical a philosopher! The sense data theory of philosophy has taken an unconscionably long time to die its lingering death. This theory assumed that perception begins by seeing abstract meaningless sense data, coloured blobs in the visual field. These are communicated to the brain for further evaluation. According to Russell the data are 'bundled' into the more complex entities which are associated with real things. Gestalt psychology is no great advance on this naïve theory even when compared with the earlier atomistic theories it replaced. Before the advent of gestalt psychology it was assumed that the sense data consisted of a pointillist mosaic. The bits and pieces were then added together into larger entities. Gestalt psychology rightly dispenses with this mosaic of sense data and suggests that perception goes out immediately towards comprehensive abstract patterns, the so-called gestalt. But a better understanding of our immediate syncretistic awareness of concrete objects is still a long way off. As before, the abstract gestalt aspects of a thing are supposed to serve as meaningless sense data waiting to be associated with the idea of a concrete object. It is not easy to understand why it is quite so difficult to envisage a perception that is guided by libido and goes straight for the total individual objects without awareness of their abstract elements. Perhaps the perennial dualism of form and content, the bugbear of aesthetics, also vitiates psychological insight, so that understanding form is said to come before understanding content. But this is simply not true. Concrete thing perception comes before the awareness of a generalized abstract gestalt. Moreover, as we have seen, our recognition of reality is disturbed, not assisted, by such abstract awareness. Thing perception, with its syncretistic grasp of a total object, has to be firmly established before the analytic awareness of abstract pattern can come into its own around the eighth year of life. By then 'latency' has stunted the child's sexual drives. The weakening of the child's libidinous ties with reality allows his perception to detach itself from its old syncretistic search for the concrete individual object and attach itself instead to generalized abstract patterns, thereby setting up a profound split in his orientation towards reality, which is never entirely resolved.

I am, of course, not decrying the awakening of the analytic

abstract faculties during latency. Far from it; the new awareness of abstract form becomes one of the most potent tools in the hands of the artist and the scientist. Scientific abstraction is a product of unconscious dedifferentiation. It is based on a mixture of images which to conscious introspection appear incompatible and so blot each other out. I will discuss this close relationship between undifferentiation and abstraction in a separate chapter. (I will speak of *un*differentiation when referring to the static structure of unconscious image making, of *de*differentiation when describing the dynamic process by which the ego scatters and represses surface imagery.) The growth of new images in art and of new concepts in science is nourished by the conflict between two opposing structural principles. The analysis of abstract gestalt elements is pitted against the syncretistic grasp of the total object, focusing on detail against complex scanning, fragmentation against wholeness, differentiation against dedifferentiation. These polarities are aspects of the same conflict between the secondary and primary process. The new technical meaning which I have given to the terms 'undifferentiation' and 'dedifferentiation' may necessitate not only a modification of the present conception of the primary process, but also of the term 'unconscious'; images are withdrawn from consciousness not merely because of the superego's censorship of certain offensive *contents*; they may become inaccessible through their undifferentiated *structure* alone. The paradox of syncretistic vision can be explained in this way. Syncretistic vision may appear empty of precise detail though it is in fact merely undifferentiated. Through its lack of differentiation it can accommodate a wide range of incompatible forms, for instance all the possible distortions of a face by a good caricature. Nevertheless, syncretistic vision is highly sensitive to the smallest of cues and proves more efficient in identifying individual objects. It impresses us as empty, vague and generalized only because the narrowly focused surface consciousness cannot grasp its wider more comprehensive structure. Its precise concrete content has become inaccessible and 'unconscious'.

2   The Two Kinds of Attention

The conscious gestalt compulsion makes us bisect the visual field into significant 'figure' and insignificant 'ground'. Yet bisecting the picture plane into significant and insignificant areas is precisely what the artist cannot afford to do. Only a bad artist will concentrate his attention exclusively on the large-scale composition and treat less articulate form elements like textures or the scribbles of artistic 'handwriting' as decorative additions that have no structural significance. A true artist will agree with the psycho-analyst that nothing can be deemed insignificant or accidental in a product of the human spirit and that – at least on an unconscious level – the usual evaluation has to be reversed. Superficially insignificant or accidental looking detail may well carry the most important unconscious symbolism. Indeed the great emotional power of spontaneous handwriting testifies to its hidden meaning and symbolism (plates 13, 16). A great work of painting stripped of its original brush work by a bad restorer will lose almost all of its substance. There was little point in restoring Leonardo's *Last Supper*.

In a work of art any element, however paltry, has to be firmly related to the total structure in a complex web of cross ties radiating across the entire picture plane. There is no decisive division between the gestalt or figure and mere background elements. The complexity of any work of art, however simple, far outstrips the powers of conscious attention, which, with its pin-point focus, can attend to only one thing at a time. Only the extreme undifferentiation of unconscious vision can scan these complexities. It can hold them in a single unfocused glance and treat figure and ground with equal impartiality. For this we have the testimony of the artists.

Paul Klee [16] spoke of two kinds of attention practised by the artist. The normal type of attention focuses on the positive figure which a line encloses, or else – with an effort – on the negative shape which the figure cuts out from the ground. Klee speaks of the endotopic (inside) area and the exotopic (outside) area of the picture plane. He says that the artist can either emphasize the boundary contrast produced by the bisection of the picture plane; in which case he will keep his attention on one (endotopic or exotopic) side of the line he draws; or else he can scatter his attention and watch the simultaneous shaping of inside and outside areas on either side of the line, a feat which the gestalt psychologists would consider impossible. According to the gestalt theory, we have to make a choice; we can choose either to see the figure; then the shape of the ground becomes invisible, or else – with an effort – to scrutinize the negative shape cut from the ground; then the original figure disappears from view. We can never see both at the same time. Of course, one can construct purposely ambiguous patterns where figure and ground are easily interchangeable. Rubin's famous double profiles (figure 3) are such a pattern. A wavy line runs down the middle of a square. It can be either read as a profile turned right – then the left half turns solid and the area to the right into empty ground; or else it can be seen as a profile facing the other way – then the right side becomes solid and the left area recedes. We can only see one profile at a time. We have to make a choice. But do we really? Ambiguous patterns of this sort are often called counterchanges. They are ascribed definite aesthetic and educational value. Some primitive ornaments can impress us as particularly incisive and vigorous because they can be as easily seen as black-on-white patterns as they can as white-on-black patterns. If the student is presented with the task of constructing such counterchanges, he may well find the task insuperable. His difficulty bears out the teachings of gestalt psychology. I have found that if art students are too rigid they make their attention jump alternately between the endotopic or exotopic areas divided by the line. In this cumbersome manner they can check that both readings make aesthetic sense. But this is not the way to achieve good draughtsmanship. Somehow – as Paul Klee postulates – a good artist must be able to hold the entire picture plane in a single undivided focus. He will, as he draws a single line, automatically give aesthetic shape to the negative which his line cuts out from the ground. Counter-changes only represent a special case in which the negative is consciously related to the positive pattern (plate 19).

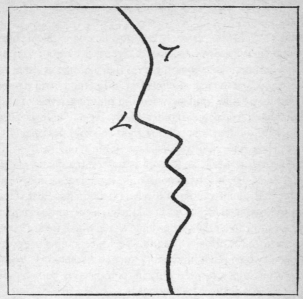

Figure 3. Rubin's double profiles. The two faces try to kiss each other, but cannot do so; as the eye focuses on one the other disappears. Counterchange ornaments have this structure; it must be assumed that the artist can unconsciously comprehend both alternative views in a single glance.

What, of course, is needed is an undifferentiated attention akin to syncretistic vision which does not focus on detail, but holds the total structure of the work of art in a single undifferentiated view. Introspection will fail us. The content of this scattered attention appears essentially blank and empty to conscious memory. The truly unconscious and potentially disruptive quality of undifferentiation is brought out by the use of ambiguous patterns for personality tests. The American psycho-analyst, Else Frenkel-Brunswik [11], found that certain rigid and badly integrated personalities reacted to ambiguous patterns with anxiety. This is not surprising. Like the rigid art student who cannot unfocus his attention, these people are incapable of a smooth rhythm between different levels of perception. This incapacity is due to a near-pathological dissociation of their ego functions. Because of this dissociation the untoward breakthrough of undifferentiated modes of vision threatens their rigidly focused surface sensibilities with sudden disruption and disintegration.

Another point: their anxiety may also be due to the id content of unconscious fantasies. Once undifferentiated perceptions have become inaccessible to consciousness they become invested with id fantasy. Then the unconscious fear of id fantasy will reinforce the already existing split between the different levels of vision and harden further the rigidity of the ego. There is only a quantitative difference between a rigid schizoid personality and the over-concrete rigidity of schizophrenic thought. In schizophrenia the unconscious fear of dedifferentiation oversteps a critical limit. The creative ego rhythm swinging between differentiated and undifferentiated levels is halted altogether. Under such extreme conditions a breakthrough of undifferentiated fantasy brings about the catastrophic chaos which we are wont to associate with the primary process. We are beginning to appreciate that the chaos is not inherent in the undifferentiated structure of the primary process, but only in its impact on pathologically rigid, dissociated surface functions.

A flexible scattering of attention comes quite easily to the artist, if only because of his need for holding all elements of the picture in a single undivided act of attention. He cannot afford the fatal bisection into figure and ground imposed by the conscious gestalt principle. How often have we not observed how an artist suddenly stops in his tracks without apparent reason, steps back from his canvas and looks at it with a curiously vacant stare? What happens is that the conscious gestalt is prevented from crystallizing. Nothing seems to come into his mind. Perhaps one or another detail lights up for a moment only to sink back into the emptiness. During this absence of mind an unconscious scanning seems to go on. Suddenly as from nowhere some offending detail hitherto ignored will come into view. It had somehow upset the balance of the picture, but had gone undetected. With relief the painter will end his apparent inactivity. He returns to his canvas and carries out the necessary retouching. This 'full' emptiness of unconscious scanning occurs in many other examples of creative work. Paul Klee's scattered attention that can attend to figure and ground on both sides of a line is of this kind. As far as consciousness is concerned, it is empty. For the gestalt principle ruling conscious perception cannot relinquish its hold on the figure.

The 'full' emptiness of attention also exists in hearing. Paul Klee himself makes the link between painting and music. He calls his dispersed attention that can attend to the entire picture plane 'multi-dimensional' (this expression happily stresses its irrational structure) and also 'polyphonic'. This too is a good name. Polyphonic hearing also overcomes the conscious division between figure and ground. In music the figure is represented by the melody standing out against an indistinct ground of the harmonic accompaniment. Musicians are loath to call the polyphonic strands of a well-constructed harmonic progression a mere accompaniment. Often the accompanying voices form parallel melodic phrases expressive in themselves. Yet the usual description fits the ordinary naïve way of enjoying music well enough. Moreover, it corresponds to the demands of the gestalt principle which exalts the melody as the figure to which the accompaniment serves as a background. In our memory a piece of music is remembered only as the sound of a melody. But as we have come to appreciate, artistic perception is neither ordinary, nor is it bound to the narrow limits of everyday attention, nor confined to its precise focus which can only attend to a single melody at a time. The musician, like the painter, has to train himself to scatter his attention over the entire musical structure so that he can grasp the polyphonic fabric hidden in the accompaniment.

Unlike the visual artists, among whom only Klee appreciated the problem, musicians have coined technical terms for the two types of hearing. The normal focused type of attention can only appreciate the loose polyphonic structure as solid harmonic chords progressing heavily below the dominant melody above. As chords are written out vertically in musical notation, this solid kind of hearing is called vertical. The second more scattered (polyphonic) type of attention is called horizontal. For in notation the polyphonic voices are written out horizontally along the five lines. This is a rather superficial, purely visual terminology. It hardly does justice to the psychological problem involved. Few musicians appreciate the 'full' emptiness of horizontal hearing.

I remember as a young boy listening awestruck to a discussion among some young musicians as to their relative capacity for horizontal hearing. The music students obviously assumed that horizontal hearing was merely the normal vertical hearing multiplied and thought that it required full conscious attention to all polyphonic voices simultaneously. One of them claimed ruefully that at best he could follow two voices sounding together. Another thought that he could include a third voice. Significantly none of them asserted that he could keep track on all four voices, the normal complement needed for a full harmonic sound. Yet the young Mozart once listened to a polyphonic piece in the Sistine Chapel, the score of which was kept a close secret of the choir. The boy, however, wrote down the score from memory. Obviously the number of polyphonic voices was no obstacle to the young genius. The experienced conductor too can pick out from the full orchestra some erring instrument without necessarily relying on flaws in the vertical sound. I think the mistake which the young musicians made was confusing horizontal hearing with normal focused attention. If we observe ourselves more closely it soon becomes apparent that it is impossible – on a conscious level – to divide one's attention even between two independent voices, unless of course one makes it jump between them in a breathless attempt to catch up with each of them in turn. But this is surely not the way to appreciate music. Polyphonic hearing is unfocused and 'empty' for the musician as it is for the layman; but from this full emptiness the musician can extract all the information he needs through the help of the unconscious scanning I have repeatedly described. So quickly is this information obtained that in retrospect the moment of emptiness is forgotten. This is why we know so little about the gaps in the perpetually oscillating stream of consciousness. In these gaps the work of unconscious scanning is carried on.

The trained musician allows his attention to oscillate freely between focused and unfocused (empty) states, now focusing precisely on the solid vertical sounds of chords, now emptying his attention so that he can comprehend the loose, transparent web of polyphonic voices in their entirety. The naïve layman may refuse to let go the dominant melody as the sole object of his (vertical) attention. He will already feel discomfort in listening to classical symphonies. There the thread of the dominant melody

can be taken up by various instruments in turn, but not a
fitting neatly; gaps occur as well as overlapping, which prev
his stable focusing on a continuous line. The result is confus
and unease. His discomfiture is not unlike the anxieties whic
ambiguous (counterchange) patterns arouse in rigid observers.
These too are due to an attack on the gestalt principle of focused
perception.

A more sophisticated listener will experience no such confusion. He has already learned how to disperse and scatter his
attention into a more horizontal type of listening. He will hardly
be aware of gaps and overlapping in the flow of the melody.
There is no hard and fast distinction between vertical and horizontal listening just as there is no sharp boundary between
conscious and unconscious processes. One mental level gradually
leads into the other. The oscillation between the two types of
hearing can be shallow; but it can also be profound. The structure of classical diatonic music alternates between the solid
harmonic fusion of chords (favouring vertical hearing) and their
temporary dissolution branching into loose strands of polyphony.
Attention keeps shifting between a sonorous melody supported
by the vertical solidity of harmonic chords and the weightless
transparency of polyphonic counterpoint. Single dissonant tones
within a chord may resist being sucked into the vertical sound.
For a moment they will stand out and divert attention to the
horizontal melodic step that 'resolves' the dissonance. There is
certainly a conflict between the two types of attention, one feed-
ing on the other. Differentiation (focusing) of attention is
achieved at the expense of dedifferentiation (dispersing) and vice
versa. The easily focused solidity of harmonic chords is weakened by the looseness of counterpoint, while the lucidity and
transparency of the counter-point is obscured whenever the
voices fall into opaque solid chords. Sometimes the voices form
good chords with every single step. This happens to a large extent in the slow moving chorales of Bach's *St Matthew Passion*.
Yet so strong and expressive are the melodies given to each voice
in the chorales that they can balance the pull towards complete
harmonic fusion. Attention can freely alternate between vertical
and horizontal modes. Conscious and unconscious mental
functioning are harmoniously integrated in a singular way.
There is no violent mutual disruption as happens so frequently

...ern music. The smooth oscillation between focused and
...used modes of perception affords a kind of mental gymnas-
which is immensely salutary for the health of the ego.

Because of this successful integration new doubts may be
...aised as to whether polyphonic hearing and Klee's multi-
dimensional vision really involve unconscious phenomena in the
technical sense. Neither displays the impression of unstructured
chaos which adheres to the primary process of the deep unconscious. This is the old intractable problem. It arises as soon
as we forget that the integration between the opposing principles
is solely due to the success of a creative ego rhythm. Without it
(as the confusion of Mrs Frenkel-Brunswik's observers and of
the naïve listener faced with polyphonic overlapping demonstrates) the antagonism between the two principles is not resolved. Without this creative effort at integration the splitting
between the two kinds of sensitivity is likely to occur. I have
mentioned how the untrained artist will split apart figure and
ground. He will dismiss textured background elements as insignificant and chaotic, possibly to be added after the main work on
the composition has been done. The full assistance of a dispersed
empty stare is needed to overcome this serious, anti-creative
split. A truly nervous, seemingly uncontrolled 'handwriting'
that resists all deliberate mannerisms and tricks is highly valued
by artists and art lovers. In some mysterious way it expresses the
artist's personality better than his more considered compositions.
Is this because these undifferentiated textures conceal unconscious symbols which are for ever beyond conscious interpretation? If, as I believe, the seemingly chaotic structure of
handwriting conceals some hidden unconscious order, such order
is destroyed as soon as it is imitated by a conscious effort, a fact
which is bound to throw grave doubt on the over-confidence of
restorers who do not hesitate to reproduce the master's brush
work in a highly deliberate way. The conflict between deliberate
and spontaneous methods of working is indeed profound. While
the artist's conscious attention may be occupied with shaping the
large-scale composition his (unconscious) spontaneity will add
the countless hardly articulate inflections that make up his
personal handwriting. Any switch of conscious attention towards
these minute distortions, scribbles and textures would interfere
with their apparent lack of structure (plate 17). It would infuse a

measure of good gestalt into them and so rob them of their most precious quality, that impression of unstructured chaos on which their emotional impact (and therefore also their unconscious order and significance) depends. We cannot define their hidden organization and order any more than we can decipher their unconscious symbolism. Their content and formal principle of organization are truly unconscious.

It is only a quantitative step from Paul Klee's multi-dimensional attention which takes in the entire undifferentiated picture plane, to the empty-handed control of inarticulate inflections and handwriting. The artist's vacant unfocused stare pays attention to the smallest detail however far removed from the consciously perceived figure. The uncompromising democracy which refuses to make any distinction between the significance of the elements building the work of art belongs to the essence of artistic rigour.

So it is in music. There the conscious articulate elements are classified within various 'systems' of scale, rhythm and harmony. Anything falling outside these systems is automatically excluded from normal attention. There are for instance the countless inarticulate inflections of the melody by *vibrato*, *portamento*, *rubato*, etc., none of which are articulate enough to be caught by musical notation. They are left to the spontaneous execution of the performer. They greatly contribute to the emotional impact of the music and are certainly part of its essential structure. Just as the bad commercial artist will ape a nervous artistic handwriting by making his hand wobble deliberately in a stereotyped way, so the commercial violinist or pop singer will make his melody wobble with indiscriminately applied *vibrato* or *portamento* for the sake of a thick sensual sound. Neither will deceive us. An inspired performer like Casals places a *vibrato* or *portamento* only in certain places, but not in others, obeying the command of some rigorous discipline which he is unable to put into words. This does not make his spontaneous discipline less compelling. If he allowed his conscious attention to control their application by conscious effort, his purpose would inevitably falter and mislead him. To conscious inspection, even by the artist himself, these inflections cannot but seem chaotic and arbitrary. Hence conscious attention would deprive the performer of the strict discipline he needs in shaping the total structure of the work. It is, of course, possible – and some good work has been done in this respect – to measure precisely the *vibrato* in good singing voices, and to arrive at certain optimal frequencies. But clearly such optimal values are subject to changes of taste as is any other element of art. Pop singers indulge in a slow *vibrato* that would be unacceptable in *lieder* singing. Measurements of this kind are bound to lead to stereotyped mannerisms. If we listen to the *vibrato* as performed by a great instrumentalist we will become aware that the rate of his *vibrato* may change even within a single performance. Spontaneously applied form elements are fragile and subject to unpredictable changes of mood. A performer may readily change the inarticulate micro-elements of his interpretation from performance to performance. But this instability does not make them arbitrary. Any change forces the performer to recast his interpretation of the whole work on the spur of the moment. This total integration can only be controlled by the empty stare of unconscious scanning which alone is capable of overcoming the fragmentation in art's surface structure. The relative smallness of micro-elements defies conscious articulation; so do the macro-elements of art owing to their excessive breadth. This applies for instance to the macro-structure of a symphony as distinct from its single movements. The much-vaunted grasp of a symphony's total structure is well beyond the capacities even of many well-known conductors. Most are content to shape their phrases only in their immediate context and this procedure emphasizes the fragmentation of the whole. On the surface the overall structure of a sonata or symphony seems to go out of its way to evade a total grasp. The single movements are tightly organized and form good gestalt structures in themselves. These are then sharply contrasted in rhythm, harmony and form. More than ever an undifferentiated empty stare is needed to transcend such sharp divisions and forge the total work into a single indivisible whole. It seems that art, almost perversely, creates tasks that cannot be mastered by our normal faculties. Chaos is precariously near.

We arrive back at our central problem, the role which the unconscious plays in controlling the vast substructure of art. Its contribution appears chaotic and altogether accidental, but only as long as we rely on the gestalt-bound discipline of conscious perception. In spite of the caution built into the foundations of psycho-analytic thinking, which makes it beware of superficial impressions of chaos and accidentality, psycho-analytic aesthetics have so far faltered and succumbed to the chaotic impression which the substructure of art so seductively presents. Once we have overcome the deception the eminently constructive role of the primary process in art can no longer be ignored.

3   Unconscious Scanning

What is common to all examples of dedifferentiation is their freedom from having to make a choice. While the conscious gestalt principle enforces the selection of a definite gestalt as a figure, the multi-dimensional attention of which Paul Klee speaks can embrace both figure and ground. While vertical attention has to select a single melody, horizontal attention can comprise all polyphonic voices without choosing between them. Undifferentiated perception can grasp in a single undivided act of comprehension data that to conscious perception would be incompatible. I have elsewhere called these mutually exclusive constellations the '. . . or-or . . .' structure of the primary process. Serial structure would be a better term. While surface vision is disjunctive, low-level vision is conjunctive and serial. What appears ambiguous, multi-evocative or open-ended on a conscious level becomes a single serial structure with quite firm boundaries on an unconscious level. Because of its wider sweep low-level vision can serve as the precision instrument for scanning far-flung structures offering a great number of choices. Such structures recur regularly in any creative search.

The superior efficiency of unconscious vision in scanning the total visual field has been confirmed by experiments in subliminal vision. 'Subliminal' is only another word for unconscious, differently named only because we are still reluctant to concede a truly unconscious quality to imagery that has become inaccessible because of its undifferentiated structure alone. It is possible to speak of a purely formal 'structural' repression which gives an unconscious quality to split-second tachistoscopic exposures and to the totally invisible subliminal images. When the still visible split-second exposure in tachistoscopic experiments is cut down below a critical threshold, the image disappears and the screen remains empty. The New York psycho-analyst, Charles Fisher [10], presented Rubin's double profiles (which I have described earlier) subliminally and asked his observers to make drawings by free association. (In this way he used the same short cut to the unconscious which Freud used after he had abandoned hypnosis as a means of tapping the unconscious.) The drawings produced a significant number of images where two objects faced each other in the manner of the double profiles. Obviously the split-second exposure had sufficed for subliminal vision to pick up the positive and negative shape simultaneously. Unconscious vision is thus proved to be capable of scanning serial structures and gathering more information than a conscious scrutiny lasting a hundred times longer. With impartial acuity subliminal vision registers details irrespective of whether they belong to the figure or to the ground. It tends to reverse the conscious preference for the figure and pays more attention to textural and background elements. Such displacement of emphasis is, of course, character-istic of the primary process. Subliminal images often enter subse-quent dreams and display full-blown traits of condensation, displacement, representation by the opposite, fragmentation, duplication and other techniques of the primary process. But this again does not make it chaotic. Once dedifferentiation has been achieved, the wider serial structure of low-level images willingly accommodates and indeed contains from the outset many such possible variations of the originally selected gestalt constellation. What matters in our context is the fact that the undifferentiated structure of unconscious (subliminal) vision is far from being weakly structured or chaotic as first impressions suggest, but displays the scanning powers that are superior to conscious vision.

Perhaps the most elegant example in art of an undifferentiated serial structure, which from the outset contains an unlimited number of variations, is afforded by the technique of serialization in modern music. In serialization the same elements are scram-bled up in every possible sequence so that their relationship becomes quite obscured to conscious hearing. Yet the composer insists that, contrary to appearances, all variations are somehow equivalent. Schoenberg, who was the first to make use of syste-matic serialization, conceded that their equivalence was only unconsciously recognized. In a classical 'variation' of a theme many elements could be freely varied, but normally the sequence of the harmonic progression was preserved. For the naïve listener the inconspicuous harmonic 'accompaniment' of the melody was thus elevated to become the essential structure of music, a rather neat reversal of naïve musical values. The close integration between melody and harmony is also made explicit: melodies become close relatives if they share the same harmonic substructure. The claim of melody to represent the conscious gestalt of music is seriously challenged in favour of a more profound meaning. Serialization discards every remnant of an identical sequence and systematically attacks every vestige of a surface gestalt. I have said that the preservation of temporal sequence is the principle of acoustic gestalt. Melodies can be transposed, their key character changed; they remain recognizable as long as the sequence of the melodic steps remains the same. But once this sequence is tampered with, for instance by reversing a melody from back to front, the theme loses its identity. Yet Schoenberg considered this back-to-front reversal as the most characteristic variation of his theme. For him the twelve tones of the chromatic scale were the eternal theme containing from the outset the unlimited number of permutations which are supposed to preserve intact the identity of the theme. We are once again confronted with the chaos of the primary process which treats temporal and spatial cohesion with the same cavalier contempt. The identity of temporal sequence as the principle of an acoustic gestalt is paralleled in vision by the identity of spatial distribution. It is difficult to recognize an object if it is shown upside down, almost impossible if the spatial relationships between its elements are scrambled up. But this is precisely what happens in Picasso's portraits and in his arbitrary conglomerations of the human figure. I have argued that a total syncretistic vision that is undifferentiated in the arrangement of the details could transcend the chaotic impression and recognize the likeness and the inviolate wholeness of the human body.

Schoenberg's or Boulez's critics quite properly complained that it was impossible by ordinary means of appreciation to recognize the submerged order of serialization. Serialization directly attacks all conscious means of continuity. These critics missed the essential point that serialization meant to defeat conscious powers of appreciation. Here is a case of the intellect turning against itself. Hence the composer and listener have to take recourse to undifferentiated visualization which can hold the complex serial structure of the possible permutations in a single glance. I will show presently that the choice of a suitable fugue subject also implies an intuitive, non-intellectual grasp of the many polyphonic combinations into which the subject can enter. It can be stated as a general psychological law that any creative search involves holding before the inner eye a multitude of possible choices that totally defeat conscious comprehension. Creativity remains closely related to the chaos of the primary process. Whether we are to experience chaos or a high creative order depends entirely on the reaction of our rational faculties. If they are capable of yielding to the shift of control from conscious focusing to unconscious scanning the disruption of consciousness is hardly felt. The momentary absence of mind will be forgotten as the creative mind returns to the surface with newly won insight. If however the surface faculties react with defensive rigidity and insist on judging the contents of dedifferentiation from their own restricted focus, then the more scattered, broadly based imagery of low-level visualization impresses us as vague and chaotic. In illness the surface faculties tend to react defensively in this way. They tend to crumble catastrophically as they try to resist the surge of undifferentiated fantasies and images. The schizoid fear of chaos turns into terrible psychic reality, as the ego disintegrates.

But let us first pursue the smooth functioning of the creative ego and observe its fruitful alternation between differentiated and undifferentiated modes of functioning. Any creative search, whether for a new image or idea, involves the scrutiny of an often astronomical number of possibilities. The correct choice between them cannot be made by a conscious weighing up of each single possibility cropping up during the search; if attempted it would only lead us astray. A creative search resembles a maze with many nodal points (figure 4). From each of these points many possible pathways radiate in all directions leading to further crossroads where a new network of high- and by-ways comes into view. Each choice is equally crucial for further progress. The choice would be easy if we could command an aerial view of the

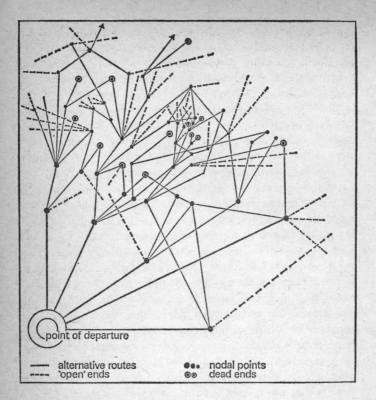

point of departure

——— alternative routes   ●●● nodal points
----- 'open' ends   ◉◉ dead ends

Figure 4. The maze (serial structure) of a creative search. The creative thinker has to advance on a broad front keeping open many options. He must gain a comprehensive view of the entire structure of the way ahead without being able to focus on any single possibility.

entire network of nodal points and radiating pathways still lying ahead. This is never the case. If we could map out the entire way ahead, no further search would be needed. As it is, the creative thinker has to make a decision about his route without having the full information needed for his choice. This dilemma belongs to the essence of creativity. The structure of a mathematical problem is a neat example. The creative thinker has to scrutinize it without any hope of a really clear view. Let us say an algebraic equation has to be transformed by a number of consecutive steps until it assumes a form that can be accepted as the solution of some unsolved problem. Each possible transformation opens up an unlimited number of new transformations, some fruitful, some ending in blind alleys. Admittedly, strict rules exist that govern algebraic transformations; but they do not say which of the possible transformations will prove fertile in the end. In order to judge the fruitfulness of each new step one has somehow to anticipate the entire route ahead. But a clear view is not possible, if only because of the great number of mutually exclusive possibilities. They add up to typical serial structures that overflow the narrow focus of normal attention. This means that the creative mathematician, as in any truly original problem in art and science, has to make correct decisions without having the full information needed for them. The mathematician, Hadamard [15], who became interested in the psychology of mathematical thought, emphatically states that any attempt at visualizing the way ahead clearly only leads astray; the decision must be left to the unconscious. This demand implies my hypothesis that unconscious visualization is better equipped for scanning the complex serial structure of a new mathematical argument. Hadamard admits that the student cannot start by blotting out his conscious attention. He has first to learn the conscious rules governing mathematical transformations and he will check each step according to these rules. But at a certain point, which has to do with the awakening of creativity, he has to abandon precise visualization. Instead of concentrating on each single step he has to reach out and grasp the total structure of the argument as compared with any other possible structure. He has to visualize syncretistically the total structure though he cannot look sufficiently far ahead to see clearly the detailed choices and decisions awaiting him. In Wittgenstein's words: his view must be comprehensive though not clear in detail. Hadamard, like Poincaré before him, states categorically that it is necessary to cloud one's consciousness in order to make the right decision. But, of course, conscious vagueness is not enough if it does not lead to a shift of attention to unfocused low-level vision.

An excessive need for clear visualization is prompted by the schizoid dissociation of ego functions. It is characteristic of a rigid uncreative personality who cannot let go his hold on the surface functions. Ironically, academic teaching usually puts a premium on the precise visualization of the working process and its result. A good craftsman in any sphere of learning is exalted for his full control of the working process. He is supposed to see the way ahead with clarity and choose the most direct route to a desired result. For the beginner such ambitions are praiseworthy. But they become nonsense and a nuisance as soon as the craftsman has to solve a new truly original task. There he can only have a comprehensive, but not clearly detailed view, in the manner of the mysterious syncretistic vision which can be precise in grasping a total structure the components of which are interchangeable.

An exaggerated need for clear visualization will even be harmful in playing a comparatively simple combination game like chess or bridge. The playing of combination games is not unlike creative work. It too requires the scanning of serial structures in order to decide strategy. A game of bridge can develop in many ways according to the distribution of the cards among the players. In order to play the right card or to make the right bid the player must evaluate the many possible distributions of the cards. The permutations in the possible distributions represent typical serial structures. I myself, being an exceedingly bad player, have to consider every possible constellation one by one and, of course, usually end up by making a wrong decision. I will fail because I cannot widen the narrow focus of normal everyday attention and can only deal with one possible distribution at a time. The experienced player, gifted with a mysterious card sense, can consider all relevant distributions in a split second, holding them in a single view as it were. If we were to ask him how he performed this feat and what was actually in his mind when he was scrutinizing the 'structure' of a particular game he would probably be unable to tell us. His attention was blank and blurred while unconscious scanning went on in deeper levels of his mind. Any attempt at a more precise visualization would be as confusing for him as it is in a creative search. If at the crucial moment of choice we try to size up a situation too clearly we will automatically narrow the scope of our attention and so deprive ourselves of the faculty of low-level scanning on which the right move depends.

Playing games is rarely a creative activity; the number of possible choices, however many, are strictly limited by the rules of the game. No such limiting rules exist in creative work; it creates its own rules which may only be known after the work is finished. The serial structure of the search must always contain unknown variables and the creative thinker must somehow be able to accommodate them without losing in precision. When I said that creative thought implied a capacity for handling imprecise material with utmost precision I had these open variables in mind. I have mentioned how gestalt perception tends to close gaps and smooth away imperfections that mar otherwise coherent and simple material. For instance, it is difficult to detect among a row of perfect identical circles that one imperfect circle which shows a small gap in its circumference. The 'law of closure' postulated by the gestalt theory will always tend to round off and simplify the images and concepts of conscious thought. It makes it difficult, if not impossible, for rational thought to handle 'open' material without rounding it off prematurely. A secondary revision will tend to impart to such material a greater precision and compactness than it actually possesses. This can lead to wrong results. Low-level visualization, by comparison, would be better equipped for dealing with open forms and so avoiding the pitfalls prepared by the 'law of closure'. Geometricians, architects, logicians, all of whom mostly handle material of almost perfect gestalt, have to learn to beware of the law of closure. They tend to 'idealize' their material, and are often intolerant of fragmentation. For instance, logicians, concerned as they are with the imperfections of everyday language, try to perfect it so as to make it an ideal instrument for describing truth and reality. In his later work Wittgenstein recognized that he had succumbed to this wish to idealize language and the almost compulsive need to give it maximum clarity. He rejected his famous *Tractatus*, the book on which his reputation still largely rests. He had first thought he could describe the inherent precision of language by comparing its logical structure to the structure of a picture. This was the famous 'picture theory' of language. He assumed – rather naïvely as a painter would think – that a picture consisted of elements whose structure could be analysed and matched against reality in an objective way. He hoped that the logical structure of language had a similarly precise relationship to reality. We know now – after Gombrich – that pictorial realism affords none of this objective one-to-one relationship between its elements and reality. It is entirely based on learning conventional 'schemata'. Later in life Wittgenstein rejected his picture theory of language. In his *Philosophical Investigations* [35] (the following quotations of paragraphs refer to this work) he substituted for it another model. Language is a 'game' the rules of which we have to make up as we go along (paragraph 83). Wittgenstein deals here with the creative use of language. We have seen how, generally, in using images creatively (words are only a specific case of mental image making), we are formulating our rules of the game as we go along. A clear view of their use will emerge only after the creative search is over. Classical logic only deals with the well-defined word imagery which is available after the search is over, and new insights have to be moulded into a clearly defined exposition in order to communicate a new discovery to others. Wittgenstein, in spite of his protest that he was not a psychologist, was really concerned with the same depth-psychology of creative thought with which Hadamard and Poincaré were concerned. Philosophy often anticipates subjects of research that are later taken up by a new developing science. I feel that Wittgenstein's later theories will only be fully understood when the depth-psychological problems implicit in his majestic struggle with language are made explicit. Let us listen to his own words. In paragraph 126 of the *Philosophical Investigations* he speaks of the structure of our thought as it exists before an illuminating discovery is made and when there are still contradictions to solve. He says that it is not the business of the logician to solve and clarify these contradictions, but to give a comprehensive (*übersehbar*) view of the disquieting state of affairs before the contradiction is resolved (paragraph 125). In my own view, the disquieting aspect of language in this state is the ambiguous serial structure of mutually incompatible attempts at a final solution. These mutually contradictory possibilities have to be held in a comprehensive (*übersehbar*) view. This fully agrees with my concept of an undifferentiated unfocused vision inherent in any creative search. It appears vague, yet must nevertheless be precise and comprehensive. How difficult it was for Wittgenstein to communicate his insights is evident from the faulty translation of the word *übersehbar* by his disciple, G. E. M. Anscombe. She renders it as 'perspicuous' or 'clear' (paragraphs 122, 125), a dangerous and misleading leaning towards the need for 'crystal-purity' and clarity which Wittgenstein was so anxious to reject as a compulsive idealization of language. The dilemma in the use of symbols in a creative search is not that their use is altogether vague or lacking in perspicuity (this is largely unavoidable), but that this vagueness in detail must not prevent us from gaining a comprehensive and precise all-over view of the problem. This formulation is almost identical with Hadamard's description of the need for grasping the total structure of a mathematical argument which must be precise though one cannot have a clear view of the single steps that compose that total structure. We are once again back at the dilemma of syncretism; a comprehensive and precise grasp of a total view in which the elements are variable and exchangeable. We *are* capable – so Wittgenstein says – of understanding a word 'in a flash', though its precise meaning is not yet definable, but will emerge only through the whole subsequent use of the word (paragraph 139). Wittgenstein's followers often made nonsense of their master's teaching by interpreting this saying as an apology for woolly thinking. But it is only a statement about how words are actually used. Even something vague can be said with precision. The meaning of a word lies in its future use; yet the meaning must already be present as we grasp its meaning in a flash, 'yet it is not present' (paragraph 197). Wittgenstein dismisses the paradox. We need not know the full use of the word in order to grasp it in a flash of understanding. Often the detailed information will be simply not yet there. The main thing is that we know how to play the language game, although – as in a real game – we cannot anticipate all the possible moves that are open according to the rules which we are still making up.

Wittgenstein's paradox is resolved by introducing the concept of unconscious scanning. Consciously we would not be able to grasp all the future usages of a word, but unconscious scanning can. The complication arises that objectively all the future usages may not yet exist at present and so are beyond unconscious scanning. We have to put it in a more sophisticated way: unconscious scanning – in contrast to conscious thought which needs closed gestalt patterns – can handle 'open' structures with blurred frontiers which will be drawn with proper precision only in the unknowable future. The lawgiver has to use words in just this way. He has to anticipate usages of his legal terms that might become necessary through social and economic developments in the unforeseeable future. The architect, in designing a service-able building, also has to anticipate a number of possible uses for the building that are partly determined by unknowable future factors. In short these open forms are able to absorb genuine 'accidents' that fall wholly outside any kind of rational planning. Tentative scientific terms, good laws and good buildings are only 'defined' by subsequent use. Yet in all these cases – the logical use of words, the formulation of legal statutes, the design of buildings – the creative thinker has to grasp in a flash the total function of his work as distinct from its more detailed uses. Playing the creative game well is all that is needed. Precise visualization or worse still a straining of one's attention to see crystal-clearness where there is in fact none, will only produce wrong or unusable results.

In teaching foreign languages we may start with training the student in grammar and syntax. This gives him precise rules for assembling whole sentences from words, the basic material of language. If the student becomes too satisfied with the mechani-cal computation of his sentences he will fail to grasp the spirit of a living language. It can only be felt by scanning the unlimitable range of constellations into which words are fitted in their daily use. This scanning, of course, defies conscious analysis and is not teachable as such. It depends on the psychological constitution of the student whether an overemphasis on detailed grammatical analysis and computation could be harmful for him and should be replaced by a more intuitive total grasp of language. Similar decisions must be taken in devising the syllabus in an art school. As long as rational analysis and intuitive work are both given their due, their combination in a particular case should not present insuperable difficulties. Ways must be found for stimu-lating low-level sensibilities and true spontaneity without neces-sarily disrupting reason and the gestalt tendencies supporting reason. However, whenever we are faced with defensive rigidity in an art student we may still have to find ways for resolving it and clearing away the rationalizations that are put forward to justify it. I mentioned a defensive attitude of this kind when I discussed the immature student's wish for a fully conscious control of the working process. We may neutralize or bypass the defences by turning the student's attention immediately to the uncontrollable factors in art, such as the emergence of pictorial space, or the hidden discipline governing those textures in music that imperceptibly distort articulate pitch, rhythm and intensity. We cannot discourage outright a young pianist's ambition to acquire full physical control over his fingers. The anatomic differences between the muscular action of the five fingers are such that it is exceedingly difficult to give them equal weight in depressing the piano keys. Daily exercises are needed for equalizing the muscular handicap of the weaker fingers. In the end the pianist is able to play scales with an absolute regularity of speed and intensity. But if he achieves too absolute a control he may fail to attend properly to the subtler irregularities of his playing. There is a 'wisdom of the body'. The pianist should never lose the habit of listening to his own finger action in the way a violinist must check his pitch or the painter must watch the spreading of his brush mark. But because the pitch of the piano strings is fixed, the bad pianist will just control his muscular action and neglect listening to the seeming imperfections in the regularity of his playing, for instance the *rubato* that imperceptibly distorts the iron rigidity of the beat. These organic distortions of rhythm cannot be taught, nor achieved by conscious control. They are part of those inarticulate textures that can only be shaped by an unconscious form discipline. The dutiful pianist wishes to acquire first the necessary craftsmanship for regularizing and equalizing the action of his fingers. If he ignores the spontaneous inflections of his playing he will kill the spirit of living music. He will neither listen to what his own body tells him nor respect the independent life of his work. He will inevitably fail as an artist. Creativity is always linked with the happy moment when all conscious control can be forgotten. What is not sufficiently realized is the genuine conflict between two kinds of sensibility, conscious intellect and unconscious intuition. One sensibility will feed on the other, whenever the ego rigidity brings about their dissociation. Bad art teaching and the wrong kind of ambition will exacerbate this dissociation.

It is not an advantage if the creative thinker has to handle elements that are precise in themselves such as geometric or architectural diagrams. Their near perfect gestalt appeals too much to the gestalt principle and its law of closure. They resist the dedifferentiation needed for fruitful unconscious scanning.

Hadamard came to the conclusion that the use of diagrams in doing geometry – I am thinking of course of creative inventions – is misleading because their neatness is apt to obscure the complexity (serial structure) of a problem. He trained himself to ignore the good gestalt of such diagrams and purposely diverted his attention to some, in itself meaningless, detail. The subjective destruction of the good gestalt is needed even if the material which is to be handled objectively possesses qualities of good gestalt.

In uncreative mechanical computation according to fixed rules, precise visualization, far from being harmful, will help the computer. Hadamard suggests that Greek geometry lost its creative impetus in Hellenistic times because of too precise visualization. It produced generations of clever computers and geometers, but no true geometricians. Development in geometric theory stopped altogether. Descartes broke the deadlock by doing away with precise visualization and the seduction of neat diagrams. He invented analytical geometry which expressed geometric relationships by numbers only. Today non-Euclidean geometry precludes the precise visualization of a stable space grid. We are faced with dynamic interaction between several shifting space systems. No precise focusing is possible. No wonder that space intuition is the rarest of gifts among mathematicians.

It is equally rare among architects. They have never fully faced up to the inherent difficulties of space visualization. Their failure in teaching good design is so great that at least one leading school of architecture has postponed any kind of drawing or design until a late stage in favour of a more general, not necessarily visual education. This is educational bankruptcy. The diagrammatic representation of an architectural structure can serve two purposes. It can serve as the exposition of a finished design or as a visual aid in search of a not yet existing solution. If used as a creative tool for invention it ought to remain vague and open-ended, so as not to pre-empt the solution at too early a stage. In other words, the uncreative use of diagrams for exposition must not be confused with its creative use in visualizing vague and tentative attempts at new solutions of a problem. A young architecture student once told me how horrified his teacher was when he began toying with a design problem by concentrating on a detail of the elevation before visualizing the ground plan. Academic teaching is wont to put a premium on powers of precise visualization, not only in the arts, but also in music or in science, and certainly also in logic, as Wittgenstein's vain battle exemplifies. I would explain this insistent demand for precision in academic teaching as a defensive secondary process in a psycho-analytic sense; the slighted surface faculties try to suppress unconscious scanning in order to retain full control of the working process. The necessary blurring of conscious focusing is felt as a danger and a threat of total chaos. This fear may be only another aspect of the more general misunderstanding of unconscious participation in creative work. As I have said, Wittgenstein's acceptance of vagueness in everyday language is often misunderstood as the advocacy of vague, woolly thinking. Hadamard's recommended procedure in the use of diagrams in geometry displaces the emphasis from important features to insignificant details. How easily could this advice be construed as encouragement of chaos! The displacement of proper emphasis is a typical primary-process technique. It is not easy for dry academicians to accept that syncretistic primary-process techniques rather than analytic clarity of detail are needed by the creative thinker to control the vast complexities of his work. Nor will my argument convince them.

Part Two
Creative Conflict

4   The Fertile Motif and the Happy Accident

Creative research proceeds in steps and stages; each of them represents an interim result that cannot yet be connected with the final solution. Even if the proposed solution is given, as happens in the search for the proof of a tentative proposition, the path to it is unknown. Euler, who had a knack for inventing new proofs, often chose the most devious routes that, on a conscious level, could have no direct bearing on the final result. He would invent obscure symbols, the precise function of which would emerge only after the proof had been completed. This use of symbols is fully in accordance with Wittgenstein's description of a creative use of language where the exact meaning (function) of words would only become known by their later use. The creative thinker has to move and make interim decisions without being able to visualize their precise relationship with the end product. I have described how he manages to extract from this half-baked material information far in excess of its face value. He keeps his conscious visualization intentionally clouded and imprecise and leaves it to unconscious scanning to guide him on his way.

An American critic once complained to me about the usual conception of action painting as being concerned exclusively with muscular action. While it was true, he said, that the action painter could not precisely foresee the end result, he was very much concerned with the state of his painting at each particular stage. Each stage imposed on him new choices and decisions that he could not have foreseen at an earlier stage. I hope that the reader has by now recognized that this description fits any kind of creative work. However, to say that the creative mind is indifferent to the final outcome obscures the real issue. The creative searcher is, of course, extremely concerned about the effect his interim decisions might have on the end result, but he must be able to bear the suspense. Stanley W. Hayter, the pioneer of modern engraving, once described in a lecture how he overcame in his teaching the narrow professionalism of traditional engraving. He would tell his pupils to work in successive stages without pre-planning the composition. Each stage introduced some new motif or technical procedure. The students were to invent first a single motif, then balance it with a counter motif that enriched the first one, and add step by step new ideas and techniques. There was a mysterious logic and cohesion in the gradual build-up of the composition. Each step was equally crucial even though its relevance could not be precisely visualized at the time. If the pupil took the right step, it would quicken the flow of ideas; if he took a wrong one, his ideas would soon dry up and bring the work to a premature standstill. As in any creative work the student had to make the correct decision though the information for making it was not at hand.

A truly fertile 'motif' – in music or drama as well as in the visual arts – often has something incomplete and vague about its structure. It bears the imprint of the undifferentiated vision which created it in the first place and which guides its use. Its open imperfect structure is far removed from the neat compact gestalt of logical, geometric, architectural material which panders to the gestalt needs of conscious vision. A fertile motif, through its undifferentiated structure, often refuses immediate aesthetic satisfaction and for its justification points to its further development in the future. A good musical theme is rarely a good and expressive melody. But once we have listened to the complete performance we may no longer be bothered, in retrospect, by the theme's frayed edges and lack of polish. The imperfections are now justified by the later developments. These were somehow already contained in the theme's original shape. As they pressed around it they prevented it from setting hard too early. The gestalt law of 'closure' ruling our surface vision will always strive to round it off and polish its structure prematurely and so may cut off its further development. It is as difficult to hold on to the imperfections of a good theme as to invent it in the first place. Fortunately, the creative thinker is at home in those deeper mental levels where the gestalt principle no longer holds sway.

For him an insignificant scrap of melody or bit of texture may contain the key to the emerging total structure far more securely than a well-rounded melody or carefully worked out composition. It is accepted as a general principle of art education that the student must learn to resist the aesthetic attraction of some happy detail achieved too early; he must be able to destroy it in order to safeguard the integrity of the whole. An aspiring poet must learn to delete the felicities of a purple phrase much as the composer must resist the lure of sonority for its own sake, which appeals to our love of beauty and in the last resort to the demands of the (conscious) gestalt principle.

A conscious analysis of the future fertility of a motif is impossible. This is true even where rules for its development exist, as in a fugue or a sonnet. Choosing a good fugue subject is of crucial importance. But no conscious rules will help in making the right choice. We have to scan intuitively the complex polyphonic textures into which it will interweave. Bach was greatly admired for his deftness in inventing or borrowing good subjects. So uncanny seemed his gift to his contemporaries that he was credited with possessing a secret recipe handed down through the many generations of the great Bach family. There was, of course, no such recipe. But the anecdote brings out our tacit acknowledgement of the fact that rational analysis of a motif cannot evaluate its future uses. We are up against the same problem which Wittgenstein faced up to so bravely in the logical use of words.

There is no definite recipe for breaking the pernicious rule of preconceived design and for setting free the diffuse inarticulate vision of the unconscious. Michelangelo, a superb craftsman, sometimes started with a wholly traditional scheme, but under his hands the scheme bulged and swelled and assumed gigantic proportions. Adrian Stokes in his book *Michelangelo, A Study in the Nature of Art* [31] put forward a convincing explanation how, unconsciously to Michelangelo, the realistic forms of his male nudes bulged and distended as an unconscious symbol of their ambisexuality, where male and female characteristics become intermingled. He explains Michelangelo's *terribilità* from this unconscious ambiguity, which defeats rational comprehension and so evokes anxiety. Beethoven is often compared with Michelangelo; yet, if we accept the evidence of his notebooks, his method of composition was often different. Like Michelangelo he finally arrived at structures on a grand scale, but he did not always start with the total structure and allow it to burst at the seams. He often adopted something like a 'tachist' method; he teased and worried little bits of inarticulate melody, insignificant in themselves, until they yielded, often after a struggle lasting years, extended phrases, whole movements and perhaps the all-over structure itself. The third (slow) movement of the *Hammerclavier Sonata* still startles me by a sudden twist that breaks into the broad beautiful *cantilena* and produces a melodic as well as an harmonic rupture. The notebooks tell us that it was not the broad adagio theme but this abrupt transition which Beethoven first noted down (figure 5). How strange: a transition between melodies not yet existing! The melodies themselves unfolded later from this rupture between them. Beethoven never revised the break while he kept on filing and refining the broad melodies. Here we have a good example of an inarticulate disruptive idea which guides and unfolds the large-scale structures. A fully articulate well-knit melody belongs altogether too much to consciousness. An incoherent fragment, a disruptive form element is better able to break the narrow focus of intellectual thought and produce a fissure in the mind's smooth surface which leads down to the depth of the unconscious.

I am not advocating the use of scraps and bits of texture as artistic motifs. Chaos as such has no merit. It is an advantage, however, if a motif lacks objective qualities of good gestalt and can repel an exclusively conscious attention more easily. The fact that a melody is well turned or an image neat and self-contained does not *per se* exclude its use as a fertile motif; but it becomes more difficult for it to resist the attractions of surface attention. In order to develop a beautiful motif of this kind it may become necessary first to fragment and distort it so that it can enter lower undifferentiated levels of image making. This is what often happens in the development section of a classical sonata movement. The theme may well be a beautiful extended melody. Developing often means tearing it to shreds with little regard for its coherent phrasing in an almost frontal attack on the gestalt principle, which fails to safeguard its integrity. It is not the objective structure of the theme that matters, nor its good or bad gestalt qualities, it is the subjective use to which it is put.

The creative thinker in contemplating the theme's all too precise and compact gestalt must be able to break it down or tease its edges open so that it becomes more malleable material akin to the serial structures of low-level vision. A textile motif has this double nature. Taken by itself in isolation it may represent a neat self-contained image giving immediate aesthetic satisfaction. Yet it has to be obliterated as an image in its own right in order to be developed into the all-over texture of a printed or woven cloth. We would be bothered if in looking at a piece of cloth we

Bar 13

Figure 5. The rupture in the third movement of the *Hammerclavier Sonata*. The high B natural after the bar line makes a complete break in the melodic line, and the grace note only emphasizes the rupture and does not bind the high B to the preceding phrase. Most pianists, even Schnabel, underplay the rupture, depriving the initial *cantilena* of its hot *appassionato* and the interrupting phrase of coolness.

were to see the same little picture duplicated wherever we look. To be effective the textile motif must be submerged and its edges blurred where it intertwines with its own replica, in much the same way as a fugue subject joins with itself to weave its rich polyphonic structure. The textural effect is qualitatively different from the aesthetic appeal of the single motif. All the creative effort goes into the invention of one single motif, but its final transformation cannot be predicted with any precision. Textile design as it is taught today as a humble branch of commercial art is not conducive to imaginativeness and creativity. It is too much concerned with the mechanical technicalities of the so-called 'repeat' (the polyphonic repetition of the motif). The student fails to realize the immense creative challenge presented by the invention of a truly original motif. The average student, concerned as he is with the neat fitting of the repeat, will feel bothered instead of delighted by the total transformation of his pretty motif as it sinks into the emergent all-over texture. What would be needed (but is never done) is to train him to look at a motif in a twofold way. He is entitled to enjoy it as a little image in its own right. But this pleasure must not interfere with its more important evaluation as a growth element from which the future all-over texture is to develop. Conscious analysis will not help him. He must blot out in his subjective vision the motif's too precise and compact gestalt and transform it into a blurred, hardly articulate scrap that wins aesthetic merit only by its final obliteration.

Motifs preserve their fertility only if their connexion with the final result remains obscure. Otherwise they turn into mechanical assembly devices. I have mentioned how architectural design is hampered by its tendency to visualize too precisely and by its abuse of diagrammatic aids (ground plan, elevation, etc.). These visual aids seem to allow a precise presentation of the architectural problem, but in fact obscure it. It is vital for good design to break down the design process into stages that have no obvious connexion with the final result. Creative bursts in the recent history of architecture managed to break the hold of mannered formulae by inventing disruptive devices that stemmed the headlong rush to some predetermined solution. For a time any newly discovered functionalist factor served this purpose. Superficially, functionalism represents a purely rational, fully conscious approach to design. But functional factors when still unfamiliar complicate the design process and make its eventual result quite uncertain. They force the designer to consider each factor in separate interim stages leading to interim decisions that are as yet unconnected with the final structure. The earlier technological type of functionalism utilized the technological limitations imposed by new materials and techniques and so arrived at new solutions. Modern building techniques soon proved so flexible that they could be made to conform with almost any preconceived structure. Today architects are casting around for sociological factors that would introduce welcome complication into their calculations. So great is their need that they are often not content to serve existing social needs, but see themselves as social reformers creating new needs for them to satisfy. I am not deprecating this new functionalism. However doubtful in their social aspirations, these factors serve their role as creative catalysts well enough. Le Corbusier's *L'Unité d'Habitation* at Marseilles may not have succeeded in creating a new community, but it certainly created a new architectural shape expressing his deep humanism.

Le Corbusier's modulor began as a true motif. It served as a growth element to be developed into an unpredictable all-over structure. As a basic architectural unit it corresponds to certain human measurements and to the cosmic order of the Golden Section. But these conscious intentions matter comparatively little. The use of the modulor prevented him from previsualizing the final solution too easily. Instead of starting from the outer shell of a building, such as a stylish façade, he had to develop his design from within in interim stages, starting from the smallest unit. For a time, Le Corbusier hoped to have invented a permanent recipe for good design. But it worked as a creative catalyst only as long as it disrupted a too-early visualization of the end result. As a disruptive device the modulor was as shortlived as the various functionalist factors before. Le Corbusier's disciples soon learned to assemble it into very much the same kind of buildings they had built before. It is not easy to block our conscious gestalt need for precise visualization for long. A defensive secondary process will soon counteract the disruption of conscious visualization and transform the originally disruptive device into a mechanical assembly device fully under conscious control. Intuition and unconscious scanning are once again replaced by rational planning and foresight. The creative conflict between the opposing principles is never resolved.

An amusing counterpart to the quick demise of the modulor as a creative catalyst is afforded by Richard Wagner's invention of the *leitmotiv*. It served the master well enough, but failed to supply the permanent recipe it was first hoped to be. The *leitmotiv* resembles the modulor in that it too broke up the traditional set pieces of grand opera and forced Wagner to reconstruct the large-scale structure of opera from within, starting with the motif as the smallest unit. The various *leitmotivs* were related organically to dramatic motifs of the plot and were spun and woven together into melody and polyphony according to the changing dramatic situation. For Wagner, the resulting melodic and polyphonic effects remained unpredictable. When in *Götterdämmerung* he used motifs he had invented in his *Das Rheingold* twenty years earlier, he felt filled with awe and wonder at the novelty of the sound he was able to elicit from the well-worn material. Not so his disciples. For them the *leitmotiv* became an assembly device for putting together another conventional operatic form, this time the teutonic music drama. All that was needed was to invent a number of suitable motifs related to incidents in the plot and string them together illustrating musically the happenings on the stage. Certainly the much vaunted unity of the music drama was assured; yet the method proved sterile. The deliberate assembly of motifs led to entirely predictable results in the sonorous Wagnerian style.

Basic-design courses which have become popular in progressive art schools all over the world are now affected by the same withering due to the reaction of the anti-intuitive secondary processes (secondary revision). Art schools usually take up advances in art after a time-lag of ten and twenty years, long after they have lost their disruptive power. The principle of 'free self-expression' still reigns in the nursery and infant schools as a residue of romantic and dada ideas that have largely lost their meaning for the art of today. The present sweeping victory of basic design in our art schools testifies that abstract art has gained an almost too decisive victory. Indeed a yearning to fill up its already empty forms with some sort of new meaning has become urgent outside the art colleges. When basic design was first introduced in the days of the *Bauhaus* and the renaissance of the *Bauhaus* tradition during the nineteen-fifties, it did not arrive as the desiccated analysis of pure empty form which it is largely today. In the heroic period of abstract art the disruption of academic cliché had a liberating and exhilarating effect. It was sufficient to cut across careful methods of deliberate composition and instead use simple 'basic' procedures without any definite aim in mind in order to produce exciting and relevant imagery. Rauschenberg recollects how it came as a revelation to him when his teacher tore up his careful composition and reassembled the bits casually. Today such physical fragmentation will neither shock, nor come as a revelation. Basic-design methods even when they use disruption of this kind lead to fully predictable results, examples of which can be seen in commercial art galleries everywhere.

The assembly of the most 'basic' shapes of all, dots, straight lines, squares, circles etc., is considered particularly beneficial in educating a beginner's aesthetic sensibilities. It is difficult to see why. After what we have found out about the dangerous seductiveness of precise forms in geometry and architecture, it becomes obvious that this is a particularly difficult exercise to handle. Through their appeal to the conscious gestalt principle, geometric forms will impede the scattering of attention needed for watching the emergent total structure as distinct from focusing on the isolated basic elements. Geometry will not easily melt into the full emptiness of low-level vision. It is certainly an advantage to make the student aware that any composition however complex can be assembled from simple elements. This makes for clean athletic design. But it could also lead to the self-deception that the designer can gain a fully conscious control of his working process by being aware of the basic elements. An excessive preoccupation with the geometric units could make the designer blind to the qualitative transformation which takes place as the units fuse into a more complex total structure. It can be intensely exciting to watch their organic growth, which cannot be predicted in any way from the nature of the single units. Without this sensibility to their growth a too deliberate handling of the elements will prevent the development of the intuitive (syncretistic) capacity needed for scanning the constantly shifting inter-relations on which their organic life depends. We should expect that, as in doing geometry or logic, intuitive scanning comes into its own only when the student learns to blot out his over-precise visualization and allows his attention to shift to lower mental levels. With geometric elements this is particularly difficult. Students already affected by a measure of ego rigidity may well be harmed by geometric exercises. They should be abandoned as a general method of basic art teaching.

Good art teaching has always intuitively disrupted the student's over-precise visualization. If he has learned to master one particular medium too well, the teacher would make him switch to a new unfamiliar technique that can still frustrate his preconceived intentions. Rigid students can be deeply perturbed by their lack of full control and could dismiss the unavoidable awkwardnesses and accidents as playful and insignificant results that had no meaning for them. Psycho-analysis, of course, has taught us to evaluate accidents differently. Freud coined the phrase a 'psycho-pathology of everyday life'; he discussed how unconscious fantasy utilizes a breakdown of conscious planning in order to infiltrate and take its due share in the business of our lives. The mature artist keeps his intentions flexible enough – by his capacity for ranging freely through the many differentiated and dedifferentiated levels of consciousness – and is able to do without a fully conscious control of his medium. The wood carver is delighted and not upset when the wood grain inside his block gradually reveals itself and by its obstinate twists compels him to modify his tentative ideas. 'Accident' is a relative term. The same unpredictable incident which may severely disrupt the planning of a rigid student and appear to him a frustrating 'accident', will come as a welcome and indeed invited refinement of the more flexible planning of the mature artist. The British painter, Heinz Koppel, has talked about the beneficial conflict between the artist's point of departure and the resisting medium. If an idea is really new, the artist can never predict how it is to be realized in a medium. A new idea will inevitably be modified through its impact on the resisting medium and conversely impose entirely new uses on the medium. In the end, by their mutual impact both idea and medium will be realized in a more profound manner. The idea will be purified of preconceived and manneristic elements unrelated to the rest of the personality and become enriched by unconscious fantasies that were excluded from the initial conception. The artist feels this need for expanding his point of departure and will welcome the independent life of his medium. Something like a true conversation takes place between the artist and his own work. The medium, by frustrating the artist's purely conscious intentions, allows him to contact more submerged parts of his own personality and draw them up for conscious contemplation. While the artist struggles with his medium, unknown to himself he wrestles with his unconscious personality revealed by the work of art. Taking back from the work on a conscious level what has been projected into it on an unconscious level is perhaps the most fruitful and painful result of creativity. In Part III, I will show that one can distinguish three phases in creative work: projection, followed by the partly unconscious integration (unconscious scanning) which gives the work its independent life, and finally the partial re-introjection and feedback on a higher mental level.

One has to explain to the student that a purely conscious control of the working process is neither desirable nor possible. The rigid art student often comes to the college motivated by the pious wish for good craftsmanship, which he misconceives as a fully conscious control of his medium. He wants to put down exactly 'what he has in mind'. It is useless to explain to him that what he has in mind are usually clichés and mannerisms which he has picked up from existing art in a life-long devotion to the master works of the past and present and that really new ideas do not allow a predictable use of the medium. True craftsmanship does not impose its will on the medium, but explores its varying responses in the kind of conversation between equals I have described. A passive but acute watchfulness for subtle variations in the medium's response is the true achievement of craftsmanship. The first brush stroke on a white piece of paper sends a shudder right across the pictorial plane contained by the four edges of the paper. It is never possible to predict which precise shape a brush stroke will form on the paper. Its juiciness, clear definition, gradation of tone depends on the varying consistency of the paint, on the changing proportion of oil and turpentine. These in turn will influence the elasticity of the brush and the pressure required. The wear-and-tear of the bristles during the work and their physical response to paint will also determine the exact shape of the mark. Hence utter watchfulness is the first demand of craftsmanship, a split-second reaction to innumerable variables which will enforce a subtle change of plan and make us respond willingly to the ever new shapes growing and interacting before our eyes. An excessive wish for control will blind the student's sensitivities to such subtle variations.

I have mentioned the shudder which every brush stroke sends across the picture plane. Its pulse contributes to the gradual emergence of a dynamic 'pictorial space', the most unpredictable and at the same time most significant result of painting. It has nothing to do with traditional perspective and its realistic illusion of depth. A Vermeer interior gives this illusionistic depth. But at the same time, like all master works, the picture plane has its own life; its elements keep heaving in and out with little regard to illusionistic realism. New American painting has made us more aware of this abstract pictorial space. It represents the secret independent life of art utterly beyond conscious planning and control. I have mentioned how any increase in the unconscious substructure of art will produce as its outward signal on a conscious level an enhanced plastic effect, much in the way in which, according to Freud, particularly vivid parts of the dream indicate a complex unconscious substructure. This explains why the miracle of pictorial space, its mighty pulse that heaves through the picture plane, must remain for ever beyond conscious control. It is the result of a well-integrated unconscious substructure and the complex cross-ties that bind all the elements together whose serial structure can only be shaped and scanned by the wider focus of low-level vision. A good pictorial space, then, is a measure of proper unconscious control as opposed to conscious planning. Hence the importance of impressing on the students the unpredictable impact of the simplest element – like a single brush stroke – on the flat picture plane. They have to realize how the first black brush mark on a piece of white paper sends a ripple right across it. The rigid student bent on complete conscious control of the working process will blind himself to the constant modulations of pictorial space while the structure of the work gradually unfolds. Conscious composition must constantly react to the heavings of pictorial space. Once the student has made himself sensitive to the dynamic instability of pictorial space he has also made contact with art's substructure. He will learn by and by how to make use of unconscious scanning for the real control of the immense complexities of art. The importance of teaching awareness of pictorial space can hardly be exaggerated. It helps to emphasize the hidden order of art and the oscillating plastic effects which are its outward signal. The illusionist perspective of the old realism opened up a vista behind the canvas. Today's pictorial space bulges towards the spectator and almost envelops him in its embrace.

The impression of a heaving, pulsating pictorial space is entirely subjective, dependent, as I have suggested, on the unconscious scanning of the enormous complexities hidden in a work of art. I once demonstrated the subjectivity of pictorial space by showing a diagrammatic map of the London Underground railway (figure 6). The design has undoubted aesthetic

merits. We do not react to them if we consult the map just for
information about train routes; it then remains flat. But if we

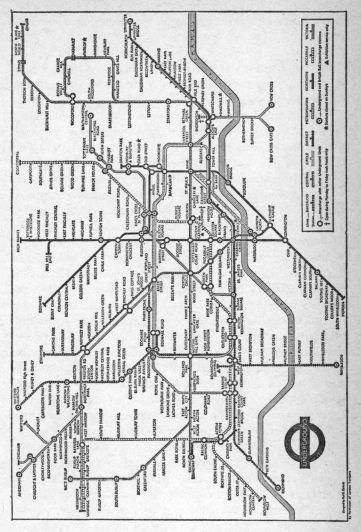

Figure 6. Map of the London Underground railway. Seen as an
informative diagram the pattern remains flat; seen as an aesthetic
design it is transformed into plastic pictorial space, with lines
intertwining and oscillating. (This is particularly noticeable if you
turn the page upside down.)

choose to look at it as a good design, the lines of the diagram will suddenly detach themselves from the surface and rhythmically intertwine and embrace each other. This change indicates that we no longer react with our reason alone, and have mobilized deeper levels of sensitivity.

Summing up, we can say that art teaching should use disruptive techniques that attack our surface sensibilities only as far as they can serve to stimulate deeper unconscious sensibilities. Accidents are useful if they displace control from conscious to unconscious levels of the mind. Pouring paint was not Jackson Pollock's invention. For a long time past tasteful book-endpapers have been produced by pouring oil-paint on water and taking monoprints from the curling strands of paint floating on the water. The pleasing decorative effects of the monoprint are not felt as 'accident' nor can they upset conscious planning in any way. Any conscious intentions are too thin, flabby and blind for that. They certainly do not help to sharpen the artist's sensibilities. Action painting underwent a similar decline into decorative texture-making only a few years after Jackson Pollock's breakthrough into a new realm of sensibilities. We can hardly muster enough historical imagination to understand why Pollock's swaying curtains and giant loops were once felt uncomfortable and engulfing. There is precious little true accident about dripping and splashing paint. Seen in this way a clever use of accident is as old as art itself. The most skilled techniques of nineteenth-century art knew how to make use of seemingly uncontrollable techniques. The clever water-colourist delights in the untamable spreading of running wet colour. The painter has hardly time to catch up with the floods of colour and to channel them into definite directions. Every touch of the brush that serves to dam the spreading may start a new flow somewhere else. The painter always remains one step behind in his effort to keep up some measure of control, quite apart from the fact that he cannot entirely anticipate the change in colour caused by drying. Yet nobody would accuse him of irresponsibility and excessive reliance on the happy accident compared with a painter who uses a drier brush. The successful use of wet colours will be considered the greater skill. Objectively the academic water-colourist will be less able to predict the exact outcome of his work than the modern artist using Jackson Pollock's technique of pouring and splashing paint. After a day or so of practice Pollock's technique can be easily mastered; not so, of course, the use of wet water-colours.

We might say that the skilled water-colourist watches the running of the colours with great alertness. He will react within a split second to the happenings on the paper. It is this sensitive reaction and instantaneous feedback enforcing ever new decisions that distinguishes the skilled painter from the irresponsible exploiter of accident. The accident is immediately incorporated into the artist's planning and to this extent becomes indistinguishable from his more intentional design. It is the subjective relation to the artist's planning that decides the character of the accident. Accidental in this sense is anything in the medium that does not conform with the artist's preconceived planning, something which is felt wholly extraneous and not controlled by him. If we make the student 'make do' with ready-made elements such as the letters of the alphabet, or collage material made up from *objets trouvés*, or if we restrict him to basic geometric elements that do not fit in with his more painterly preoccupations, he is faced with extraneous factors that are 'accidental' and alien to his intentions. But as soon as the student has become familiar with their effects they will have lost their former disruptive effect and easily become part of his planning. The teacher will have to think up a new, still alien situation for which the student has no ready-made solution. Many basic-design methods have become obsolete and ineffective often after very short runs. It is doubtful whether it is still useful to invent new disruptive devices. Students have become wise to the blessings of accidents. They almost wait for surprises and disruptions knowing well enough that the techniques will soon become usable as new gimmicks. Perhaps disruption itself as a teaching technique had its cutting edge worn off and should be discarded. It is closely connected with the self-destructive disruptive tendencies that underlay the recurrent revolutions of modern art during the first half of this century. Any innovation necessarily disrupts existing sensibilities. But the surrealistic spirit of modern art went out of its way to twist our rational sensibilities and attack our reason. What may have happened in the second half of the twentieth century is that this deliberate twisting no longer excites. We have learned to expect and welcome it. Modern art was largely based on surrealist techniques of surprise and disruption. I will argue that modern art has already become an historical style in the way in which 'art nouveau' is no longer novel, as its name implies, but has turned into museum art. The same thing seems to have happened to art education. Disruptive techniques in teaching no longer surprise us and so fail to cut through our expectations and preconceptions. Nor are they capable of shifting the control of the working process to lower levels of the ego and stimulating unconscious scanning. They have lost all meaning. Possibly art and art teaching will have to revert to more constructive, intellectually controlled techniques, which nevertheless do not exclude the participation of the unconscious. Certain motifs have proved curiously independent of changes in style and sensitivity. They reflect in the most direct manner the temporary decomposition of the surface functions which creativity must always bring about. In the second half of this book I will discuss the motif of the 'dying god', which has shown itself incredibly persistent throughout the history of human civilization. I will maintain that this perennial theme gains its catalytic power from its capacity to induce the critical shift of control to the deepest levels of the ego. The creative mind must identify itself with the fate of the 'dying god' in order to surrender control to the powers of the deep.

5   The Fragmentation of 'Modern Art'

Before the advent of modern art, there was no open conflict (dissociation) between surface and depth sensibilities, between intellect and intuition. In the past the conscious surface gestalt remained flexible enough to accommodate, without undue stress, the contributions of the primary process. There was no experience of chaos or disruption. We have discussed the easy integration of vertical and horizontal structure in classical music. Nor do we feel disruption when the articulate melody is shot through with inarticulate inflections of pitch, rhythm and loudness. In painting the deliberate large-scale composition is not disturbed by the subtle distortions and textures infused by a nervous artistic handwriting.

But even in old art disruption looms near the surface and becomes fully apparent if we refuse to let go of normal gestalt-bound sensibilities. I have mentioned the distorting forces in Michelangelo's and Beethoven's work. Beethoven, in his late work, seems to have paid less and less attention to surface continuity. (I will show later that this applies also to Goethe's late work.) Conductors, for the technical reason of controlling the orchestra, often play down rhythmic irregularity. A review of several editions of Verdi's operas has proved that rhythmical shifts tended to be eliminated by the editors of later versions. This, of course, is not possible with Beethoven's work. The first movement of his *Ninth Symphony* falls apart rhythmically as a matter of design. Conductors with their addiction to a clearly defined beat have found it impossible to render the rhythmical shifts with a natural transition, and they slur over the ruptures in the musical fabric. The movement starts with a slow cosmic weaving followed without obvious transition by the sharp thunderclaps of the main theme. Furtwängler hung on to the dumb slowness of the cosmic weaving and distended the thunderclaps into a heavy rumble, Toscanini anticipated the thunderclaps and hurried the pace of the cosmic weaving. What would be needed, but is hardly ever attained today, is the magic of the artistic illusion which makes the different tempi feel the same. Then the disruption rising from deeper levels of sensibility is contained. In a way the old Beethoven already belongs to the climate of open deliberate disruption that dominates the turbulent history of modern art. To feel the submerged depth coherence we must, almost with an effort, abandon the conscious need for logic, order and sequence. Then the superficial fragmentation will not be felt and will be replaced by a feeling of inner necessity far more potent than the needs of conscious reason and logic. I will discuss later how the ageing Goethe purposely abandoned conscious logic in order to serve the necessities of a more profound continuity. We are far too intolerant of superficial fragmentation. A modicum of surface fragmentation is always needed in order to bring into action the usually starved low-level sensibilities. Conductors who cling to a steady beat will even ignore the quite excessive fragmentation characteristic of Mozart's late music. There, manic and depressive moods oscillate with utmost rapidity even within the same phrase. These changes of mood constantly break the thread of an easy melodic flow. The conductor has to accept or rather to accentuate the fragmentation of the surface to give the alternating moods of elation and melancholy their proper weight. But, of course, today Mozart has become a symbol of balanced musical construction. His submerged turbulence is conveniently ignored. If the inexorable sequence of manic and depressive episodes were brought out – by accentuating rather than levelling their contrast – the superficial fragmentation would disappear for the sake of a deeper continuity. As it is, most conductors slur over the breaks for the sake of superficial fluency. Perhaps we have become intolerant of fragmentation in the enjoyment of classical works because our modern art is so openly fragmented in a deliberate and savage attack on our surface sensibilities. The haters of modern savagery and self-destruction like to turn to the serenity of Mozart's work in order to find relief for their lacerated sensibilities.

Modern art is all intellect or all spontaneity, hardly ever both at the same time. The modern artist attacks his own rational sensibilities in order to make room for spontaneous growth. A vicious circle operates. The attacked surface faculties fight back in self-defence and overnight the spontaneous breakthrough from below is turned into another deliberate, manneristic device. This in turn stifles further spontaneity and has to be overthrown by another burst from the depth. It is difficult to decide whether an initial defensiveness of conscious control or the disruptiveness of low-level functions is the first cause of the vicious circle. One reinforces and provokes the other. The surface crust of mannerisms does not allow the spontaneous depth functions to breathe and so has to be disrupted totally. This total victory of the depth functions leads to an equally drastic defensive action on the part of the surface functions. I will later comment on the definite schizoid tinge of modern art, which explains the occasionally extreme dissociation of the surface and depth functions.

Action painting is a good example of an almost total disruption of conscious composition. When I first commented on the spontaneous character of artistic handwriting, I suggested that much modern art allowed the inarticulate structure of artistic handwriting to intrude into the main composition. The subsequent arrival of American action painting bore out my tentative diagnosis in the most spectacular manner. Jackson Pollock blew up the microscopic network of scribbles of which ordinary texture and handwriting consists. The enormous loops and driplets dazzled the eye, at least as long as this kind of painting was new. At the time, action painting represented a sudden eruption of art's unconscious substructure. My evaluation of inarticulate textures as the product of the unconscious could have been taken as a proof that action painting, more than any other type of painting, was a very direct manifestation of unconscious form principles. This may have been true as long as action painting was still young and raw. But after a few years or so the inevitable defensive reaction of the secondary process set in. Today fashionable action painting is little more than a very deliberate exercise in decorative textures with little sensitivity to the unconscious form discipline that first animated it.

There had been earlier eruptions of unfocusable inarticulate form elements. Sir Herbert Read, as far back as the nineteen-thirties, said that much modern art contradicted the teachings of gestalt psychology. The gestalt psychologists had maintained that art more than any other human activity documented the fundamental striving of the human mind towards the stable, compact, simple organization of a 'good' gestalt. Sir Herbert had only to point to what he called the eye-wandering effect of Picasso's Cubism to refute this claim. Cubism went out of its way to deny the eye stable focusing points round which the rest of the composition could be organized. Instead, the eye was sent on a fool's errand. When it fastened on one feature the cubistic fragments fell into a new pattern, which was shattered again as soon as the eye wandered on and was caught by another feature. The picture kept heaving in and out as the eye tried to infuse some measure of stability into the pattern.

The first impact of Cubism attacked conscious sensibilities and the gestalt principle ruling them. We have to give in to this attack in order to enjoy the pictures and become aware of the new highly mobile space that Cubism created. The weaving in and out of the picture plane was perhaps the first manifestation of a new abstract pictorial space which later became fully revealed in the painting of Jackson Pollock and his associates. Our attempt at focusing must give way to the vacant all-embracing stare which I have described as the conscious signal of unconscious scanning (plate 18). This kind of low-level scrutiny can overcome the superficial impression of chaos and disruption and appreciate the stringent formal discipline underneath. This hidden order redeems the near-schizoid character of the excessive fragmentation found in so much modern art.

One could trace the true beginning of disruption in modern art back to French Impressionism. Classicistic painting had stressed the coherence of line and surface and had blossomed in the linear harmonies of Ingres. The Impressionists blew all coherence of line and surface to bits and stressed the significance of the single brush stroke. They freely indulged in the fragmentation of the picture plane by scattering these isolated brush strokes across the canvas. We are no longer quite so aware of the severity of the attack on conscious sensibilities which the Impressionists mounted. We may only guess its vehemence from the reaction of the academicians and their circle. After a decade or so the attack became muted, partly due to the good services of the critics who supported the new movement. They found they could gather up the scattered brush strokes into stable patterns by stepping back from the canvas and allowing the brush marks to congeal once again into solid surfaces and outlines. The art critics proclaimed that the Impressionists, far from scattering the coherence of the picture plane, had in fact constructed a new kind of atmospheric space that was in no way less precise or stable than the space constructed according to the rules of Renaissance perspective. Many post-Impressionist painters succumbed to deliberate space construction and so brought to an end the spontaneous treatment of a freely oscillating picture plane. Only the ageing Monet broke through the barrier. In his late *Lily Pond* paintings he resurrected the old vibrant pictorial space. Once again loose clusters of brush strokes were allowed to oscillate freely throughout the picture plane. No wonder that Monet was later acclaimed as a precursor of modern sensibilities.

We have seen how Picasso's Cubism, by using near-geometric elements instead of painterly brush work, re-mounted the attack on our conscious sensibilities. Cubism in turn degenerated into an academic exercise in space construction. During the nineteen-twenties and -thirties academic teaching everywhere put to the test Cézanne's remark that we can see nature in (cubistic) elements of spheres, cylinders, etc. Even today virtue is attributed to a kind of life-drawing which automatically converts the organic forms of the body into rigid cylinders, cubes and the like, a particularly boring exercise in constructing a geometric space lacking all the former fragmentation and eye-wandering effects. Almost all painters of the inter-war period went through some phase of Cubist space construction. This decadence explains the profound experience of exhilaration when Jackson Pollock once again blew up the solidified academic Cubism and spun his gossamer curtains of space. They kept swaying in and out as once again the eye was sent wandering in search of stable focusing points. The reaction of the secondary process against this most violent of all attacks was equally swift and ruthless. Within a few years the dazzling effect wore off. The mobile space curtains duly fused into a solid thick texture that afforded a most undisturbing background for the display of elegant domestic furniture.

The dazzling effects of optical painting organized the attack on the gestalt principle in quite explicit, almost scientific terms. Its dazzle defeats focusing on any single element altogether even for the shortest time. One art critic suggested that a painting by Bridget Riley, now in the Tate Gallery, could only be tolerated in a domestic setting by hiding it behind curtains. I very much doubt this. The secondary process will undoubtedly succeed in overcoming even this latest attack on conscious gestalt perception and convert these pictures into comfortable decorative pieces. Once the secondary process has done its work, we will understand contemporary reports on their uncomfortable dazzling quality as little as we now understand Kandinsky having been so dazzled by Monet's *Haystacks* that he was unable to pick out the haystacks from the welter of the brush work. Will there be yet another wave of attacks against our surface sensibilities? I very much doubt it. Modern art is dying.

It has been said that the spirit of surrealism begot every new movement in modern art. This is another way of saying (as we did) that modern art aimed at disrupting or twisting one's normal sensibilities as a matter of principle. A negro musician in the United States told me that in his opinion ragtime had inspired every new departure in jazz. Ragtime literally 'ragged' existing tunes, twisting them in a hurtful way. Whenever a new jazz idiom became jaded it was simply given another turn of the screw to make it sound incisive and disturbing. Somehow the ragging of jazz also had its day. One feels that the surrealistic spirit of deliberate disruption has gone flat on us. Rauschenberg and his friends have sometimes been belittled for not having revived the true revolutionary spirit of Dada. I do not think that this was either possible or desirable. Rauschenberg's dreamy concoctions no longer attack us. To my mind they may be the harbingers of an altogether new, friendlier art that I feel is in the air. Something more positive may be needed, aiming at constructive results rather than demolishing existing formulae and clichés.

The modern art of any period, of course, could not but disrupt conventional standards of seeing and listening. Any artistic innovation does that. But before the advent of our modern art innovations could be accepted as an enrichment of existing tradition, not as self-conscious outright attacks on conscious order and reason. Even sixteenth-century Mannerism did not purposely destroy Renaissance conventions. The manneristic painters despaired of emulating the great of the past and rather tamely set out to twist sensibilities in order to get highly sophisticated effects. They certainly lacked the destructiveness of our modern art and its avowed primitivism. With rousing manifestos our modern art tried to sweep aside all pre-existing art as no longer meaningful for modern times. This hubris has worn thin. Paradoxically, the avant-garde of today turns against the nihilism of past 'modern art'; it is groping for a new, still very unsure traditionalism, a new reverence for older values which our fathers thought to be shattered for ever. This new traditionalism may be another symptom of what I would like to consider as the friendlier, less aggressive spirit of the present avant-garde. The old 'modern art' exhibited the creative shift towards dedifferentiation as aggressive fragmentation. We have seen how the reaction of the secondary process set to work with equal vehemence, debasing the fragmentation techniques into manneristic assembly devices almost overnight.

Slower secondary processes have always existed. Much of the serenity of classical art is due to them. Such secondary processes have mellowed the innovations of older painting and music. All new art at its inception must have appeared less solid and more dispersed than it now appears to a later generation. In music, dispersed polyphony is gradually bundled up into solid harmony. The freely converging and scattering voices are fused into the stately progression of harmonic chords supporting a single dominant melody. Uncomfortable horizontal hearing lacking a proper rallying point for our attention turns into the more comfortable vertical hearing of solid chords. This is not an altogether unwelcome process. Throughout history new music has been blamed for its lack of melody. Schoenberg hoped that some time in the future his allegedly unmelodious and fragmented work would yield up some expressive singable melody. There is every reason to expect that it will. We know that even Mozart's music was criticized for its confusion by the Emperor Josef II of Austria. He complained that the music was overloaded with too many notes. His displeasure was probably caused by the richness of the polyphonic structure that obscured the clean line of the melody. Mozart, in his later works, purposely strengthened the more inconspicuous middle voices by giving them a melodious expressiveness of their own (thus giving food to horizontal listening). He hoped that their intricacy would escape the naïve listener and please the connoisseur. The Emperor's discomfort shows that Mozart failed in deceiving the naïve listener. Today there is no such difficulty. Most people will hear Mozart and Haydn, particularly Haydn, as a pleasant coherent melody lightly underscored by a few now hackneyed chords. It is difficult to imagine why the Emperor should have rejected such feather-weight, lucid music as overcomplex and confusing.

Sir Thomas Beecham had a certain mannerism in conducting Mozart's late works by which he tried to counteract the secondary verticalization of polyphonic complexity. He gave more than ordinary weight to the inconspicuous middle voices and tried to make it more difficult for the listener's attention to remain fixed on the dominant main melody. But even so, the average listener refuses to let go his iron grip on a single melody. It needs the savage attacks of modern art and music to dislodge such comfortable habits.

The secondary verticalization process is speedy enough to act within a lifetime. One needs only a clear memory to bear witness to its unique powers of transformation. It seems, however, that few people can hold on to the initial impact of a work of art once its edge has worn off. This is why art critics will never learn, and go on condemning every new departure in art for its confusion and incomprehensibility. Only after the secondary processes have made a new work more palatable for their appetite will they accept it and simply feel that they had missed its clarity at the first hearing. They will not realize that their perception has undergone a qualitative change. Something similar happens if we meet a person with a repulsive face for the first time. As we get to know that person and learn to love him his face will be transformed and assume more agreeable features. We will then tend to forget the first repulsive impression and simply think that we had seen wrongly and now know better. This is not so. The first unpleasant impression was as real and true as the later pleasant one. Neither is the initial confusing impression of new art misleading. It conforms with its objective, still undifferentiated structure. Schoenberg's music, whether he liked it or not, did lack and still largely lacks traditional melodiousness. But once his scattered polyphony has thickened into solid harmony supporting a clear melodic line, it will have turned into something else that is qualitatively different. Most probably by then the original more diffuse impression will be forgotten. My analysis of the unfocusable substructure of art was only made possible by my obstinacy in holding on to uncomfortable initial impressions even after they had been superseded by more pleasant and unexciting experiences. I might be able to convince only those readers of the reality of secondary processes who might be prepared to resuscitate similar memories. Some people of my own age may have shared the transformation that Brahms's and later Stravinsky's music has undergone within our own life-span. I can still clearly remember when half a century ago I got to know and to love the harsh music of Brahms. He was then considered a modernist in the largely conservative musical circles of Vienna. Brahms's music still sounded acid and brittle, and lacking in smooth finish; his intricate and widely spaced polyphony produced a hollow sound that failed to support the thin flow of the melody. I loved this uncompromising music for its masculinity. It seemed to go well with Brahms's forbidding and lonely personality. As time went by, the hard edges of his music were smoothed down. Today there is a luscious velvetiness, an almost erotic warmth about his melody that makes the same music almost too rich and sweet a fare. The once hesitant melody has duly thickened into broad, solid song. We cannot reverse this transformation by any means, any more than Sir Thomas could restore Mozart's lost complexity. I myself can quite clearly remember the harsh and hollow sound of the Brahms of my youth; but I cannot, however hard I try, associate this memory with the sweet, lush sonority which meets me when I listen to the same music in the concert-hall today. I am left with a memory of a sound that no real experience can now duplicate.

No wonder that most people will not care to retain such haunting visions and immaterial sounds. Still, something can be retrieved through the consistent unity of a great man's life work. The late Beethoven quartets were left unperformed for almost a century. Perhaps Richard Wagner was able to become a largely self-taught revolutionary because he alone among his contemporaries could tolerate the fragmented structure of Beethoven's late works. Today we are beginning to understand the unity beneath their loose improvisation and apparent fragmentation. Once we have accommodated our sensitivities to these low-level linkages, his earlier music can be heard with a better understanding of its original ruptures and sudden transitions which are now largely lost. Familiarity has trained us to slip too lightly over obstacles that formerly must have been felt as deep abysses and steep ridges. Schubert's late works still have a hollow, loose sound not unlike that of Brahms. If we grasp the strange harmonic twists in these works his earlier music may shed its misleading impression of easily flowing melodiousness and we may suddenly hear the faint echo of subterranean rumblings. Generally, late half-forgotten works of masters which by some lucky chance have escaped the secondary transformation process can, through the unity of a great man's life work, help us to retrieve some of the lost edge even in the earlier hackneyed works. In this rehabilitation lies the main achievement of great conductors and performers. The ruptures of the *Ninth Symphony* or fragmented great plays like *King Lear* or *Faust* still serve as a challenge to performers to dive below the obvious surface discontinuities and tap the hidden unity below.

It is only in really new art that we can fully appreciate the attack on conscious sensibilities and the anxiety which all artistic innovation entails. There, the secondary rationalization process has not yet pulled together the superficial disruptions. If we hold on to our ingrained habits of seeing and listening which are formed in appreciating traditional art, we are bound to feel attacked and experience the acute discomfort connected with unconscious anxiety. In fairness it must be conceded that only certain psychological types can easily relinquish the conscious need for stable focusing and rational coherence. Lowenfeld [19] explained the difference between the so-called haptic and visual types of artists by pointing to the discomfort that people of the visual type feel in looking out from a moving railway train. They have an overwhelming need to connect up the scraps of landscape carried past the window in chaotic sequence, while passengers of the haptic type are content enough to watch empty-eyed the constant change of scenery. Haptic artists would largely work from an unconscious need and care little for surface coherence, while visual and more rational types need surface coherence and stable focusing.

Extreme examples of action painting such as the unending loops of Jackson Pollock could not but cause discomfort in people of the more rational visual type. To avoid discomfort we have to give up our focusing tendency and our conscious need for integrating the colour patches into coherent patterns. We must allow our eye to drift without sense of time or direction, living always in the present moment without trying to connect the colour patch just now moving into our field of vision with others we have already seen or are going to see. If we succeed in evoking in ourselves such a purposeless daydream-like state, not only do we lose our sense of unease but the picture may suddenly transform itself and lose its appearance of haphazard construction and incoherence. Each new encounter now comes as a logical development and after a while we feel that we have grasped some hidden all-over structure which is contained in each nucleus of colour (just as I have assumed that for Beethoven's inner vision an incoherent scrap of melody could stand for the all-over structure of a whole symphony). Conscious surface coherence has to be disrupted in order to bring unconscious form discipline into its own. As this unconscious form discipline cannot be analysed in rational terms, we are thrown back on our low-level sensibility which alone can distinguish irresponsible arty-crafty gimmicks from truly creative art ruled by an inner necessity.

Boulez's experiments in serialization have been criticized on the grounds that the regularity of their construction was not consciously apparent; it was not realized that psychologically this was just the aim of this exercise in fragmentation. As in action painting, any attempt at consciously organizing such music was bound to end in acute discomfort. Any continuity of melodic line or harmonic progression seemed missing; the instrumental sounds tumbled like the tinkles of an Aeolian harp responding to irregular gusts of the wind. But just as we allowed our eye to drift through an action painting without sense of time, so we must listen to this music without trying to connect the present sound with the past and future; again after a while the sounds will come with the feeling of inevitable necessity, obeying an unconscious submerged coherence that defies conscious analysis.

The re-creation of old music in the spirit of modern art may come dramatically, with a sense of shock and suddenly disrupt comfortable habits of listening. Once the young British composer, Alexander Goehr, played a most unsettling joke on me, which was, however, very instructive. Goehr claimed that he could demonstrate to me that Boulez, in spite of his deliberate destruction of traditional forms, really worked within an established French tradition. He played first the full recording of Boulez's *Le Marteau sans Maitre* which was still unfamiliar to me at the time. This naturally conditioned my attention to the diffuse disconnected type of listening that this very new music required. Afterwards without much warning he continued with Debussy's *La Mer*. I did not recognize this well-worn piece of Impressionistic writing! Normally Debussy's tone-poem produces realistic associations, like the roar of the waves and the wind. Now I heard for the first time a constant variation and mixture of tone-colours so subtle and fleeting that they forced me to live eternally in the present as Boulez's music had done. Obviously the realistic associations with nature's noises tend to coarsen our sensibility and we fail to accord to Debussy the place among the greatest that is due to him. The experiment came as a shock because I was not prepared for this twist of my sensibilities. I felt driven to compulsive laughter. Such laughter may occur when we are suddenly forced to acknowledge a hidden identity between very distant objects, such as animal forms transformed into a human face and the like; here I was suddenly confronted with the hidden affinity between a familiar piece of musical Impressionism and a modern exponent of twelve-tone music. I have said that Debussy's disconnected tone-colour mixtures and contrasts had been dulled and coarsened by too realistic interpretations. We might remember that exaggerated realistic reinterpretation did the same dis-service to Claude Monet's Impressionist painting of the same period. In either case the sharpened modern sensibility for disconnected textures in tone and colour helps us to regain some of the lost original tensions. In this way the action painters rediscovered Monet; and in this way Boulez allows us not only to reassess Debussy's true achievement, but also explains the immense antagonism which his disruption of traditional harmonic cliché aroused at a time when his loose tone-colour sequences were not safely tied together into crudely naturalistic sound.

I do not maintain, for a moment, that sensitivity for modern art allows us to restore the original impression of an historic work of art; far from it. In my view, the secondary rationalization process, once imposed on art, is irreversible and the original experience is lost for ever. Monet and Debussy were, after all, realistic Impressionists, only not quite as much as later rationalization and verticalization has made them appear to us. Monet did paint lily ponds though he was obviously not very interested in producing easily focused coherent forms. By imposing the disruption of action painting or Boulez's music on Monet and Debussy, we simply blow the entire hardened surface of their realism to bits. We expose the raw diffuse matrix below and re-interpret it according to our own contemporary form feeling. This is of course quite arbitrary, but not more so than the shallow rationalizations of previous generations. It is the glory of great art that it can tolerate this arbitrary manipulation of its conscious surface, because its real substance belongs to deeper untouched levels. We do not really mind that we cannot reconstruct the conscious intentions of the Stone Age cave painters or of the old Mexicans, because we feel instinctively the relative unimportance of the artist's conscious message. It is perhaps due to the fact that our own modern art is often content to work from low irrational levels of the mind alone, that our civilization has become so receptive to the art of other civilizations, prehistoric, historic, primitive and exotic. What alone seems to matter to us is the complex diffuse substructure of all art. It had its source in the unconscious and our own unconscious still reacts readily to it, preparing the way for ever new reinterpretations. The immortality of great art seems bound up with the inevitable loss of its original surface meaning and its rebirth in the spirit of every new age.

6   The Inner Fabric

The undifferentiated inner fabric of art can never be fully appreciated. We transform it into something more solid and definite by the very act of perceiving it. This difficulty amounts to a genuine epistemological problem, like that involved in our incapacity for observing both movement and position of an electron. The ray which we are forced to use for observing it throws the electron off its course. In either case the means of observation interferes with the phenomenon to be observed so that it can never be caught in its original state. The hidden structure of art is created on lower levels of awareness that are nearer to the undifferentiated techniques of the primary process. But once it is created it can only be observed on a higher level of awareness. For instance, the integration of art's substructure is only observed through its conscious signal: pictorial space. In this way we are forced to observe the unconscious structure of art with the gestalt techniques of the (conscious or preconscious) secondary process which will automatically infuse a more solid and compact structure into it.

This secondary process also occurs as the so-called secondary revision of a dream memory. The original structure of a dream has the apparent incoherence and chaos of the primary process. When after waking we try to recall it we will inevitably project a better gestalt into it, iron out seemingly superfluous detail and fill in incoherences and gaps. We simply cannot remember the dream in its original less differentiated structure. The same epistemological problem is involved. Freud could recapture some of the dream's lost substance by drawing on his patients' free associations, but he could not thereby alone restore the dream to its original unrevised structure. That structure was lost through the shift of attention from a dispersed dreamlike level to the narrower focus of everyday vision.

Freud also noticed that the secondary revision of the dream was steered by the superego in order to polish off the unconsciously most significant symbolic details which like to masquerade in the disguise of unimportant and superfluous details. There is little doubt that the secondary revision of art is steered in the same way. It tends to ignore and polish off irregularities and textural elements that seem insignificant, but which contain the unconsciously most important symbolism. I have suggested that the undoubted emotional power of a nervous artistic handwriting is best explained by a symbolism which is unconsciously understood. It remains withdrawn from conscious detection owing to the crudeness and over-simplification of secondary process techniques which our conscious analysis of art has willy-nilly to employ.

Art is a dream dreamt by the artist which we, the wide awake spectators, can never see in its true structure; our waking faculties are bound to give us too precise an image produced by secondary revision. The work of art remains the unknowable *Ding an sich*. Our impressions amount to illusions, possibly even hallucinations of non-existent data. We have seen that the superego's censorship benefits from the repression of art's unconscious substructure. The superego may also play a part in preventing our perception from regressing to the exact level of undifferentiation on which this substructure was originally produced so that a secondary revision becomes inevitable. But fundamentally the shift between differentiated and undifferentiated modes of perception is inherent in an ego rhythm that underlies all creative work.

The process of secondary revision belongs to the third and last phase in this rhythm. I will distinguish a first phase of fragmented projection, 'schizoid' in character. It is followed by a 'manic' phase of unconscious scanning and integration when art's unconscious substructure is formed. The secondary revision occurs in the ultimate 'depressive' feedback and re-introjection of the work into the surface ego.* This introjection is often painful and beset with doubt. Because the introjected material was shaped on a lower (less differentiated) level it must appear to the artist

* See Appendix, p. 303ff.

more fragmented and chaotic than it actually is. The work of secondary revision is never complete. The artist himself is cast in the role of the spectator faced with the chaos of newly created art. He is often afflicted with the same doubt, possible misunderstanding and insensitive destructiveness. This is the reason why art teaching must be so much concerned with helping the student in his self-doubts and his resistance against understanding his own work. The secondary process of revision will only partly transform art's substructure into more intelligible, easily palatable gestalt. The student must learn to rely on his low-level sensibilities that alone can overcome the superficial impression of chaos and fragmentation and the depressive anxieties attendant on it. To this extent secondary revision must be resisted.

I have shown how pictorial space – the surest sign of unconscious integration below a fragmented surface – is liable to be solidified and verticalized through secondary revision. Hence perhaps the most important task of art teaching is to weaken the student's need for constructing a precise solid space and to become sensitive to true pictorial space. He ought to understand that pictorial space serves as a signal of the countless form relationships by which every single element of the work is tied to every other element in the structure. Even the simplest geometric construction has a complexity that is beyond conscious scrutiny and has to be scanned on an unconscious level. As a reward for the proper unconscious integration the conscious superstructure is stirred into intense plastic life. One of the best tests for assessing a student's low-level sensibilities is to ask him whether he is sensitive to that shudder which the first brush mark on a white piece of paper sends right across the picture plane. Being able to see these ripples proves that he has fully sensed the tensions set up between the black mark and the white expanse of the picture plane, dammed up by the four distant corners and the four rigid edges limiting the expanse, and many other responses of this kind. The student has to accept the paradox that hardly any of his marks will stick firmly to the flat picture plane. Any new element he puts down will shake the entire pictorial space along new ridges and furrows. Of course, there are some rules. A small square wedged into one of the corners of the picture quadrangle is parallel to the four edges and will be firmly held by them. To this extent it will be comparatively less mobile than other shapes that do not relate in such a simple way to the picture quadrangle. Generally speaking any shapes that incorporate or reflect the edges of the picture plane will be held flat and taut by them. But they will still partake in the upheavals of pictorial space and their relative stability will only dramatize other areas of greater mobility. Something similar holds good for the interaction of colours, which is equally unpredictable. Each new colour dot added will throw the interaction between the other colour areas out of gear. There will also be certain colour areas which will resist interaction up to a point so that their relative stability highlights the instability of the other colour areas.

In music the secondary verticalization process also impinges on an experience of a more mobile musical space. The translucent plastic quality of the strings in a quartet may well be deemed superior to the solid sound of the full orchestra. A late fugue by Bach comes nearest to the experience of a pure musical 'space'. As we keep our attention dispersed over the whole structure of the polyphonic web we become aware of the constant flux in the density of its fabric, alternately constricting, swelling and opening up. There is no need to look out for the fugue subject as it re-appears in the various voices. The volume of the musical space will be eloquent enough. At times the vertical tension between the voices will tighten up and demand to be resolved by another reappearance of the subject. The actual intonation of the subject, even in the hidden middle voices, will announce itself by a sudden change in the vertical density. The fabric of the voices will open up and expand into the infinite, an experience not dissimilar to the mystic's oceanic feeling as described by Freud. Time will seem to stand still. We begin to live eternally in the present and are given the infinity of true musical space.

Musical space is quite comparable to pictorial space in painting. Like pictorial space it is constantly converted into a more solid vertical sonority. We have seen something of this kind in the secondary verticalization which has befallen Haydn, Mozart, Brahms and Debussy. A similar secondary solidification process has converted the mobile pictorial space of Impressionism and Cubism into precise almost measurable space illusions. Even the most insubstantial transparent painting is not immune. An admirer of Rothko's work once spoke of its transient space illusions. The once lucid film-like transparency of the colour bands has now thickened into almost solid cloud banks several miles deep as it were. He concluded that Rothko's work could no longer help him in making a dynamic use of colour.

I have spoken of the secondary processes that healed the recurrent fragmentation of surface coherence during the history of modern art. In healing the fragmentation they also solidified the original more fluid pictorial space in the manner in which Rothko's transparent films have been solidified.

The battle for the flat picture plane has been lost over and over again in the history of art. The painter's first duty is towards organizing the flat canvas. As he proceeds, the increasing complexities of his work will stimulate unconscious scanning and true pictorial space will emerge as the conscious signal of a well-knit unconscious substructure. The artist may welcome the new plasticity of his work as a reward for work well done. But soon a secondary process of solidification may take over. I have described how the Impressionists had turned away from constructing a rigid illusionist space and instead paid homage only to the flat picture plane. But in due course the art critics convinced them that they had invented a new kind of illusionistic space, a new atmospheric space created from colour and light. The action painters and Tachists once again discovered the primary significance of the single brush mark on the flat canvas. But as a sure sign of academic decadence, American painters were told that they had discovered a new space built only from abstract elements of form, tone and colour. The hard-edge painters, by deliberately constructing an ambiguous space, only paid homage to the same craving for crystallizing and measuring the felicities of pictorial space. Some American art schools have introduced the deliberate construction of a precise abstract space into their curricula and so deprived abstraction of its vigour and curiosity. When I tried to trace the origin of these curiously old-fashioned ideas I was referred to the illustrious name of Hans Hofmann, whose own work I had come to admire greatly for its vigorous freshness. Checking more carefully on Hofmann's own teaching I heard that Hofmann himself had always insisted that the artist's first concern was with organizing the flat picture plane. The final effect of a resonating pictorial space comes as a welcome reward for a well organized composition.*

A composer who is overconcerned with the vertical sonority of his composition may fail to recognize that his prime concern ought to be with knitting the inner fabric of polyphony and counterpoint. I remember how a composer mocked his academic critics by saying that he did not really care how his composition sounded. He was satisfied if he had carried out his purely formal ideas of serialization. This off-hand treatment of final sound effects is liable to shock academic music teachers, but is nevertheless quite to the point. True musical space comes as a signal of unconscious integration and cannot be aimed at as a conscious effect. Academic teaching in all spheres of learning cannot tolerate the fact that so important an effect should be withdrawn from conscious control and not be directly teachable.

I do not want to be misunderstood. I am not advocating a cult of spontaneity at the expense of intellectual control. The cult of spontaneity belongs to a bygone era of romantic self-expression and is rightly rejected by the sober young artists of today. If anything, I would advocate a maximum of intellectual control, but at the same time a clearer recognition of the limits of such a control. Pictorial and musical space, as I have described it, is definitely outside direct conscious control.

The most intellectually controlled of modern techniques, optical art, clearly shows the limits between conscious control and uncontrollable pictorial space. Some optical artists claim that for the first time in the history of art the structure of art can

* In recent years a new academic mannerism has developed as part of the intellectual study of colour interaction. Students try to defeat the innate tendency of colours to recede or to advance, and to keep them at all costs attached to the flat picture plane; for instance by making a receding blue overlap on top of an advancing red, the blue is pulled forward and the red pushed back. I think this kind of exercise is valid, but only as a brief study. What matters is the fact that the linear (graphic) composition may create spatial effects that can contradict the spatial illusion produced by colour. This conflict is most fruitful; it demands a resolution for which there is no intellectual recipe. I would maintain that the conflict between incompatible space experiences, for instance the experience of limitless expansion contradicting a simultaneous claustrophobic feeling of being trapped, may belong to the emotional subject matter of abstract art as it is now developing. As subject matter, the experience of space cannot come as a late by-product of good work, but is part of the artist's initial conception of his work. Yet it remains true, as part of the great paradox of artistic illusions, that the artist's formal concern must also be with organizing the flat picture plane.

be built by coolly intellectual calculation alone. Its composition needs none of the intuitive, non-intellectual sensibilities which have gone into the making of earlier art. One can respect the attitude behind such claims and regard them as a wholesome reaction to the old cult of spontaneity and happy accident. Yet the claim is based on self-deception. In any kind of creative work a point is reached where our power of free choice comes to an end. The work assumes a life of its own, which offers its creator only the alternative of accepting or rejecting it. A mysterious 'presence' reveals itself, which gives the work a living personality of its own. I have already discussed and will say more about the conversation-like intercourse between the creator and his own work and the need of the artist to treat his work like an independent being with a life of its own.

The systematic fragmentation of the surface gestalt that characterizes the history of modern art since French Impressionism has made sure that the final space experience can never be predicted. Optical painting has made this fragmentation into a fine art. Like serialization in music, optical painting is a case of the intellect destroying its own modes of functioning. The single elements of an optical composition are serialized in so smooth a gradation that the eye fails to pick out any stable gestalt pattern. Any attempt at focusing is punished by eye-twisting and an often unpleasant glare. Our vision is conditioned to give up focusing and to take in the entire picture plane as a totality. It is at once directed to highly mobile and unstable patterns of pictorial space and its fluttering pulse. In this manner the initial total intellectual control of optical serialization leads without transition directly to the experience of uncontrollable pictorial space. The dissociation of intellectual and spontaneous sensibilities that characterizes so much modern art could not be more complete. I once discussed with Bridget Riley her method of working [9]. She is keenly aware of these two separate phases in her work. She has, up to a point, some control over the emergent pictorial space (plate 20). There are areas of 'stability' where the dazzle effect is minimal and which afford the eye almost, but never entirely, some stable centre of attention. There, the elements appear least distorted and almost detach themselves from the continuum of the dazzle pattern. In adjacent areas the elements gradually become absorbed into a series of imperceptible variations. At last an area of 'crisis' is reached where the element is fully submerged by a maximum dazzle effect. The critical area is also in danger of becoming isolated from the rest of the picture plane and threatens to break the continuity of the picture plane. Bridget Riley's conscious concern is with the gradual variation (serialization) of the single element which represents her theme. Its effect on the continuity of the flat picture plane and the danger of disrupting it by isolating certain detached areas of maximum 'stability' and 'crisis', can only be tested by trial and error. When the picture plane holds without breaking under the opposing strains, then the final unpredictable transformation takes place to which Bridget Riley looks forward with impatience. A 'presence' comes through, which she likes to compare to an hallucination. A mighty pulse skims through the entire picture plane, now lifting this or the other area to form a fleeting and swiftly crumbling pattern which need not have any correlate whatsoever in the objective composition. It is this presence and not the optically dazzling effect which matters to her. No wonder that the optical artists resent the label of optical art. After all, the dazzle is shared, or rather was shared at one time, by Monet's *Haystacks*, or by the first impact of Cubism and American Expressionism. It may well be that through the good services of the secondary process the dazzle effect of optical painting will also wear off. The surface faculties will refuse to be attacked and disrupted. We will be content to treat the glare as a pleasantly decorative texture, without attempting to articulate single units and patterns.

The fusion and obliteration of the single element within an over all texture is not unlike the absorption of a textile design unit into the all-over texture of a printed cloth. No wonder that textile design was the first among the commercial arts to seize on optical effects. In textile design the same formal problem exists. The single textile motif may be pleasant in itself, but it must never detach itself from the broader textural effect so as to become an isolated unit. If we lie sick in bed and look at the single motif in wallpapers or curtains we may, through the pressure of id fantasy, endow the motif with a stronger significance than it ought to have; for instance we could read threatening devil masks into some semi-abstract flower motif. Then the mask will start to stand out from the all-over texture wherever we turn our eye to avoid it. Our eyes will become strained and 'dazzled' not altogether unlike the effects of optical art. I wonder whether this manuscript will go into print soon enough before fashionable optical art has lost its dazzling effect. Then the reader could in his personal experience confirm my prediction that it will be transformed into decorative textures like all the other fragmentation techniques of modern art before.

One expects from exact science verifiable predictions, or to put it more precisely, predictions that can be verified by anyone who cares to take the trouble. However, hypotheses of the kind I am proposing are really only verified by introspection into one's past experiences and through holding on to memories that can be exceedingly fleeting. This requires unusual gifts of introspection. Speaking for myself, I feel that my researches can only be supported by holding on to 'first impressions' in modern art such as most people are liable to forget. In this manner one is able to neutralize the effects of the secondary processes which obscure the originally undifferentiated structure of creative work. But will my readers care to retrace their steps to the first transient experiences which the modern art of any period affords? Many people like their art mellowed and seasoned by the action of secondary processes and will therefore reject the raw modern art of their own period. Will they be able to accept my arguments?

There is perhaps another important reason why we want to forget 'first impressions'. Perception, particularly vision, secures our hold on reality. This is probably why we are so unwilling to accept that perception is unstable, its data shifting and subject to the interplay of the uncontrollable forces within our mind. The most sceptical philosophers have accepted uncritically the sense data theory, which considers the data conveyed by perception as a secure unquestioned basis for our understanding of objective reality. Yet perception has a history; it changes during our life and even within a very short span of time; more important, perception has a different structure on different levels of mental life and varies according to the level which is stimulated at one particular time. Only in our conscious experience has it the firm and stable structure which the gestalt psychologists postulated. We have seen how, as we penetrate into deeper levels of awareness, into the dream, reveries, subliminal imagery, and the dreamlike visions of the creative state, our perception becomes more fluid and flexible. It widens its focus to comprehend the most far-flung structures. These different levels of differentiation in our perception interact constantly, not only during the massive shifts between dreaming and waking, but also in the rapid pulse of differentiation and dedifferentiation that goes on continually undetected in our daily lives. It is extremely difficult to hold on to the interludes of dreamlike ambiguity and broader focusing that are interspersed among the sharper images of conscious memories. It requires perhaps singular powers of introspecting into the stream of consciousness to remember or rather to reconstruct the innumerable twilight states strung out between the more sharply crystallized gestalt structures of our memory. Freud thought that memory only registers the periodic (gestalt) crystallizations in the stream of consciousness and that the undifferentiated interludes are altogether lost, a strange assumption for the founder of psycho-analysis, who proclaimed the persistence of long lost memories and the timelessness of the unconscious mind. It is possible to train one's powers of introspection to hold on to the less articulated states of consciousness and to earlier phases in the history of perception where its gestalt structures were not yet fully crystallized. But it is very difficult to recall an earlier less structured phase of a perception once it has matured into precise gestalt. William James called it the 'psychologist's fallacy par excellence' to forget earlier less articulate states of consciousness. The difficulty is very evident in the appreciation of art, where our impression of the same work of art regularly undergoes very drastic changes. It was through my persistence in not wanting to forget my first experiences of unfamiliar art that I arrived at my dynamic theory of perception in general, and the laws of differentiation and dedifferentiation that rule its dynamic changes. I have illustrated the difficulty of memorizing superseded stages of perceptual experiences by a more familiar example: the repulsive look of a person who later turns beautiful in our eyes after we have made friends with him. We then feel that the first repulsive experience was simply misleading and mistaken, and prefer to forget it. But in fact it was as real at the time as our new more pleasant impression. It is extremely difficult or even impossible for most of us to reconstruct it in our memory or, more difficult still, in our present contemplation of our newly won friend. We can never imagine that reality can look different from the way in which we see it here and now; hence the naïve gullibility of the sense data philosophers. Our tenuous hold on reality may require that we should dismiss all other possible ways of looking at it as mistaken or fictitious and unreal.

The creative artist, however, more than any other person, must resist being seduced by final appearances and by a determined effort must seek out the half obliterated substructure of art in the raw. We have seen how in his own work he has to forego the wish to visualize precisely the final appearance of his work. An inordinate desire of this kind will only detract from eventual success. Bridget Riley once told some of my students how she was impatient to visualize the total impression while she was shaping the transformation of single elements. The effect was that her eyesight failed her altogether; she gave up, had a hot bath and returned to her work duly chastened.

What I am trying to say now is in a way only a paraphrase of my earlier description of creative work. It is work done in interim stages involving interim decisions that cannot yet be connected with the final solution. We begin to suspect that even the final result, the work of art as it leaves the artist's hands, is an interim result, only an 'inner fabric' still to be outwardly clothed with plastic effects and to be animated by a mysterious presence which is partly in the eye of the beholder. The artist may not even care for the final result. An opera composer once confided to me, rather shamefacedly, yet with enough conviction of his rightness, that he wrote his notoriously complex counterpoint first. He would later check its sound quality on the piano, a procedure which is anathema to the academic teachers. They like to intimidate their students with the awe-inspiring figure of the deaf Beethoven who could write revolutionary music in spite of his infirmity. But there are indications that Beethoven did not care all too much about the sound qualities of his late work. In his maturity he took lessons in counterpoint and paid increasing attention to the polyphonic inner fabric. Accordingly his late music is often lacking in sensuous sound quality and melodiousness. It can be tinny and hollow. His late piano sonatas often make the player's hands move far apart, so that the metallic jingle of the right hand fails to fuse with the rumbling bass, a disagreeable experience for the average music lover who likes his fare rich and sonorous. So great is our need for a rounded sound that even eminent conductors think it necessary to re-orchestrate passages in the *Ninth Symphony* which lack a well-balanced harmonic texture. Doing this they pander to the common craving for full sonority. They may well detract from Beethoven's intentions. Beethoven seems to have cared less and less for spinning rounded melodic phrases (he disliked his early adagios) and instead sustained a dispersed unfocused polyphony for long stretches. Depriving the listener of his customary vertical sonority may help him to follow Beethoven's own way of listening. It would require great temerity to explain the lack of sonority from Beethoven's deafness. He was too accomplished a pianist not to be able to envisage, had he cared, the precise sound of a piano. In the *Ninth Symphony* he invented new orchestral sounds, such as the unprecedented use of the double-basses in the opening bars of the choral movement. When they sing their harrowing *recitativo* melodies and answer the tentative quotations from the previous movements, they come as near to the singing of a human voice as a dumb instrument can. So it comes as an inevitable development when the singing voice at last intervenes to give tongue to the orgiastic spirit of joy. It is truly astounding that the deaf Beethoven could shape this transition from orchestral tone colour to the human voice by his inner hearing alone. He certainly had great powers of visualizing precise sound qualities. It is all the more preposterous that music teachers dare to criticize what they call his 'awkward' orchestration.

Composers must accept that an unwanted sonority is sometimes thrust on them. Chopin, for one, chafed under the wrong praise of his music. He certainly made the piano sing as it never sang before or after, but performers who indulge too much in its sweet sonority tend to obscure the complex inner fabric. If we look closely we find that the specific Chopin sound is bound up with the rhythmical independence of the accompaniment. The left hand never 'accompanies' by producing lush vertical sound, but has an independent rhythmical structure that often has a thematic significance of its own. Chopin's incomparable sound quality results from the recalcitrant fusion between the two superimposed rhythms. Performers must forego a lush sweet sound and instead ought to emphasize the harshness of the rhythmical clash.

Chopin was aware of his bad fortune. His friend, the painter Delacroix, wrote in his journal how Chopin, in spite of his sweet temper, could become angry when his music was praised for its sonority. Delacroix was somewhat puzzled and added apologetically that Chopin spoke of course only as a pianist, not as a composer. The reverse is more likely. Chopin must have resented that his music's complex inner structure was drowned by solid sonority.

We must be grateful that late, rarely performed works by great masters sometimes fail to be corrupted by sonority. I have mentioned the hollowness of some of Schubert's late works. The absence of thick sonority in Beethoven's late quartets is another example. There, we can perceive the spare inner fabric of great music before it is overgrown by solid sound. Performers should present it with all its uncompromising bareness without trying to clothe it with spurious sonority.

The secondary solidification of musical space in classical works can mislead the composer, particularly if he is egged on by academic teachers to pay excessive attention to sonority and a particular vertical sound quality. What Hofmann says about pictorial space in painting also goes for musical composition. The composer's first duty is towards the inner fabric of the music. If he has worked it with sufficient care, the sound can well look after itself. It is fatal for him to aim first at some specific sound and then bolster it up by sundry padding, *arpeggi*, *glissandi*, or devices like the Alberti bass. The ultimate failure of Delius is perhaps explained by his excessive dependence on certain sound qualities. If the conductor fails to produce them, the meaning of the work evaporates. Good art should be able to withstand a worse beating. Puccini's works, in spite of appearances to the contrary, do not depend on sound alone. The fabric of his music has an inner logic which is only now being discovered. His harmonies are simple, but so are Janáček's, whose music was also considered over-simple for too long a time.

Sometimes the inner complexity of a work seems to contribute nothing to the ultimate sound. I remember a conductor poking fun at Wagner because he would give an instrument drowned in the mighty surge of the orchestra its own little *leitmotiv* to play. It merely seems a pedantic allusion to a dramatic idea which is only discovered by reading the score. But who dares to accuse

Wagner of sound padding? The little motif is meaningful in the way in which the parallel fifths and octaves in the full organ are meaningful; this parallel movement of the voices which is considered ugly in other contexts. When Schoenberg pointed out the presence of parallel fifths and octaves in the full organ sound he was answered that they were only padding and were not heard as such. Schoenberg calls this a priceless (*köstlich*) objection. One adds the forbidden parallels because they are not heard. Why, on earth, does one add them at all? Why not quotations from the bible or cannon shots? He goes on to say that it does not matter that they are only heard as increase in sonority. How, he asks, should one hear a change in sound quality other than as just a change. It is precisely the point, of course, that all laws of harmony concerned with the hidden polyphonic fabric, such as the law governing the preparation and resolution of a dissonance, deal with horizontal (polyphonic, melodic *Stimmführung*) events solely in terms of good or bad sound. If Wagner gives a little instrument drowned in the full orchestra a little motif to play instead of bible quotations and cannon shots, he certainly affects ultimately only the resulting sound quality. What Schoenberg does not say, however, is that great composers never manipulate this plastic sound quality as their first and primary concern. The shaping of the inner horizontal fabric comes first. Only ears that have become dull and blunted by too great an addiction to solid sonority will not detect the decisive difference which this makes for the final beauty of sound and the plastic quality of an expanding musical space.

The composer could not but fail if his music were dependent on achieving some precisely visualized sound effect. I have mentioned Delius, whom perhaps only his friend Sir Thomas Beecham could keep alive. Musical notation is notoriously ambiguous and open to many interpretations. This crudity is sometimes deplored because it does not allow the composer to lay down his intention precisely. It gives the performer great latitude and, of course, almost full discretion in suffusing the music's bare structure with the countless inarticulate inflections on which its life and also its final sonority so largely depends. But is the ambiguity of musical notation really a disadvantage? Does it not enforce the fuller deployment of the composer's creative faculties, which, in any medium, have to be capable of handling imprecise open-ended material with utmost precision? The ambiguity of musical notation imposes on the composer the wholesome duty of providing in advance for a multitude of mutually incompatible interpretations. The composer must somehow take into account all possible interpretations, all of which should preserve the validity of his work. This in more technical terms means scanning serial structures that cannot be limited. The composer thus leaves his work uncompleted, a bare inner fabric that has to be clothed by many possible sound qualities, an interim result to be completed by the performer over and over again. Contemporary composers, like Stockhausen or Cage, have been much maligned for their 'indeterminacy', that is to say, their explicit decision to leave the completion of the work to the performer. Stockhausen's most notorious work merely supplies the performer with disconnected bits which he can piece together *ad libitum*. Critics generally have little understanding for the powers of creative scanning and control of an unlimited number of permutations and serial structures. John Cage's indeterminacy is more subtle. He attacks definite sound effects by leaving open the exact timing in which the melodic lines of instruments will fall on each other. This is perhaps a more significant use of indeterminacy. It certainly has a long tradition behind it. Chopin's large passages of rhythmically quite free melodies fall on the other voices with a large degree of indeterminacy. Up to a point this is also true of any really powerful polyphony of expressive melodies. Each strong melody demands its own rhythmical irregularities. These will pull it away from precisely synchronized chords. Bach's work is now sometimes performed in this looser expressive way. This produces a woolly texture not unlike the whispering voices (representing God's voice) at the beginning of Schoenberg's opera *Moses and Aaron*. Vertical indeterminacy, seen in this way, is not a wilful modernistic fashion but deeply embedded in musical sensibilities. In all these cases the composer has detached his attention from a precise vertical sound (which he ought to do anyway) and is solely concerned with creating partly independent events. As they fall on each other they produce each time a wide variety of possible fusions of a very different sound quality. Merce Cunningham has also introduced a kind of polyphonic indeterminacy into choreography with a true counterpoint of dance movements.

The dancers have to go through a limited number of possible movements. But within this repertoire they are free to choose any sequence. It can vary from performance to performance. The overall pattern fused from several simultaneous events will vary in an enormous number of possible permutations (serial structures) which the choreographer has somehow anticipated. The interaction between the dancers also impressed me deeply in purely human terms. Each dancer spun and wove an invisible cocoon. He built a protective (womb-like) space around himself, not unlike an animal taking possession of a territory that is to belong only to him. To allow each dancer the freedom to complete his sequences, the other dancers had to move along and around the invisible frontiers. These continually changed; they shrank, expanded, intersected for meaningless or dangerous encounters until, in a blessed moment, the separate spaces opened and fused in a sudden union. The ritual space could express the full gamut of human relations: loneliness, self-protection, fear and aggression, doubt, recognition, loving and losing. Is this not the same kind of 'space' with which we were concerned in painting and music? Pictorial space and musical space have the same capacity for compression and simultaneous expansion, stability within constant change, envelopment and repulsion. The pictorial space of great painting repels and envelops us. We may feel trapped and lost in the infinite at the same time. These contradictory yet compatible experiences of space reflect the undifferentiated substructure of art. There a womb is being prepared to receive, nurse and ultimately return the artist's projections, an inner space that both contains and repels the spectator. One suspects that we are not really dealing with purely formal and technical aspects but with art's innermost content, which recurs in any profound aesthetic experience. For once form and content are one and cannot be separated by any artifice. In a later chapter I will analyse the 'poemagogic' imagery of art, which allows us to dissect this minimum content of art in greater detail. Ultimately it has to do with creativity in basic human relationships and so transcends the realm of art.

Part Three
Teaching Creativity

7 The Three Phases of Creativity

Indeterminacy has an important social aspect; it requires the cooperation of others. Indeterminacy is also built into the writing of an opera libretto. Great poets are rarely good librettists, because they want to put everything into the words and do not leave the composer enough elbow room. There must be something sketchy, skeleton-like about a good libretto which challenges the composer to clothe the bare bones with living flesh. A well-made libretto is an interim result that must be open to many, possibly even contradictory, realizations by the composer. His music will always be more powerful than the librettist's words. Mozart's *Cosi fan Tutte* ceases to be cynical when Fiordiligi in her surrender breaks into deeply felt, heart-rending melody. The last act of *The Marriage of Figaro* is replete with light-hearted disguises, practical jokes and a certain aggressive coarseness of feeling. Yet both Susanna in her last aria and the Countess in her final words of forgiveness reach heights of emotion, the purity of which must not be doubted. Mozart's librettists for his two greatest works, *Don Giovanni* and *The Magic Flute*, were an odd pair; Da Ponte a not undistinguished literary man, Schikaneder a suburban impresario not unlike modern music-hall hacks who order their music for easy effect. Yet both works inspired Goethe in writing his *Faust*. Goethe, barely musical, reacted mainly to the literary content of the operas transfigured by Mozart's music. (I will later show how Goethe's emotional reaction to *The Magic Flute* allows us to understand better the unconscious meaning of his *Faust*.) Perhaps I should not have spoken of music 'transfiguring' the words; 'transforming' them would have put it better. Music has the power to recast and even to destroy completely the words to which it is set. This fact is often misunderstood. We can hardly understand the words when they are sung, the plot is silly and overcomplex; so why bother about them? Is it not better to listen to opera as though it were abstract orchestral music? This seems a sophisticated attitude very much in line with our liking for abstraction, but it is rather naïve and shows little respect for the composer. How eager are composers for plots or words that have the power to move and involve them! These allegedly unimportant words often hovered in their minds for a long time before the music rose that came to replace them. We must know plot and words precisely in order to re-experience in ourselves the same transformation. Once we have felt how the music took the words into its flesh and blood, we can safely forget about them. The music now expresses everything. It seems hardly credible that there should be controversy in English literature – largely inspired by the late E. J. Dent – whether or not *Don Giovanni* is a tragedy or merely a comedy. Like Faust, Don Giovanni dares the powers of the underworld. His knavish servant, Leoporello, may be funny, but not more so than Faust's helpmate, Mephistopheles. Both represent the dark self-destructive aspect of the hero, his defiance of heaven and hell. In the penultimate scene Leoporello's anxious chattering does not detract from the enormous dramatic power of the meeting between Don Giovanni and his hellish (or heavenly?) guest of stone.

I think modern abstract art has made us too willing to ignore the artist's conscious intentions. For this the artists are partly themselves to blame. They used to tease the public by denying them any information about their intentions. The picture was all there was to it, so they said. This was only true as long as the ambiguity of abstract art still had a disturbing quality. The spectator who wanted to use his sharply focused reason was faced with a dreamlike ambiguity which was indeed part of the content of abstract art. That content has now evaporated, due to the usual services of the secondary process. The public has accepted ambiguity as a self-indulgent game. The spectators of today like to project any meaning they like into an abstract picture. They are quite happy with somewhat amorphous patterns that serve them as a neutral backcloth for projecting their private daydreams. This is not good enough. As so often in the history of modern art a complete turn-about is now in the making. As part of this re-orientation opera libretti may again receive their due. The artist may well demand from the spectator a more definite exercise of his reason in relation to the content of art. The artist today often divulges the detailed reasoning that went into the making of his work, in the way in which Duchamp wants us to study the reasonings in his *Green Box* (figures 7, 8). We no longer expect that art must totally explain itself. The spectator should work his way through the artist's private reasoning, as he once had to read Bernard Shaw's interminable prefaces in order to appreciate his plays. A new kind of cooperation between the artist and his public may spring up, which paradoxically rests on a diminution of art's ambiguity and indeterminacy.

The social bond inherent in creative communication can take on very different and sometimes contradictory forms. Artists vary in their ability for making a creative use of other people's independent cooperation. Merce Cunningham, John Cage or Duke Ellington certainly have been capable of benefiting from such cooperation, which lesser people would have felt as gross interference with their artistic freedom. The mutual responses are sometimes so tightly knit that it becomes impossible to decide individual contributions. It is an idle question to ask how far Duke Ellington inspired his performers or how far he was inspired by them. They are artists who can work through others who sometimes seem to act quite independently. Diaghilev, for one, had few professional qualifications, yet he revolutionized ballet by working through a succession of choreographers whom he shaped and educated. One after the other left his company without impairing further progress and innovation. It became clear that the principal creative impetus came from the impresario, Diaghilev. In much the same way a good art teacher paints through his pupils. He uses them as his 'brushes' as it were. The main point is that he, like Diaghilev and Ellington, educates the creative power of his executants so that they seem to work quite independently. There is nothing wrong in a teacher claiming the work of his students as his own, although in fact he has only developed his pupils' free creative imagination. It seems incontrovertible that good teachers lose some of their energy to work as independent artists. Hans Hofmann, who taught generations of American artists, gave up full-time teaching late in life.

Progress (improvement)

~~Journey~~ of the illuminating gas up to the planes of flow. (continued)

24

the capillary tubes

A
{
each malic form terminates at the head in

3 capillary tubes, (the 24 therefore) were supposed

to cut the gas in bits and would have led it

to disguise itself as 24 fine

solid needles so that they will become when reunited

2
once again, in the demi-siphons, a fog

made of a thousand spangles of frosty gas.

B
↓
At the head, [at the summit], of each malic mould

3 capillary tubes, (24 in all): to cut the gas

in bits, to cut the gas in long needles

(already) solid, since before becoming an explosive liquid,

solid
it takes the form of a fog of spangles of frosty gas, all

this by the phenomenon of stretching in the unit of length

(refer to figure)

When the 2 demi-siphons (letter in fig.) would have been filled

with the fog of spangles which

are lighter than air, the operation of

began
the liquefaction of the gas through the sieve and the horizontal filter:

each spangle of solid gas strives (in a kind of spangle

derby) to (pass) the holes of the sieve

with élan, reacting already to the suction of the pump.

Figure 7. Page from Richard Hamilton's typographic reconstruction of Duchamp's *Green Box*, originally published in 1934 in the form of facsimiles of handwritten notes. Richard Hamilton wanted to make the notes more widely available to the public because they constitute an integral part of the *Large Glass*; Duchamp, at one time, planned to incorporate written texts into the *Large Glass* itself. He was a conceptual painter; he lived with his concepts for a long time and studied their functions and interactions. However intangible and abstract they were in the beginning, they became completely realized objects to him with little surrealistic and irrational qualities. The spectator too should enter this imaginary world by studying the contents of the *Green Box*.

Is this perhaps the reason why he is still not given the position in the front rank of the pioneers who made the great break-through for American painting at the end of the nineteen-forties? Another great teacher, Josef Albers, made his full impact as an

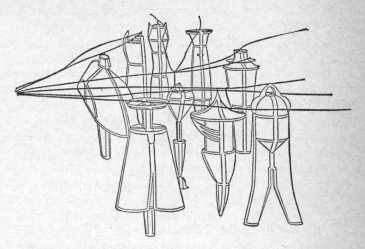

Figure 8. Working drawing for 'Nine Malic Moulds' in Richard Hamilton's reconstruction of Duchamp's *Large Glass* (full title: *The Bride Stripped Bare by her Bachelors, Even*). It is necessary to realize that Duchamp's terms represent very precise intellectual concepts. It is generally understood that the word 'malic' refers to the maleness of the 'Bachelor Apparatus'; the term 'moulds' is to be taken literally: they mould the 'lighting gas' and give it specific individual properties before it is carried away by the 'capillary tubes'.

artist only after he retired from teaching at Yale. It seems that it was a fairer arrangement centuries ago when a master could claim the work of his disciples as his own without further ado. The line is difficult to draw anyway. The examples of Diaghilev and Ellington show this. These artists work better with 'living tools' possessing their own minds and making their own seemingly quite independent contributions. Such artistic personalities have an increased capacity for keeping their planning wide open, ready to absorb to advantage outside interference that to other more rigid artists may appear as rude accident or disruption. I myself have acted as a screen-printer for the young Eduardo Paolozzi, who has since become a sculptor second only to Henry Moore. Paolozzi made silk screens that could be overprinted on top of each other in almost any position. They would always produce meaningful results. I freely overprinted the screens to his satisfaction. Once Paolozzi printed rolls of ceiling paper in ever varying overprints (plate 4). He left it to the workmen who were papering the ceiling to put up the printed paper rolls according to chance. Again any result always made sense. Paolozzi made good any small roughness in the joins. He certainly thrived on living tools possessing their own aesthetic judgement; and equally well on accident-inviting media that cannot be fully controlled. His early sculptures were highly textured and went through many stages of transformation, wax impressions, plaster casts, new wax shapes that were cast in bronze and so on. Later he preferred living tools. For his first aluminium sculptures of the *Mars* series (first exhibited at the Waddington Gallery in London) he had not yet found or trained technicians with whom he could truly collaborate. They worked according to his precise working drawings. The result was machine-like and almost hostile, and this went well with some aspects of Paolozzi's personality, but somehow was lacking in organic life. It also seemed incapable of further development. As time went on he found a technician who could prefabricate elements without consulting precise drawings. He welded the prefabricated pieces under Paolozzi's personal instruction (plates 5, 6). Paolozzi's ideas had to be kept fluid so as to accommodate technical advice offered by the technician. I have spoken of the creative capacity for manipulating precisely imprecise matter. Some artists like Paolozzi are not merely capable of working in this way, but need the stimulus of uncontrollable and unpredictable results in order to realize their true vision.

When I recently organized an experimental course for training art teachers at the University of London Goldsmith's College [7] I was not yet fully aware of the more general significance of what I had learned from these artists. I knew that it was important to loosen up the students' ego rigidity, which would prevent them from responding freely to the work of their own pupils. I assumed that the teacher trainees by doing their own work with less rigidity and anxiety could be made aware of the complex problems that attend the blocking and release of imagination in general. But soon a significant correlation emerged. Those teachers who were unable to tolerate their own spontaneity and the loosening up of their rigid planning could not tolerate the spontaneous and wilful reaction of their young pupils during their teaching practice either. They were upset, instead of delighted, when children disregarded their too narrow and restrictive instructions and 'did not do what they wanted them to do'. Of course, good teacher training has always tried to discourage the trainees from a too disciplinarian attitude. They were encouraged to welcome spontaneous ideas on the part of the children even if they ran counter to their own. But what has perhaps not been sufficiently realized is the close correlation between the two kinds of ego rigidity, the trainee's intolerance of the independent life of his own work of art and his intolerance of his pupils' independent contributions to his teaching programme. The unconscious fear of losing control underlies both.

Any work of art functions like another person, having independent life of its own. An excessive wish to control it prevents the development of a passive watchfulness towards the work in progress that is needed for scanning half consciously its still scattered and fragmented structure. We have seen how 'accidents' that crop up during the work could well be the expression of parts of the artist's personality that have become split off and dissociated from the rest of the self. Fragmentation, to a certain extent, is an unavoidable first stage in shaping the work and mirrors the artist's own unavoidably fragmented personality. The artist must be capable of tolerating this fragmented state without undue persecutory anxiety, and bring his powers of unconscious scanning to bear in order to integrate the total structure through the countless unconscious cross-ties that bind every element of the work to any other element. This final integrated structure is then taken back (re-introjected) into the artist's ego and contributes to the better integration of the previously split-off parts of the self. The creative process can thus be divided into three stages: an initial ('schizoid') stage of projecting fragmented parts of the self into the work; unacknowledged split-off elements will then easily appear accidental, fragmented, unwanted and persecutory. The second ('manic') phase initiates unconscious scanning that integrates art's substructure, but may not necessarily heal the fragmentation of the surface gestalt. For instance the systematic disruption of the surface faculties in much modern art remains partly unresolved in the final result. But the unconscious cross-ties still bind the single elements together, and an unbroken pictorial space emerges as the conscious signal of unconscious integration. In the third stage of re-introjection part of the work's hidden substructure is taken back into the artist's ego on a higher mental level. Because the undifferentiated substructure necessarily appears chaotic to conscious analysis, the third stage too is beset with often severe anxiety. But if all goes well, anxiety is no longer persecutory (paranoid-schizoid) as it was in the first stage of fragmented projection. It tends to be depressive, mixed with a sober acceptance of imperfection and hope for future integration. (This hope corresponds to psychic reality as the exposed seemingly chaotic substructure will gradually be covered up by secondary processes.) I will show that the dual rhythm of projection and introjection can be conceived as an alternation between the paranoid-schizoid and depressive positions as described by Melanie Klein.* But what about the intermediate (second) stage of unconscious scanning when art's undifferentiated substructure is formed? Then creative dedifferentiation tends towards a 'manic' oceanic limit where all differentiation ceases. The inside and outside world begin to merge and even the differentiation between ego and superego becomes attenuated. In this 'manic' stage all accidents seem to come right; all fragmentation is resolved. Because of the manic quality of the second stage, the following 'depressive' stage is all the more difficult to bear. Who has not experienced the grey feeling of the 'morning after' when having to face the work done on the day before? Suddenly the ignored gaps and fragmentation and the apparent chaos of undifferentiation push into consciousness. Part of the creative capacity is the strength to resist an almost anal disgust that would make us sweep the whole mess into the waste-paper basket.

It is astonishing to see how artists after finishing their work may begin to study it in great detail as though it were the work of somebody else. Something happens that is like awakening from a dream, when we try to recall the dream with our gestalt faculties fully restored. A measure of secondary revision and a

* See Appendix, p. 303.

projection of a better gestalt is then unavoidable. The artist in scrutinizing his work certainly falsifies its objective structure in the way in which we spectators falsify it. We cannot help solidifying (or verticalizing) its objectively looser, more open structure. But how else could we integrate the different levels of the ego functioning? The artist, for his part, is in a happier position. He can revert to his creative dreaming and to the less differentiated near-oceanic states of consciousness where the bulk of the creative work is carried out. He will set into motion once again the triple rhythm of projection, dedifferentiation and re-introjection.

It is the third phase of re-introjection when the independent existence of the work of art is felt most strongly. The work of art acts like another living person with whom we are conversing. The theory of projective identification as developed by Melanie Klein and her followers suggests that all human intercourse involves the projection of scattered parts of one's self into another person. In a good personal relationship the other is willing to accept the projections and makes them part of his own self. The good nursing mother, according to W. R. Bion [3], is capable of reverie (an undifferentiated state of consciousness akin to day-dreaming) in which she literally 'nurses' her child's projections. The child has felt this split-off material to be dangerous and persecuting. His mother is better able to assimilate it, due to her more mature personality. The child can then re-introject them in an enriched, more integrated form which he can tolerate. Projection does not lead to ego impoverishment, but to growth and greater strength of the ego. This good personal relationship fully corresponds to the artist's relationship with his work. In the first (schizoid) phase of creativity the artist's unconscious projections are still felt as fragmented, accidental, alien and persecuting. In the second phase the work acts as a receiving 'womb'. It contains and – through the artist's unconscious scanning of the work – integrates the fragments into a coherent whole (the unconscious substructure or matrix of the work of art). In the third phase the artist can re-introject his work on a higher near-conscious level of awareness. He so enriches and strengthens his surface ego. At the same time secondary processes of revision articulate previously unconscious components of the work. They thus become part of art's conscious superstructure. In this manner a full exchange occurs between the conscious and unconscious components of the work as well as between the artist's conscious and unconscious levels of perception. His own unconscious also serves as a 'womb' to receive split-off and repressed parts of his conscious self. The external and internal processes of integration are different aspects of the same indivisible process of creativity.

One can also say that all good personal relationships contain an element of creativeness. This entails a measure of generosity, humility and a lack of envy. We must not only be able to give away parts of our self to a loved person, but must be willing to take them back into ourselves enriched by the accretions stemming from the other's independent personality. Taking back, in a way, needs more generosity and lack of envy than the initial free projection. If a neurotic person has to dominate and control another person in order to love him, he can only take back from him what he himself had deliberately put into him. Possessive parents love their child in this sterile and sterilizing way. An immature artist who is hell-bent on exerting full control over his work is incapable of accepting that a work of art contains more than what he had (consciously) put into it. To accept the work's independent life requires a humility that is an essential part of creativity; it also presupposes a lessening of the persecutory fears of taking back into oneself split-off parts of one's personality. A psycho-analyst once told me how difficult it was to make his artist patients realize how bad their work was; they tended to idealize it in order to escape from persecutory anxieties. He was somewhat taken aback when I maintained that it was infinitely more difficult in art teaching to make neurotic students realize how good their work was. Alan Davie once said how easy it was for him to make completely inexperienced, untaught adolescents (he taught very unsophisticated silversmith apprentices for a time) produce near masterworks, and how difficult, if not impossible, it was to make them realize how good they were. Alan Davie, like all good teachers everywhere, could draw astonishingly strong and original work from unsophisticated students by putting them into an unfamiliar situation which allowed of no ready-made solution. The students had to fall back on their spontaneity and so mobilized (low-level) sensibilities not ordinarily at their command. Alan Davie's pupils produced work of a quality that deeply impressed him and left a permanent mark on his own work. One of his methods was almost literally polyphonic. He asked his pupils to work on eight designs at once; they were to insert in turn into each some simple element, a square, two circles, herring-bone patterns and the like, with the sole stipulation that they should vary their size and position every time. They had to go ahead with each design piece-meal without being able to make elaborate plans for the future, like a chess player who has to play several chess games simultaneously. Undoubtedly, of course, unconscious scanning, which can hold mutually exclusive serial structures in a single focus, can contemplate all designs in a single act of comprehension. This dispersal of the sharp focus of ordinary concentration helped to stimulate low-level sensibilities, which was the aim of the exercise. But the pupils were not aware of this and did not accept the result as their own achievement. They did not really know what had happened to them and could gain nothing.

The walls of final-term exhibitions all over the country are hung with impressive work in which the students have served as blind tools for their teachers. These exhibits prove nothing about the effectiveness of the teaching. The students did not really assimilate their work. Alan Davie's apprentices, at best, thought the whole affair a huge joke that had little to do with them. They were right. The process of assimilation or of re-introjection is the most difficult task of the teacher and is hardly ever attempted with a purpose. Putting up work of the student on the wall does help. It is an implicit invitation to realize what effect their work can have on the atmosphere of a room. Making the student choose the work to be hung on the wall forces the student to face up to what he has done. But this is not nearly enough.

Ego rigidity and insistence on full conscious control of the work blinds the student from seeing what he has done. He can only see what he has purposely put into the work. Showing him that there are other more important features in his work which he had not premeditated is tantamount to making him face his own fragmented personality. When we point out the unintended effects in his work – and they are the greater part of the artistic structure – he will feel them as alien and hostile, and the work now appears to him fragmented and falling to bits. It is difficult to convince him that this is not so, that there existed a complexity of cross-links and submerged harmonies which he had shaped spontaneously on an unconscious level and for which he was fully responsible. The contrast of surface fragmentation and low-level coherence is common to most really new art on which the secondary processes have not yet set to work. The teacher must, by his example, demonstrate to his student the open-eyed empty stare which is needed for scanning low-level integration hidden below the fragmented surface. In this way he may help the student to overcome anxiety. He may point out to the student that the same kind of 'accident' or any other failure of conscious purpose has a fatal propensity to recur in later work. The laws of chance speak against such an accumulation of accidents. They are rather the protest of unconscious and unacknowledged parts of his personality and as such have to be accorded meaning and significance. Accepting their significance does not mean a psycho-analytic interpretation of their symbolism, but requires from the teacher empathy and aesthetic appreciation on the highest level, such as is accorded only to the greatest master works of the past, which have achieved wholeness in spite of superficial conflict. Every student deserves to be treated as a potential genius. The teacher cannot expect gratitude for his effort. The student may well resent his teacher's reading into his work so much of which he himself is not yet aware. The usual kind of art teaching, concerned as it is only with correcting details according to good taste, is so much more comfortable because it panders to the student's conscious needs for good gestalt. It is not essential that what the teacher says should be true; what matters is the deeper level of experience on which the discourse between teacher and pupil should be carried on. Even a wrong, if sincere, reaction of the teacher will achieve its purpose if it makes the student react with more profound sensibilities, so that he himself can resolve the conflict between surface fragmentation and a submerged low-level coherence. Facing up to one's work will always be apt to evoke intense anxieties and often enough irreparable destructiveness. The teacher must learn to handle these anxieties and the deep disgust that may accompany them. The least he should be able to achieve is to induce the student to postpone judgement on certain features of the work which he has refused to acknowledge and wants to eliminate outright. Learning to postpone judgement is altogether an important ability which every artist (and certainly every teacher) must try to possess.

Some students once complained that my teaching was really psycho-therapy in disguise. I had to explain over and over again that I was only concerned with their work in purely formal terms, in a manner that contradicted the aims of psycho-therapy. For instance, I welcomed it if a student pursued an image in an almost compulsive, obsessional way. This ensured his honesty as well as his deep involvement and industry. Obsessional images are often split off from the rest of the personality. A psycho-therapist might well wish to keep them so because of their possible pathogenic effect. My own aim is to dissipate the compulsive image throughout the student's personality and make it flexible enough to be able to interact freely with the entire range of the student's aesthetic and emotional sensibilities. As compulsive behaviour usually fends off anxiety and is repeated unchanged with ritual rigidity, any attempted wider dissipation of the image may bring on overpowering anxiety. In that case the teacher has to hand over to the therapist. Good art teaching (and creativity itself) is dependent on a greater than usual tolerance of anxiety because of the need to work through one's total personality. This requires a more than average strength of the ego. It is wrongly thought that creative people thrive on neurotic illness. This is not so. The philistine can ignore his illness by living with only a part of his personality and can keep his illness from showing. The creative person faces his illness and its attending anxieties so that they noisily dominate his behaviour. But he is not more neurotic for this reason; rather the reverse is true. If satisfactory human relationships are proof of mental health, as is universally accepted, then the creative mind is healthy through establishing at least one good object relationship: with his own work acting as an independent being. He is able to accept what Adrian Stokes has called the 'otherness' of the work of art [30]. This acceptance requires the entire apparatus of projection, integration and introjection, which is part of any good relationship. The link between creativity and good object relations also works in the reverse direction. The continuous growth and nursing of a human bond requires a modicum of creative imagination, the receptive watchfulness needed in creative work. In a good marriage we constantly have to re-create the relationship as the partner changes through maturation, age or illness. A neurotic person cannot tolerate this need for re-making human relationships. He needs a measure of imagination to enjoy doing the continuous creative work needed in renewing a well-established relationship. In this sense the artist's creative attitude towards his work is only a particular instance of a more general social adaptation. It could be that doing good work as an artist also influences one's social adaptation in general.

It is sometimes said, with a wrong slant, that art's social aspect lies in its ability to communicate. This demand is directed against the narcissistic artist enclosed in his ivory tower who refuses to communicate in conventional language. But does he really refuse? If he is capable of intercourse with his own work in a free give and take, he learns to communicate with submerged parts of his own personality. If he allows his work to talk back to him as an independent being, his work will also be capable of talking to others with the same eloquence. But the communication between the artist and his work comes first.

The observation of artists and art students during their practical work allows us to study mainly the third phase of creativity, the feedback and introjection of art's substructure. The fragmentation of modern art and its resolution on an oceanic-manic level (to be discussed in more detail in the following chapter) permits further insights into the schizoid and manic-depressive phases of creativity. To see the complete stratification and interaction of all three phases we have to rely on the testimony of the vast poemagogic imagery around the motif of the dying god which permeates great myths and works of art. There we can clearly discern the three separate levels and their different functions in the creative process. In this way our more theoretical discussion of poemagogic imagery in the second half of this book will be capable of illuminating our present more practical discourse.

8 Enveloping Pictorial Space

Unless it is for political reasons, such as a demand for social realism, we have little cause to criticize an artist for not wanting to communicate some intellectually understandable message. Admittedly, the anti-intellectualism of surrealism and kindred movements is now on the wane and a new need for an intellectual enjoyment in art is growing. But a more intellectual enjoyment of art need not be directed towards some definite literary meaning. As I have suggested, art's main communication occurs on a deeper psychic level where the artist's conversation with his own work is carried on, that level of unconscious scanning and integration which tends to appear chaotic and meaningless to a purely intellectual scrutiny.

However, modern art's lack of intellectual content is anomalous. The periodic disruption of its rational surface prevented the emergence of traditional 'schemata' (Gombrich) that could be gradually expanded and refined. Modern art was revolutionary also in the sense that its recurrent upheavals destroyed its own children. Incipient styles and self-fertilizing ideas were discarded as soon as they were born. There is something near-pathological and schizoid about these periodic attacks against its own imagery. It is saved from being truly pathological through the submerged depth coherence that redeems the laceration of the rational surface.

Traditional realism was saner. Gombrich, in *Art and Illusion* [12], has shown how the development of traditional realism preserved an unbroken continuity lasting centuries. It was dependent on creating conventional 'schemata' which by a potent artistic illusion (I have spoken elsewhere [5] of the 'externality' illusion of realism) were accepted as precise descriptions of reality. It is Gombrich's great achievement to have finally broken the 'externality' illusion that had invested the conventional schemata of Western realism with objective validity. (One wonders whether Wittgenstein would have tried to give objective validity to the logical structure of language had he not – somewhat naïvely – accepted that the elements of a picture had the desired objective structure, which, of course, they had not.) According to Gombrich the coherence of a picture rests on entirely conventional schemata which the artist has learned to read as though they were as objective and real (realistic) as reality itself. The rules of realistic picture making were the rules of a game played according to certain conventions that were constantly modified like the rules of a game. Had Wittgenstein known Gombrich's ideas he would have been able to synthesize his older 'picture theory' of logical language with his final 'game theory' of language. Understanding the flexible rules and learning to play the game accordingly is all there is to the objectivity of images both in the visual arts and in language.

What the history of Western realistic art can show so clearly is the way in which the rules of the game are gradually modified. Gombrich speaks of Constable's war against a venerable schema that represented closeness and distance in a landscape by warm golden colours in the foreground and cool atmospheric blues in the background. In such a schema the vegetation in the foreground would always wither into the golden brown of a violin. There is an anecdote about Constable putting a violin on a patch of green grass in order to demonstrate the difference in colour. By rejecting the old schema Constable could introduce the local colour of green also into the foreground of his landscapes, a most daring innovation. It could have easily led to a boring uniformity of local green colour and to a loss of depth. This danger is amply demonstrated *ad nauseam* by the green 'salad' paintings produced by countless amateur landscape painters ever since. Constable has much to answer for. Gombrich uses the anecdote for showing Constable's difficulty in reconciling local colour with the conventional gradations in tone or colour needed for representing depth. 'Matching' art against reality often needs a large arbitrary compromise between several conflicting conventions. Of the two matchings the older schema representing depth by gradation from warm browns to cold blues is perhaps the more profound. It requires the spectator to scan the total colour field whereas the matching of local colour can easily become what the word suggests, a purely local isolated comparison.

According to Land's recent experiments, colour matching depends on the structure of the total field of vision. He projected two slides of the same photograph but taken with different colour filters on a screen. Through this superimposition these two colours were mixed in different proportions in various areas of the picture. Yet this limited range of coloured light was able to produce a full spectral range of colours. Obviously the distribution of colour in the field of vision is quite as important for matching as a painstaking imitation of local colour dot by dot. The incredible success of the Impressionist colour revolution testifies to this. It is syncretistic in spirit because no analytic matching dot by dot, brush stroke by brush stroke, can 'match' its colours against specific perceptions. Only the total syncretistic vision based on unconsciously scanning a complexity of colour interrelationships produces the desired match. This completely free and spontaneous handling of colour eventually crystallized into a new Impressionist 'palette', a new conventional colour schema that was accepted as realistic and as true to nature as other realistic schemata before. I have written elsewhere how the German physicist, W. Ostwald, offered colour-conscious artists instruments for the precise matching of local colours. An awkward silence answered his indiscreet offer, which exposed the lack of interest on the part of the artist in a really scientific analysis of local colour. What is important psychologically is the ability of a dying realistic tradition to have absorbed into itself even the wild disruptive onslaught of Impressionist syncretism in colour. At one point in the history of modern art this assimilation broke down irrevocably. The Fauves revived the original attack on an analytic use of colour by making the most arbitrary colour combinations come right in a total view. But their freedom soon degenerated into a decorative play with brilliant colour. Sir Herbert Read proved against Matisse's own dicta that his free distortions of line and colour were a true presentation of reality as it is seen in a split-second (non-analytic) act of total comprehension. R. Arnheim claimed for Picasso's form distortions a power to match reality on another level of awareness. But the syncretistic total vision broke all conventional rules. It could no longer be assimilated into the old unbroken tradition of schemata. We cannot analyse them rationally. I myself have written elsewhere [5] that we have to believe Cézanne when he says that he felt himself part of the old realistic tradition and that nature was his only guide. I have tried to show that his distortions make sense if they are experienced as part of the total (undifferentiated) visual field rather than a wandering pinpoint of precise focal vision. Peripheral vision that fills far the greater part of the field of vision can easily distort the stable gestalt shapes of our ordinary awareness much in the way in which Cézanne made his apples bulge and his table tops topple, and fractured the edges of a table. Seen in this way Cézanne painted realistically. But modern art was in the air. The climate of art had changed and was ripe for the anti-traditional cycles of constant twists and disruptions that have marked the erratic progress of modern art ever since.

The important difference between traditional realism and modern art was the flexibility and 'openness' of the traditional schemata. They allowed rational analysis and so satisfied the requirements of the secondary process. At the same time they were not rigid and defensive. They could be distended and modified when primary process fantasy required new spontaneous growth and invention. There was no need for disruption. In other words there was not yet the fatal dissociation of sensibilities which smashed the traditions of Renaissance realism and led to the battle between intellect and intuition (secondary and primary process) characteristic of modern art. Flexible schemata and gradual innovation were replaced by defensive and rigid mannerisms that yielded only to periodic catastrophic disruption.

The destruction of tonality in Western music followed the same path. The rich harmonic system of tonality resembles in its gradual expansion the smooth growth of realistic schemata in the visual arts. The system of harmonic chords current at a particular period was never entirely rigid and self-contained. Schoenberg showed how new chords appeared first in the disguise of melodic 'accidents'. Gradually they were picked out as new dissonances that still required to be explained away as melodic accidents; they had to be prepared and resolved horizontally. This part-disguise softened the harshness of the dissonances, which would otherwise have disrupted the integrity of musical space. Gradually they gained in smoothness and finally could discard their melodic context and be acknowledged as fully fledged consonances. A gradual secondary process turned initially 'accidental' textural elements into fully articulate components of the current harmonic system. The various systems of musical thought never closed up to prevent further accretions. Thus a continuous unbroken tradition of tonality became possible. More and more chords were assimilated into the existing harmonic system without disrupting tonal sensibilities.

Even rigid clichés can help in new harmonic invention. Schoenberg comments on the rigid accompaniment to a Viennese waltz which, in a seemingly insensitive way, repeats the same primitive chords. The free dance of the melody does not deign to pay heed to the obvious harmonic cliché below and so often combines with it – as though by accident – into exciting new sound combinations. Perhaps the most rigid accompaniment of all was the Alberti bass, invented in the eighteenth century. It served to sustain the sonority of the short-breathed keyboard instruments of the time. It breaks up a chord consisting of three notes into a rapid alternation of four notes. The device proved extremely long-lived and is now held in justified contempt by musicologists. They have even dared to censure Mozart for a lapse from grace when he used the Alberti bass in his Piano Sonata K.545. (He is sometimes excused as having written this light-weight sonata as an exercise for beginners.) But a genius like Mozart will make use of cast-iron clichés as a welcome cover for bold experiment. Already in the first bar of the second movement the hammering accompaniment grates harshly with the melody by moving with it in three parallel sevenths, which would have been unacceptable in a more flexibly moving accompaniment (figure 9). Harshness turns into extreme sweetness of sound. The performer must feel the conflict between the rigidly moving bass figures and the freer flow of the melody. Elsewhere the melody acquires the rhythmical character of the Alberti bass: it succumbs fully to its rhythm in the surprising almost abrupt conclusion of the movement. Or else the bass suddenly frees itself and blossoms into true melody, as happens in the sixth bar of the movement.

In the right aesthetic climate, even unimaginative repetition, imitation and rigid clichés need not act as straitjackets inhibiting the play of the imagination. Artistic traditions which bind the

Andante

(a) Bar 1

parallel
sevenths

(b) Bar 73

Figure 9. Alberti bass in the slow movement of Mozart's Piano Sonata in C major (K.545). This conventional harmonic padding device is here used by Mozart for original harmonic and melodic effects. Its rigidity allows the melody and accompaniment to move in parallel sevenths in the first bar of the movement (a); and in the last three bars the structure of the Alberti bass penetrates into the main melody itself (b). Here the Alberti bass must be accorded full melodic significance. A similar case is the famous opening of Beethoven's *Moonlight Sonata*, where the melodic line of the broken chords takes over the main melody; the broken chords have to be played as true melody from the start.

artist both in content and form can give him more freedom than the forced over-originality of our time. Byzantine icons are fixed both in form and content. In the Byzantine Museum at Athens one can see the same icon repeated in many examples, one looking like an almost exact copy of the other. Yet what differences in power! Because we come to know the common schema of the composition, the slightest deviation will be all the more telling and expressive. The provincial icons of Macedonia and Crete lack classical serenity and can strain convention almost to breaking point; the inner tension coils up like a spring. Yet the schema is never really disrupted. I was amazed to hear from learned monks on Mount Athos that they considered El Greco's contorted and elongated style as being wholly in the Byzantine tradition. This casts a new light on the endeavours of Western art historians to explain these distortions solely in terms of Italian Mannerism. We know how Dutch painters of the sixteenth century also became absorbed in Italian manneristic influences. But in their maturity and old age they went 'native' and threw off the borrowed plumage. El Greco, the Greek, certainly submitted to Italian elegance, but in his old age he recaptured the spirituality of the Cretan icons he had painted in his youth. Byzantine clichés once again grew through the manneristic surface, another example of a schema or cliché acting creatively when it collides with another equally unyielding cliché.

The general acceptance of schemata and clichés certainly makes for more effective communication. Critics of modern art refer to communication theory in order to prove that modern art, lacking in tradition and convention, cannot communicate. This may well be true. I think the sickness of modern art lies deeper. I have spoken of the vicious circles operating in modern art. Innovation sweeps away all existing schemata so as to make a completely new start, only to be solidified by an equally vicious secondary process which turns it once again into a rigid cliché. As such it will stifle all further spontaneity so that a new eruption from the depth becomes inevitable.

What was the beginning of this vicious circle? Was it the public's refusal to read Cézanne's syncretistic form distortions or Matisse's colour distortions as a new realistic schema in line with the Renaissance tradition? They could have done so if they had wanted to. Today it seems strange that El Greco's Spanish contemporaries should have accepted his far more extreme distortions as realistic enough in the spirit of the far more alien Byzantine tradition. There was no public outcry comparable to that which greeted Cézanne's allegedly anti-realistic work. I feel that had Cézanne won the day during his lifetime his syncretistic handling of free form would have been accepted as a logical extension of the earlier Impressionist experimentation with free colour. No catastrophic disruption of conscious sensibilities need have occurred. However, the time was ripe for open self-destructive irrationality. The greatest modern painter, Picasso, did attack conscious sensibilities in an outright deliberate manner. His systematic fragmentation of pictorial space at the height of his Cubist experiments comes perilously near to schizophrenic fragmentation and its self-destructive attacks on the ego. The schizophrenic literally attacks his own language function and capacity for image making. He twists, contorts words in the same weird way in which he draws and paints his images. He attacks his own ego functions almost physically, and projects the splintered parts of his fragmented self into the outside world, which in turn becomes fragmented and persecutory. The sorcerer's apprentice in Goethe's poem vainly hacks the magic broom into pieces. Each fragment turns into another whole broom to continue the work of devastation. His bid for magic control is in vain. We begin to understand why the initial impression of fragmentation which characterizes any work of art in progress can evoke such anxieties and even destructiveness in the artist, particularly if he clings to his illusion that he can gain full conscious control over his working process. Such magic is beyond his power. For some reason Picasso (to my mind the supreme embodiment of the spirit of modern art) savagely attacks his picture; he literally dismembers his imagery and scatters the fragments through the picture plane and pictorial space. The conscious experience of his work retains much of the theme of attack, destruction and death. Where, of course, he differs from schizoid aggressiveness, is in the coherence of his tough pictorial space. This remains integrated on an unconscious undifferentiated level. Bion has said that schizoid splintering of the language function does not prevent a creative use of language if unconscious linkages are preserved. James Joyce's splinter language is of this kind. His fantastic word conglomerates are not just violent compressions of language splinters, but establish counterpoints of dreamlike fantasies that run on below the surface and link the word clusters into an unending hypnotic stream.* Similarly the fragmented, violently condensed picture

* It seems likely that the hypnotic state also dedifferentiates the ego, involving possibly also the superego.

plane of a ripe Cubist painting is held and animated by a dynamic pulse. It draws the fragments together into a loose yet tough cocoon that draws the spectator into itself. Again this space experience does not lack a hypnotic, almost mystic quality (plate 25).

The new American painting has ground down all splinters into tachist shreds and textured fragments. I have mentioned how it represents the climax of a long development of splintering that probably began already with French Impressionism. But again the picture plane withstands the attacks. Its continuity is emphasized and ripples with a unitary pulse acting right across the entire surface. It was said of the first impact of Jackson Pollock's painting that it sucked and enveloped the spectator inside the picture plane. This is another instance of the hypnotic quality of fragmented art. Aestheticians speak of the ambiguity of the 'aesthetic distance' between the spectator and the work of art. It is found in most kinds of art. In the extreme cases of 'envelopment' in modern art this distance is at last annihilated altogether. The distinguished artist and writer on the depth-psychology of art, Adrian Stokes, has rightly emphasized the near-mystic quality of much modern art. It often gives one the experience of being 'enveloped' [32]. The artist feels at one with his work in a mystic oceanic union, not unlike the nursling on his mother's breast who feels at one with his mother. Stokes contrasts this (manic) enveloping experience of 'oneness' with the more mature experience of 'otherness' [30]. Then, the artist feels the work as an independent organism beyond his control placed at a definite distance from him. Stokes rightly thinks the experience of oneness and otherness are present in any creative experience in varying degrees, only that in extreme examples of modern art the feeling of envelopment has almost ousted the more mature feeling of otherness. This is another way for saying that in modern art the third phase of creativity remains rudimentary. Manic envelopment by 'oneness' and depressive detachment by 'otherness' characterize two different stages in creative work. I have distinguished the three phases, schizoid projection, unconscious integration on an undifferentiated manic level and a final depressive introjection. It is in this final depressive stage that the work of art assumes independent existence and 'otherness'. In the preceding manic stage of unconscious integration the artist has not yet detached himself from his work. It is to this aspect of creative work that the manic feeling of oneness, envelopment and mystic union belongs. Because in modern art the third phase of depressive introjection has become attenuated, the manic experience of mystic oneness persists in the finished product. This however only presents a quantitative difference between traditional and modern art.

We started our analysis of undifferentiated imagery with a highly technical discussion of unfocused attention and the ambiguity of counterchanges. But already the concept of Paul Klee's multi-dimensional attention where inside and outside areas become one had mystic overtones. As we reach the deepest oceanic levels of dedifferentiation the boundaries between the inside and outside world melt away and we feel engulfed and trapped inside the work of art. The initial stages of dedifferentiation (that are still near the surface level of attention) could still be called preconscious, though the beginning blur and vagueness indicate the lapse of the surface functions. The deepest oceanic experience, however, dissolves space and time itself, which are the very modes by which our reason works. It could not be called preconscious by the widest stretch of the term.

We meet with a similar progression and gradual dissolution of all definite space experience in the so-called dream-screen as described by B. Lewin [18]. Stretched behind the more precise (gestalt) images of the dream there is an indistinct cloud-like screen that cannot be precisely located in space. In some dreams (obviously belonging to a lower level of differentiation) the figures in the foreground dissolve and the mysterious dream-screen remains open to the eye. Once the dream-screen loses substance it approaches a totally empty 'blank dream' which, in spite of its apparent emptiness, leaves behind a memory of intense emotional experience. The dream-screen is evasive. It may roll itself up and disappear in the infinite (I would guess this happens when the futile attempt at more precise focusing is made) or else advance towards the dreamer, intrude or envelop him. Lewin also reports a dream where the dreamer stood opposite a wall stretching into the infinite. While facing it he also felt inside the wall. This is truly undifferentiated oceanic envelopment, not unlike Paul Klee's multi-dimensional space. An experience of being physically engulfed appears to me already due to secondary revision that tries to solidify immaterial abstract space. Parallel to Lewin's investigations of the dream-screen are G. Róheim's [26] speculations about a basic dream conflict which can be formulated in terms of differentiated and undifferentiated space. He explicitly speaks of a spatially undifferentiated 'dream womb'. The dreamer enters his own dream womb while at the same time he leaves this inner space through the 'gates' of the dream. This is truly undifferentiated language. As he leaves the inner space he reconstructs a more tangible space outside as the dramatic stage on which the conscious dream events are being played. Róheim thinks that the basic dream conflict between differentiated and undifferentiated space underlies all creative work. In this he comes very near to my concept of a creative ego rhythm that swings between focused gestalt and oceanic undifferentiation.

The London psycho-analysts, D. W. Winnicott [34] and Marion Milner [22], have stressed the importance for a creative ego to be able to suspend the boundaries between self and not-self in order to become more at home in the world of reality where the objects and self are clearly held apart. The ego rhythm of differentiation and dedifferentiation constantly swings between these two poles and between the inside and outside worlds. So also does the spectator, now focusing on single gestalt patterns, now blotting out all conscious awareness in order to take in the undivided whole.

In modern art the ego rhythm is somewhat onesided. The surface gestalt lies in ruins, splintered and unfocusable, the undifferentiated matrix of all art lies exposed, and forces the spectator to remain in the oceanic state of the empty stare when all differentiation is suspended. The pictorial space advances and engulfs him in a multi-dimensional unity where inside and outside merge. We see now more clearly why it would be misleading to call this near-mystic experience of modern art in any way pathological; what is anomalous is the disruption of the ego rhythm on its way back to a more differentiated state. The elusive pictorial space is a conscious signal of an unconscious coherence and integration which redeems the fragmentation of the surface gestalt. Seen in this way, the oceanic experience of fusion, of a 'return to the womb', represents the minimum content of all art; Freud saw in it only the basic religious experience. But it seems now that it belongs to all creativity. In modern art it has the more specific function of counteracting the violence and destruction wrought by the periodic self-destructive attacks on the ego, such as the twisting of its surface sensibilities, the destruction of stable focusing points and of all coherent melody and line. This self-destructive attack on the ego is mirrored in the conscious themes of much modern art, which are hardly ever love, rarely pity, more often death, devastation and the hatred of life and the human condition. We have to have strength enough to stand the experience of schizoid self-destruction. As the ego sinks towards oceanic undifferentiation a new realm of the mind envelops us; we are not engulfed by death, but are released from our separate individual existence. We enter the manic womb of rebirth, an oceanic existence outside time and space.

Without the depth coherence warranted to us by oceanic envelopment, surface fragmentation indeed turns pathological. True schizophrenic art only offers the surface experience of fragmentation and death without being redeemed by low-level coherence. Cubist painting resembles schizophrenic art almost too closely. There are the same glassy all too rigid splinters that refuse to join into bigger entities, the same proximity of fear and sweetness, of laughter and tragedy. But there the similarity ends. In schizophrenic art no oceanic envelopment heals the surface fragmentation. Oceanic dedifferentiation is felt and feared as death itself. I once visited the studio of a talented schizophrenic painter on the invitation of a common friend who knew about his illness, but failed to warn me. As is my wont, I looked at the pictures with a minimum of preconceptions and anticipations, anxious to allow the work to speak for itself. I failed to spot the very obvious symptoms of the illness. The large paintings were covered with geometric glass-like splinter forms done in strong colours. Minute ant-like figures were placed on various levels of the broken planes and gave them enormous scale. I mentioned tentatively that the paintings looked like cartoons for enormous murals and that they seemed apocalyptic in content. The artist did not disagree. We went on for a while until I suddenly discovered paintings of a quite different naturalistic kind leaning against the wall. They showed huge grimacing figures with hideously distorted features. When I asked the artist about them, he answered casually: 'Oh, these are only my sketches!' The truth dawned on me. The poor man began by painting these persecuting life-size figures and then, in self-defence, cut them up into a thousand splinters allowing the figures to reappear ant-like among the huge broken fragments. The sweet colours contradicted the agony of the work. Schizophrenic painters like to connect horror with sweet decoration, probably another palliative for their fears. Their incongruity adds to the general impression of fragmentation.

The schizophrenic painter clings to his surface faculties however savagely he may attack and mutilate them; he does not allow them to melt into undifferentiated emptiness. To him the suspension of the surface faculties stands for total annihilation and death, much in the manner in which some neurotics dare not fall asleep because for them, too, letting go of the waking faculties means death. However fragmented a schizophrenic painting, the splinters remain strangely alone and rigidly isolated, and in a way still invite the focus of conscious attention to dwell on them. They do not press the eye to wander on in search of unity as the great Cubist paintings do. The gestalt process, wounded and almost paralysed, still functions and allows the sick man to cling to the scattered fragments that still remain of normal reality. The shift to lower levels of image-making so essential for creative work never occurs.

It seems that the schizophrenic's incapacitation is even more crucial. Dedifferentiation is part and parcel of the process by which the ego gives unconscious quality to certain images. In other words, dedifferentiation may be the structural (ego) aspect of repression (otherwise repression is guided by the censorship of the superego). The psychotic, in not being able to dedifferentiate his imagery, has also lost the capacity to repress and so to develop and nurse a rich unconscious fantasy life. W. R. Bion [3] seems to have something of the kind in mind when he says that the psychotic lacks the proper 'contact barrier' between his conscious and unconscious fantasy life. Normally this barrier is easily permeable, it affords contact as well as separation. Inarticulate material passes through the barrier on its way up to consciousness, while other material sinks down through the barrier towards the unconscious. In my view the functioning of the barrier involves structural changes such as I have described. Bion does not use the concept of dedifferentiation; but the consequences which he describes as due to a breakdown in the contact barrier are eloquent testimony for the struggle of the psychotic who tries to make do without dedifferentiation. He is only capable of the first phase of creative thought: schizoid fragmentation. But as he cannot melt the fragments down into undifferentiated and more malleable material, he simply compresses and telescopes them into what Bion calls 'bizarre' images. These bizarre compressions must not be confused with the harmless condensations of the dream work. Condensations are secondary products gleaned from unconscious dedifferentiation. On the truly unconscious level the undifferentiated dream images could freely interpenetrate without doing each other harm or violence. But on being brought up to the surface their serial structure repels the narrow focus of conscious attention. A secondary revision teases from the medley of incompatible images a few isolated cues and features, and condenses them into a single nonsensical mixture. These dream condensations are not bizarre. They still carry the stamp of the undifferentiated vision that created them in the first place. Bizarre forms are directly due to fragmentation and compression; they are hard and fragile, prone to fragment further, and at the same time they are flat and dead, which dream condensations are not. All characteristics of psychotic imagery may have to be explained from a lack of unconscious dedifferentiation.

The sane creative mind has created in his unconscious a 'womb' in which repressed and dedifferentiated images are safely contained, melted down and reshaped for re-entry into consciousness. The psychotic lacks this womb; he feels inside himself a hostile nothingness. For him to be trapped in his inner void means annihilation and death. It has so far proved futile to deal with these overwhelming fears. The void in the unconscious obviously corresponds to psychic reality. The schizophrenic's fantasy of being buried alive, of being trapped in a dead inner world is a true picture of his empty ego which has not prepared an inner receptacle below the barrier of consciousness for its own regeneration and rebirth. It may not be much use to sidestep this stark fact and try, as has been done, to interpret the fear of being trapped as a defence against some other deeper anxiety, such as the oral fear of being dependent on the mother's breast. The sane artist faces his fear of an inner void openly. He accepts the temporary loss of ego control which is often unconsciously experienced as the destruction of the ego. Psychosis and creativity may be two sides of the same coin. Both are in a sense self-destructive. But while creative man can absorb the ego's temporary decomposition into the rhythm of creativity and achieve self-regeneration, the psychotic is left only with the first schizoid phase of creativity. He has not learned to dedifferentiate the scattered fragments of his surface ego.

Jung noticed how often creation myths resemble schizophrenic fantasy. So do the countless variations on the 'dying god' theme, which Frazer collected in his monumental work *The Golden Bough*, and the many rites of passage. Frazer was never quite successful in accounting for the ubiquity of the 'dying god' motif. Nor has psycho-analysis been more successful. I will suggest that the motif can make sense as an account of the creative process. It refers to the heroic self-surrender of the creative mind. Death has to be faced absolutely without any sly anticipation of possible resurrection. Because of the dissociation of his ego the schizophrenic does in fact suffer final destruction as soon as he lets go of his flimsy hold on concrete reality. When his illness worsens, his over-concrete, rigid images do not dissolve gradually, but disintegrate catastrophically into the genuine chaos with which the concept of the primary process has been associated for far too long. The schizophrenic's tendency towards confusion, his doubts about his identity, about the proper distinction between the sexes, give psychic reality to his fear that undifferentiation can only signify the final destruction of his reason.

I have met with many schizophrenic border cases in the art school. At least one of them has become an acknowledged artist. His work is now in public collections. When he came into my care his work displayed full-blown schizoid traits. Some work done during his adolescence was indistinguishable from extreme schizophrenic art. It was highly excited, trying to express violent motion, yet freezing the turmoil into dead rigidity. Moreover it showed the usual intolerable admixture of sweetness with horror. He was fortunate enough to be taught by two artists of front rank. Both artists worked with a deceptive casualness and unconcern that were at first deeply disturbing to the young man. What he had to learn was to face the deep anxiety attendant on a partial loss of conscious control. He sometimes attacked his work with a ferocity which was a measure of his fears. Collage of *objets trouvés* and torn bits of paper, cloth, string, etc. suited him best, and he assembled the fragments with the utmost delicacy. But his work easily degenerated into manneristic decorativeness. He had repeatedly to change his method of working and each time had to expose himself to new attacks of anxiety. But he was brave and went on. In tearing his material (this part of the work became less and less aggressive as time passed), he already anticipated the possible ties that would join them together in the subsequent re-assembly and collage. To the schizophrenic the fragments would still remain isolated individual bits, too concrete for mutual attraction and their ultimate fusion. His need for splintering them further and further partly serves to overcome the concrete separateness of the bits. Instead of melting the bits, he can only tear them into even smaller fragments. By comparison, the artist can somehow scan in advance the undifferentiated serial structures into which the bits could combine in the future. His view is 'comprehensive' (Wittgenstein's *übersehbar*) and syncretistic rather than analytic in every detail. No specific constellation of the collage fragments need come into his mind.

This comparison between psychotic imagery and creative vision is of inestimable importance for psycho-analytic ego psychology. When we watch the schizophrenic's rigid fear of undifferentiated imagery, his intolerance of the ambiguity un-differentiation brings about, when we observe the chaos that ensues from the disruptive impact of low-level imagery on schizo-phrenic art, then we can hardly doubt that we are witnessing the rise of the normally unconscious chaos which we are used to associate with the primary process. It is difficult for us to recog-nize the same primary process in the undifferentiated yet orderly imagery of creative work. As soon as we find that the creative mind can fit the undifferentiated bits into controlled serial structures that can serve a highly rational purpose, we feel in-clined to deny undifferentiation the status of being truly un-conscious and so part of the primary process. But we cannot have it both ways. The continuity between the two aspects of un-differentiation becomes apparent in the border cases which I have mentioned and in the often severe schizoid-paranoid fear which the sane artist must tolerate during the first phase of creativity, before the chaotic fragmentation of his raw material has been melted down into low-level undifferentiation. The apocalyptic fears of the psychotic are of the same stuff as the unease which Mrs Frenkel-Brunswik's subjects experienced in the face of ambiguous patterns that dazzled their normal focusing tendencies. Tolerance of these initial paranoid-schizoid anxieties is part of the creative equipment. Even a psychotic can become an artist if he can bear the apparent chaos of the primary process. Creativity can almost be defined as the capacity for transforming the chaotic aspect of undifferentiation into a hidden order that can be encompassed by a comprehensive (syncretistic) vision. Then, schizoid anxiety will turn into the manic elation of the undifferentiated oceanic state.

9 Abstraction

There is a close nexus between the power of abstraction and the creative capacity for dedifferentiating the concreteness of surface thinking. Modern art and modern science have both achieved very high degrees of abstraction. This alone, if it were at all necessary, proves the supreme mental health of our highly creative civilization.

Though abstract art is already degenerating today into mannerism, its origin in deeply unconscious layers of the mind is beyond question. E. H. Gombrich [13] has tried to debunk the much-vaunted power of abstraction which modern art claims by pointing out that it bears a fatal resemblance to the child's weak powers in differentiating reality. When Picasso pares down the naturalistic shape of a bull into a mere cipher he does little else than the child who with his syncretistic vision can equate a wooden stick with a hobby horse. Nor, so Gombrich was quick to notice, is it an increased power of abstraction that makes the drunkard lift his hat politely to the next lamp post. Drink has so much weakened his powers of discrimination that he can no longer make the proper distinction. From a psycho-analytic point of view, Gombrich does not really debunk abstract art, but concedes it deep roots in the unconscious. The psycho-analytic concept of creative sublimation implies that the highest human achievement should be linked very directly with what is lowest and most primitive in ourselves. Our pleasure in music, according to Freud, is nourished by an infantile enjoyment of the flatus. Psycho-analysis does not drag the sublime through the mud by making such connexions. On the contrary; once we have accepted the dynamic model of creative sublimation which psycho-analysis has introduced, we can only expect that the most sublime be joined by a short-circuit with what is most debased in human nature. Nothing else will do, and squeamish readers who cannot bear such juxtapositions should keep away from depth-psychology. My own double concept of the primary process fits into the dynamic model of sublimation. Primitive undifferenti-ation turns into an instrument of high efficiency. The dynamic tension between the extreme poles of sublimation is often bridged by an arc of tenuous fragility. A schizoid dissociation of the ego is never far when distant ego functions are yoked together in testing creative tasks. Such ego dissociations need not always be taken as a pathological symptom; they could be due to a tempo-rary snapping of the highly tensed links within the creative mechanism. We have seen how again and again creative imagery is cut off from its matrix in the deep unconscious and turned into conscious mannerism and cliché. It may well be, then, that the frequent dissociation of sensibilities in modern art and the recurrent need for disrupting its mannerisms and clichés is not so much pathological as the price to be paid for the enormous tension created by its conjunction of distant ego functions. The close cooperation between precisely focused reasoning and al-most totally undifferentiated intuition has, to my mind, made our time so abundantly creative, both in art and science.

In our abstract art there is a dramatic short-circuit between its high sophistication and love of geometry on the one hand and an almost oceanic lack of differentiation obtaining in its matrix in the unconscious mind. The 'full' emptiness of great abstract art may be dependent on its close link with a cluster of incompatible images (serial structures) pressing around it on the level of un-conscious vision. These conflicting images cancelled each other out on their way up to consciousness and so produced the mis-leading superficial impression of emptiness and abstraction. Abstraction becomes truly empty whenever it is dissociated from its unconscious matrix. It will then turn into a vacuous 'generali-zation'. Empty generalizations can be handled with such facility because they have cut themselves loose from their anchorage in the deep.

The first abstract art of mankind was the art of the New Stone Age, which coincides with the two greatest advances in human civilization, the invention of agriculture and permanent settle-ment. The severe geometry of its pottery is never far from an undifferentiated vision that projected human form into the most unpromising abstract material. A smooth pot may suddenly sprout two tiny breasts to reveal its origin in a vision for which a pot was indistinguishable from the body of a woman (plate 2). Used as a funeral urn its 'womb' had to receive the bodies of the dead waiting for rebirth. Neolithic man projected human form and human agencies into almost all natural events. Their nature religions seem to us an unending fantasy of poetic metaphors. These nature religions are neither due to a specific animistic conception of reality, nor to a sudden burst of poetry. This is too specific an explanation. It is rather due to an undifferentiated vision in which the boundaries of the inside and outside world have become uncertain. So a triangular mountain or pyramid or stone slab could turn into a genuinely realistic representation of the great goddess (plate 1). The earth herself received into her great womb the dead and the scattered seed of the corn.

Professor Gilbert Murray speculated on the power of an abstract triangular shape to symbolize the great Mother goddess and her womb. He suggested that her pyramidal shape stands for a woman squatting on her fat haunches. This will hardly do, though we cannot exclude the possibility that this unattractive idea could be one of the many undifferentiated images mingling into any severe geometric form if unconscious fantasy so wishes. The power of Neolithic nature fantasy was enduring. When pious Greek monks in the Middle Ages searched for a sanctuary to be dedicated to the Mother of God they were attracted by the huge white pyramid of Mount Athos. Its triangular marble cliff rises steeply at the end of a long narrow peninsula. The holy mountain in itself already represented a shrine for the great mother. When I went to the other Greek sanctuary of the Madonna, the island of Tinos, second in importance only to Athos, I could hardly believe my eyes. There was on top of the island another small roughly triangular cliff. Of course a triangle can also stand for the phallus with its two testicles, and many other things as well. This multiplicity of symbolisms belongs to the essence of the great mother. Her womb contains the whole world of things in oceanic fusion. She herself is ambisexual and can have her progeny without the help of a husband. The naturalistically crude representations of the goddess give her enormous breasts and buttocks, but usually only a small featureless head on an elongated neck. It was recognized long ago that she thus represents the phallic mother; the small head on the long neck grows from the breast like a penis. All these mixtures of images point to an extreme of undifferentiation which is only to be expected in semi-abstract art. The images of the great mother and her dying son-lover touch on the innermost workings of the creative mind, where the differentiation of sexes, of death and birth, love and aggression ceases to make sense. The Neolithic nature religions dedicated to the cult of the earth goddess express this fusion between inner and outer world.

Adrian Stokes, in a recent lecture, pointed to the fact that the contemplation of nature favours a libidinous withdrawal from concrete reality. In my view, the dehumanization of Western art began when the contemplation of landscape replaced the representation of the human body. The undifferentiated background blotted out the human actors and took over the leading part. From then onwards it was only a comparatively small step to the total abstraction of modern art.

Psychologically, abstraction in modern scientific thought is not merely reminiscent of abstraction in modern art, but is due to the same phenomenon of dedifferentiation. Again its apparent blankness and lack of definite imagery is only due to the coarseness of conscious focusing that cannot do justice to the richness of images crowding round an abstract scientific concept. Again, their mutual contradictions will cancel each other out into blankness as we direct the focus of conscious attention on to them. Something similar also happens in the secondary revision of a blank dream. We remember that the original dream was quite clear and well-defined. But if during the transition from sleeping to waking we try to hold on to that vision, we become aware uneasily of certain contradictions. We feel that several mutually incompatible things were contained in its all too wide frame which now refuse to be caught in a narrow focus. As we train the focus of fully awake attention on the vague image it will recede and eventually disappear into a white fog. If, however, after our abortive attempts at precise recollection, we allow our attention to relax so that its narrow focus can open up just a little, then as from nowhere the mocking dream may return with some of its outlines a little more defined, only to vanish again into blankness as we hopefully train our inner eye on it.

A truly potent abstract concept has the same full emptiness. Henri Bergson once described intuition as a faculty for visualizing several incompatible images occupying the same spot in space. In true intuition the normal differentiation of time and space is suspended and events and objects can freely interpenetrate. Such intuition is needed in order to overcome any contradictions and inconsistencies that will still exist in our fragmented pictures of the world. In order to create order in chaos, the scientist extracts from the fragmented, possibly incompatible things or concepts some common property or denominator and turns it into a unifying abstract concept. While the search for unification of the incompatible is still on, the thinker has to hold on to the incompatible entities in a single comprehensive view. This 'seeing together' of a cluster of fragmented images and concepts involves a high degree of near-oceanic dedifferentiation, much in the way in which abstraction in art needs an undifferentiated matrix. A new abstract concept at first sight seems empty of all mental imagery, but empty only in the way in which a blank dream of subliminal image appears empty, filled as it is with unconscious fantasy. I am of course speaking only of truly creative abstraction which is still potent enough to beget new ideas and new searches. Scientific abstraction differs from an empty generalization in the way in which potent abstract art differs from empty ornament. A fertile abstract concept is supported on an unconscious level by a multitude of incompatible images that gave it birth in the first place and which blotted each other from view on the way up to consciousness as its narrower focus set to work on them.

The blankness of an abstract concept, then, is the work of the secondary process. Its hidden richness depends on the flexibility of the creative ego. Consciousness must allow the abstract concept to sink back to its unconscious matrix to seek new linkages in a new unity with other concepts and ideas similarly undifferentiated.

The need for seeing incompatibles 'together' is more easily discerned in periods of transition when science is still groping for new models to accommodate still existing contradictions and inconsistencies. Ernest Hutten, a physicist friend of mine, gave me a hypothetical example of an 'abstract' vision reconciling inconsistent images. Light is today visualized by two contradictory models; it is either conceived as a wave motion or else as a stream of solid bodies. Hutten suggested that a future physicist equipped with superior powers of abstraction might have no difficulty in individualizing light in terms of a new model that is neither wave nor body, but both at the same time. For unconscious vision with its limitless power of dedifferentiation such an image would not present any difficulty. But the secondary process cannot as yet transform this elusive serial structure into an abstraction based on a disciplined scanning of its complementary cross-ties, transcending the present distinctions. As long as we have not achieved this high degree of abstraction, an image that is wave and body at the same time seems as abstruse to us as is the undifferentiated world of the child.

The awakening of the child's powers of abstraction coincide with the full onset of latency around the eighth year of life. From then onwards the sexual urge and the physical growth of the organs is kept dormant until the onset of puberty. Freud was the first to draw attention to this typically human predicament of having to make two attempts at reaching sexual maturity, one abortive attempt during infancy and a second successful one during puberty. Freud speculated on the possibility of a prehistoric sexual crisis that forced mankind to postpone its earlier maturity at the end of infancy, which corresponds to an age when near-human animals become adults.

The full powers of abstract thought that come available for the child with the onset of latency have only of late been realized. It was thought previously – wrongly – that a young child was incapable of handling abstract concepts and symbols and that, for instance, the use of abstract symbols in mathematics was only feasible after puberty. This is not so. The child can treat abstract symbols with the same feeling of reality which he accords to concrete things. Admittedly in infancy, his syncretism is still entirely concrete. It is undifferentiated, but not abstract. What seems abstract in the infant's art is quite concrete to him. That circular scrawl is his mother in her entirety. Only the rise of analytic vision around the age of seven or eight brings the power of abstraction, and also simultaneously – this is most important theoretically – a lessening of interest in concrete objects. It could be said that latency of the sexual urge also diminishes the child's libidinous interests in objects generally and so allows the rise of abstraction. Two young London art teachers, Mr and Mrs K.

Mines, made a full and exciting use of the new possibilities. They rightly stretched the possibilities of the new analytic vision to its limits. They introduced the children right away to the technicalities of Renaissance realism. They suggested to their eight-year-olds the use of viewfinders in order to frame semi-abstract patterns cut out by the viewing frame from their context. The carved-up objects often became unrecognizable as such and fused with parts of the background into fantastic mixtures. Here the diminution of the child's libidinous interest in concrete reality becomes an asset. This kind of teaching at least makes a virtue out of a loss. If nursery teaching had supported the old syncretistic vision of reality before the onset of latency, the infants would have learned to equate their still intense libidinous interest in concrete objects with beautiful strong shapes and saturated colours, which they would tend to prefer anyway. If they were already aesthetically aware, the beginning of latency would not be able to dull the children's fresh colour sense and desiccate their bold shapes. Mr and Mrs Mines, by making the best of the abstract powers of the child during latency, could fortify him at least against the second and potentially more damaging crisis during puberty when often all artistic work ceases. Going on during pre-puberty with thoughtless encouragement of free self-expression does little to sustain the child's weakened spontaneity and nothing to prepare him against the impending shock of puberty. Self-expression, if it still exists, must dry up when it comes to expressing the confused sexual fantasies of the adolescent. Objects are once again, as in infancy, cathected with an urgent libido seeking the concrete object rather than abstract pattern. Yet we know that the adolescent cannot find a form strong enough to organize the urgent pressures. His love poems are notoriously unoriginal and laboured. What is needed – and Mr and Mrs Mines were doing this – is to provide the child in pre-puberty with some measure of intellectual control which can then be pitted against the new rush of sexual libido. As it is, art education fails the children all along. There is still some time left at the beginning of the secondary school to train the children in incisive pattern making (for instance, by the use of the viewing frame). Equipped with this kind of intellectual control adolescent girls under Mrs Mines's care gradually infused into their abstract patterns a growing erotic tinge. The new preoccupation with adorning their bodies fused with their new concern for more seductive pattern making in their art. Adolescent boys, I suppose, would spontaneously introduce some of their teenage mythology of power, speed and space exploration into their pattern making. Puberty, far from stifling the child's imagination further, could enlist the re-awakening interest in concrete reality to give a new edge to the tired pattern making of pre-puberty.

We tend to underestimate children's intellectual powers throughout, just as we like to underestimate the intellect of animals. In art education we throw away all the opportunities offered by the periodic shifts between libidinous syncretism and formal abstraction because we fail to spot the alternative advances of these sensibilities. The mistake is the same at every stage, a failure to train intellectual awareness and control, particularly in earliest infancy when syncretism is at its strongest, but hardly less so when the powers of abstraction awaken around the age of eight. For a long time the teaching of mathematics refused to credit children of this age with a capacity for using abstract mathematical symbols. Yet it is now becoming apparent that children take to the use of abstract symbols most naturally and endow them with as much reality as concrete objects. Similarly the course of contemporary art education is a treasure trail strewn with opportunities missed.

Abstraction has two aspects. Its *id* aspect is represented by the libidinous withdrawal from concrete objects, its *ego* aspect by the unconscious dedifferentiation; concrete objects are robbed of their individuality and merge – on an unconscious level – with other images similarly undifferentiated. Syncretism works in the opposite direction. It goes straight for the 'physiognomic' cues which stand for concrete objects and ignores uncharacteristic abstract patterns that are shared by other objects. This is why resemblance and difference in abstract appearance does not matter to the young child. But this indifference does not exclude aesthetic appreciation. There are profound differences in quality between different syncretistic representations. The young child could easily be made aware of them. The later pattern making around the age of eight is more generalized and to this extent abstract. The gestalt principle tends to iron away small individual differences. In drawing a portrait it is most damaging to draw the facial features purely in terms of abstract shapes. One is bound to miss individual cues. I have mentioned how portraitists have tricks of their own to overcome the regularizing effect of the conscious gestalt principle. They may project animal shapes into a human face and even whole landscapes with a definite 'physiognomy'. In this manner we take recourse to the neglected syncretistic vision with its superior sensibility for the unique and the individual. Drawing abstract gestalt patterns runs against our usual libidinous interest in the individual form of real objects and tends towards uncharacteristic generalization.

The extreme libidinous withdrawals from concrete reality which modern abstract art entails started many centuries ago and has only now come into the open in modern art. In my book *The Psycho-analysis of Artistic Vision and Hearing* [5], I suggested that Renaissance realism was not really interested in the objective properties of individual objects. Old Egyptian painting had represented objects with their exact properties, for instance with arms and legs equally long, their natural local colours, etc. The Renaissance painters withdrew from objective reality into a narcissistic introspection (inward looking) into their subjective sensations. The properties of the individual object hardly mattered, its perspective foreshortenings as seen from a particular spot did; so did distortions of its local tone by accidents of illumination that might cast the greater part of the object into deep impenetrable shade. In the last century Impressionism at last attacked constant local colour for the sake of a free play with colour, which dissolved all definite boundaries between objects.

In order to study one's subjective sensations one has to forget about one's interest in real form, tone, colour, and look at the external scene as though it were already a flat canvas. Otherwise the so-called constancies of normal perception will counteract the accidental distortions of perspective, chiaroscuro and open-air illumination, and will give us an immediate awareness of the true dimensions, tone and colour. For instance, we are immediately aware that all soup plates on the table are in fact circular, though in their projection they shrink into all sorts of ellipses. We have no doubt that both arms of a figure are of the same length though one of them appears foreshortened. Only emotional detachment, almost amounting to depersonalization, will allow us to overcome this constancy of the objects and see them as ever-changing flat patterns. In this sense the trend towards abstraction had already started during the Renaissance.

There were other ominous symptoms. The libidinously most important object is in reality, of course, another human being. Humanism in art ceaselessly extols the importance of the human appearance. The gradual recession of its importance over the centuries foreshadowed the anti-humanism of modern, particularly of abstract art. The rise of landscape painting had already replaced humanism as the main subject of art.

I owe to a friend, Mrs O. M. Bell, the suggestion that Wordsworth, a contemporary of Constable, needed the contemplation of nature as an escape from his attachment to his sister Dorothy. Sometimes in his poems, as in 'On Nature's invitation do I come', the beauty of nature and the beauty of his sister become indistinguishable. When he married, he found another escape from his infatuation and his poetic genius from then on began to wither and ended in the prosaism of his old age. His personal tragedy happened to fit into a particular phase during the long libidinous withdrawal from the object. Arnheim once wrote that a nineteenth-century painter who would choose as his subject either a Madonna or a cabbage without particular preference for either as long as he could practise his painterly gifts, was in a way already an abstract artist. I personally hate the impersonal term 'model' for describing a human body; model for what? For making a pattern? In schools the nudity of the model must not be associated with an individual person. The art student rises above any emotional involvement with the nude woman as a person; he is encouraged to study her abstract form with the depersonalized detachment of a true artist. What a debasement of a living human being! Life painting has to be discarded in today's art schools for this reason. It has become a soulless exercise in which it matters little whether the model is attractive. It was supposed to improve the student's draughtsmanship. Why this should be so is difficult to guess. One assumes, of course, that the emotional interest of one human being in another will sharpen his formal sensibilities. This must have been what it did in bygone times. But today our emotional detachment from reality has gone too far. Living models will do little to resuscitate a true involvement with reality. The relentless attack which art has waged against our libidinous involvement in reality has ultimately led to the self-destructive attack on our own surface functions which link us with outer reality. To escape from this impasse art has somehow to be reconnected with the dissociated intellect, and also be involved with real objects which we can love and hate.

Perhaps only a genuine hunger for catching the permanent likeness of some precious object to preserve it for eternity may have the power to defeat empty pattern-making after models and still-lives; nothing less than the young child's unconcern for aesthetic detail and his headlong rush for the syncretistic whole will do. We should be able to do this without necessarily disrupting patterns, rather should it be a positive, constructive search for a true syncretistic equivalent. There have been in the history of modern art enough attempts at syncretism of some kind. Picasso could destroy all analytic likeness of abstract form details; yet his scrambled-up portraits could achieve a good syncretistic likeness of the sitter. Matisse, in his young Fauvist days, could freely distort local colour and yet in a global syncretistic whole arrive at naturalistic colour. But – and this is the weakness – we still feel the painful twist of our abstract analytic sensibilities. Distortion of abstract form still hurts and like a caricature attacks, rather than preserves, the object. It is sad that Dubuffet's early syncretistic art was called by himself an 'art brut', a brutal art, a word which calls to mind the meaning of 'Fauves' – beasts. To be bestial and brutal, then, to attack and fragment beautiful form and colour still fits the authentic spirit of our self-destruction rampant in modern art.

The naïve urge towards finding free equivalents can be found only in popular art, graffiti and lavatory drawings. There they are inspired by the strongest human drive towards an object, sexual love. Another equally potent instinct is hunger. It is said that the marvellous calligraphy of prehistoric cave drawings was inspired by magic ritual of the Stone Age hunters striving to increase the fertility of their game animals in times of scarcity. The freedom of these drawings lacks even the slightest trace of wilful and manneristic distortion, yet it is in no way a precise analytic copy. Purely aesthetic considerations could have played only a very small part in decorating some of the hidden recesses in the caves. They are often scattered and superimposed all over the walls without apparent regard for an aesthetic result, yet not lacking in feeling for the three-dimensional protrusions and hollows in the cave walls. Sir Herbert Read [25] contrasts their principle of untamed (syncretistic) vitality with the measured (analytic) beauty of abstract art in the subsequent New Stone Age. Then analytic vision seems at last to have overcome the old unconcerned syncretism. The submerged syncretism of cave art, or at least its shadow, emerges whenever the hold of analytic abstraction was broken. Sir Herbert rediscovers a reminiscence of the freedom of Palaeolithic animal drawings in the short transitional period in Greek vase painting which followed the severe geometricity of the archaic period. Strangely elongated animal forms curl and wreathe themselves between the remaining abstract ornaments (plate 7). Nobody to my knowledge has yet attempted to explain their flowing shapes from style influences, say, from Siberian animal sculptures. Their freedom does not feel in any way manneristic or contrived. It has the unselfconsciousness of free distortion in the service of the object, which we ourselves have lost.

A parallel and perhaps even more transient interlude of syncretism interrupted the tough tradition of formalized Egyptian art. A caricature-like vitality broke through a millennia-old barrier of careful measurement. I am referring to the heretic king Akhnaton's reforms. He encouraged his court artists to represent his neurotic face with an almost cruel distortion. The scenes depicted are meant to convey serenity and contentment; for instance they represent the pharaoh with his family united in domesticity (plate 8). It is inconceivable that the artists should have dared to distort the features of their divine king intentionally and with an aggressive purpose. Perhaps an informal popular art (of which no examples survive) was allowed to intrude into the official court art. Only a naïve approach of this kind could have given the artists the courage for unselfconscious distortion. We latecomers can unfortunately read their work only as caricature. This is our loss. Syncretistic spontaneity of this kind is easily lost and is not open to a teachable tradition. Some freedom of line seems to have lingered on in Classical Greece. To judge from the unparalleled lightness of touch with which the sculptors shaved the flow of their drapery out from the marble, we can surmise a similar lightness of line in their painting, which has not survived. Some Hellenistic murals, for instance the paintings at Dura Europos, and the earliest Romanesque and Byzantine frescoes, retain some measure of an old freedom of line, until, in the West at least, the Classical tradition was finally extinguished by the analytic rigour of the Renaissance. It may seem paradoxical that the Renaissance artists, anxious as they were for the resurrection of the Classical spirit, should in fact have destroyed the thread that still connected the Western world with the libidinous art of antiquity. But self-conscious imitation often destroys the meaning of the original.

Neither can we latecomers pick up the thread by a mere wish to renew a lost tradition. We ought to give up all self-conscious attempts at regaining our innocence by copying child art or primitive and prehistoric art. I feel that our hunger for the object must still grow for quite a while until a great artist arrives to satisfy it and show us the way. A metaphysical longing for a truly life-giving and life-enhancing pictorial space (unconsciously standing for the fertile womb) may prove as potent a stimulus as a more direct libidinous eroticism. Perhaps a mixture of both the sublime and the crudely sexual may prove potent enough to stir into action our dormant syncretistic sensibilities. Who is really in a position to prophesy about the future of history? Sir Karl Popper has poured unmitigated scorn on such attempts. But it is legitimate to try to analyse trends existing in the present pointing to an unknowable future. Dynamic developments are most easily described by their static targets in the future. Our everyday language lacks the vocabulary for describing dynamic processes such as the needs, pressures and trends inherent in a given historical situation. Karl Marx described the economic and social factors obtaining at his time most accurately by predicting a future situation when the impoverished workers were to expropriate the few remaining monopolistic capitalists. This is now unlikely to come to pass. But Karl Marx's Utopia still stands as an accurate analysis of the main trends existing in his own time. In this sense I venture to suggest that a cyclical movement towards abstraction, dedifferentiation, a weakening of the libidinous interest in reality has recently come to a close and that a new trend in the opposite direction moving towards a new syncretism and object love may now be in the making. What I am trying to express is only the frustration and confusion in the air, the tired response to further self-destructive twists of our conscious sensibilities, the weariness of the overworked themes of aggression and death, the failure of abstract art to produce more than flat ornaments and the repeated loss of a dynamic pictorial space. All I want to do is to voice a growing hunger for a form of art not yet existing, a longing that is made only harder to bear when it is mocked by the empty posturing of an academic abstract art.

10 Training Spontaneity through the Intellect

The old cult of free self-expression still lingers on in art schools; but it has thoroughly exhausted itself as a stimulus for the student's imagination. Once upon a time the slogan of free self-expression came as a liberation, carried along by the yearnings of the Romantics and later the Dadaists who chafed against externally imposed conventions and restrictions. The individual pitted himself against society. By disrupting and shocking conventional sensitivities he released in himself highly individual and potent sensibilities. By one of the many ironical turn-abouts in modern art (due to a secondary process), today self-expression has become a social duty forcibly imposed on the student by teacher, parents and the public alike. More ironically still, some students therefore feel greatly relieved if they are told that there is no need for them to express their personality and that any laboured attempt to do so can only fail. The Dadaists themselves would have enjoyed this situation. They always refused to be caught in any final statement or style knowing well enough that the formalization of their maxims would destroy their meaning. And so it has indeed come to pass. Individual self-expression has turned into another social convention. If we were to formulate a new maxim that today could replace the platitude of free self-expression, it would be the opposite demand. Instead of straining too hard to discover his inner self, the student should objectively study the outside world. Because objective factors are alien to the inner self they are better able to act as extraneous 'accidents' and so cut across preconceived and defensive clichés. In this way they will be able to tap hidden parts of the personality which have become alienated from the conscious personality. Cool 'alienation', then, has to fulfil the function which hot self-expression once filled [6]. Since I first wrote on this fundamental change, the French anti-novel and Antonioni's alienated films have brought out the same point. The old psychological description and expression of inner states is replaced by a seemingly detached and objective description of man's outer environment. Somehow – and this is the paradox – our involvement with outer events is far better able to express our real preoccupations than a direct attempt at looking inside ourselves or into the minds of other people.

Today the artist is involved with objective reality in order to reach his own self. Abstract Expressionism in spite of its romantic name began as an impersonal involvement with the objective effects of paint, with its dripping, pouring, splashing, smearing, running, spreading, opaque, transparent etc., qualities. No attempt was made at expressing anything beyond. The term action painting brought out the new detachment, a wish to act rather than contemplate some inner meaning. Constructivism, although at the other pole of modern art, can serve the same alienation. The artist submits to the seemingly alien rules of number and geometry. Serialization in music, too, seems to explore an external discipline of numbers. In all these cases the seeming unrelatedness of the objective – mathematical or physical – factors to any preconceived form, will set into motion unconscious scanning which can deal more effectively with such complex and unpredictable factors. This explains the paradox why Boulez has been able to write his most moving music when all he has seemed to be doing is to carry out mechanical serializations, according to a complex mathematical chart. When he relented in this uncompromising acceptance of alienation, his work lost some of its emotional strength.

If my prophecies are correct the present irresistible trend towards objectivity and alienation is only part of a more general reorientation of art from introspection towards reality, no longer occupied with studying inner subjective sensations but inspired by a quite new libidinous interest in the objective outer world, in the things and concepts that really concern us and not merely with their picturesque subjective appearance and patterns. Our under-employed syncretistic faculties that go straight for the object without regard to its abstract pattern could be enlisted within this general reorientation. I have explained how an excessive awareness of abstract pattern while we are looking at a concrete thing proves that we are emotionally detached from it. We contemplate its flat pattern at the expense of paying attention to its real objective properties, shape and meaning. Conversely, our growing concern with objective meaning and content can override the awareness of abstract gestalt pattern. Any formal distortion is potentially 'realistic' if the syncretistic concern with the concrete object is strong enough.

It seems to me possible to train the stunted syncretistic faculties by a deliberate intellectual effort. We can give the student a task that has nothing to do with pattern and everything with content and meaning. Fortunately there are conventional situations where attention to meaning and content overrides attention to pattern. Any transition from one medium to the other, any change of size, requires us to invent a new pattern in order to retain the same old content. If we execute a two-dimensionally conceived drawing in terms of a three-dimensional sculpture we have to change its pattern radically so as to preserve the idea behind it. Interpreting a truly two-dimensional drawing as a photographic projection will hardly do. Giacometti's sculptures and paintings look very different when seen as abstract patterns (plates 11, 12). The sculptures are stick-like, as though tightly compressed by surrounding space; the paintings and drawings have far more volume. But they too are enclosed, this time by a net of furry lines. Perhaps the working processes felt the same to the artist. Kneading the plaster into insect-like sculptures may feel the same as filing down the space around the faces and bodies in the drawings. In any case the onlooker can, if he has syncretistic sensibility, feel the identity of content behind the diversity of formal pattern.

In teaching, one has to appeal to the student's interest in ideas behind the pattern, in order to mobilize his syncretistic faculties, which watch over the integrity of an idea as he realizes it in different media. It is important for him to forget about sculpture and three-dimensional space while attending to the two-dimensional work. For instance, the strong pictorial space of good counterchanges has nothing to do with three-dimensional illusion. It rests squarely on the unconscious struggle between several possible readings. The change-over of such strong pictorial space into sculptural space requires complete rethinking of the formal pattern, as obviously the space illusion of sculpture is determined quite differently. The British sculptor, Dalwood, during a short course under Harry Thubron, asked his students to forget about doing sculpture and scan illustrated magazines for any motif that attracted them. He then asked them to work over the motif in a series of drawings and to refine that aspect that was significant for them. Drastic formal changes already occurred during this purely two-dimensional transformation. When this was done to satisfaction he challenged the students to turn the essence of the drawing into sculpture. He insisted, rather drily, that a truly professional sculptor ought to make into a sculpture anything that really mattered to him however far removed its appearance seemed from the formal requirements of sculpture. Many students were puzzled, as one would expect in the climate of the academic art teaching of today.

Dalwood's challenge went against a deep-seated taboo of academic teaching. It is often impressed on the young sculptor that he has to learn to think primarily in three dimensions and give up working out ideas in the flat. This exhortation is none other than our old friend, the academic demand for precise visualization. There must be no interim stages and interim decisions as yet unconnected with an end product. But are there really separate sculptural and pictorial ideas? It is a great advantage to work out a three-dimensional idea in two-dimensional drawings if only because of the spatial ambiguity of most drawings. The ambiguity prevents a preconceived idea from setting hard too early. Keeping the final realization of an idea wide open allows the artist to engage the whole range of his sensibilities and his whole personality while he struggles with a flexible and unformed vision. The difficulty remains that the students have to re-invent new forms all the way in order to refine and in the end retain the essence of their ideas. They have to call on their stunted syncretistic faculties to control each new transformation and to check whether the idea has not got lost during the changes of formal appearance. To develop the syncretistic faculties is a slow and painful process. It cannot be done in short refresher courses. There is no teachable recipe for controlling transformations just as there is no recipe for transforming a photographic likeness into a caricature. There too we have to fall back on spontaneously controlled syncretism. The students must be taught – by coercion if necessary – not to wait on their inspiration and rushes of spontaneity, but to work hard at being spontaneous through choosing tasks that cannot be controlled by analytic vision and reasoning alone. This learning may take months, years or a whole lifetime. In this lies the momentous difference between the present teaching of spontaneity by self-expression and disruption and a possible constructive teaching of spontaneity. We would no longer disrupt reason but call on intellect and reason in order to sting into action the powers of the deep.

Art teaching shares the fate of 'modern art'. Intellect and spontaneity have been kept apart for too long. Twisting and disrupting surface sensibilities have lost their liberating effect. Unfortunately art teaching usually keeps out of step with the general course of art by a time-lag of ten or twenty years. Basic design has today become an academic exercise in the tired sensibilities of abstract art. Abstract art once came as a liberation. It was no longer necessary to copy external objects, the artist could freely invent new forms that could express ideas in purely aesthetic terms. Today abstract sensibilities have largely become more restrictive than the academic realism of old. For instance, it would not be good form to mix Constructivist and Tachist styles. Once the painter has chosen one kind of texture there remains only a limited range of other textures from which he can choose. Still the young painter can throw such demands of good taste to the winds, though he can only do so at his peril. I have mentioned how the battle for a vibrant pictorial space has been lost many times over and how the construction of a precise pictorial space is now being taught at some art schools. When I once criticized the academic construction of an abstract pictorial space I was immediately accused of advocating anarchy. A British art critic, now in the United States, pronounced that without precisely controlling space abstract art would turn into a 'mess'.

But why not a 'mess'? Any creative thinker who ventures into new territory risks chaos and fragmentation. According to my theory of creativity, an initial state of fragmentation and the not inconsiderable (paranoid-schizoid) anxieties attendant on it must be tolerated. Abstract art has become such a tired exercise in empty sensibilities because it has become so tidy, so precise, so well ordered according to teachable academic conventions. If

1 Cycladic idol of the Mother Goddess (*c.* 3000 BC). Headless and limbless, her violin shape was certainly not abstract to worshippers.

2 A bronze-age pot (*c.* twelfth century BC) could suddenly sprout two breasts, making clear that the pot's 'belly' really stood for a woman's body.

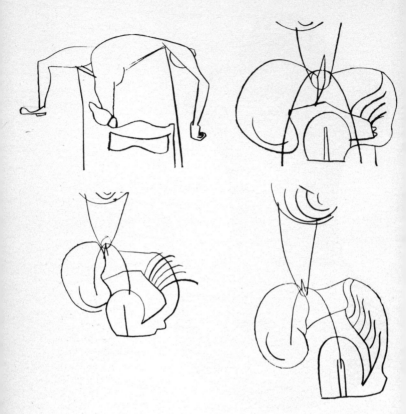

3 David Barton, Variations on the theme of the 'dying god' (Experimental course for art teachers, Goldsmiths' College, 1965). Constructivist exercises and life drawing spontaneously fused into images of self-sacrifice ('the vulnerable suppliant').

4 (*opposite*) Eduardo Paolozzi, screen-printed ceiling paper for the offices of Ove Arup and Partners, London (architects: Alison and Peter Smithson). Paolozzi printed the paper by superimposing semi-realistic images, a double profile, an aeroplane insect and an architectural grid. He allowed the workmen to put up the rolls of paper at random so that 'accidental' joints were produced. Paolozzi touched up only a few roughnesses.

*Creative
Accident*

5 Eduardo Paolozzi, Welded aluminium sculpture, Towards a new Laocoon.
Paolozzi thrives on creative accidents imposed by medium, tools and
collaborators. For a time he restricted such accidents. In his earlier series of
aluminium sculptures he often prepared precise working diagrams to be
executed by engineers with the same precision.

6 (*opposite*) Eduardo Paolozzi, Welded aluminium sculpture (*Medea* series).
Certain elements were prefabricated and assembled spontaneously without
resort to precise working drawings. The 'legs' of this sculpture were made up
from prefabricated tubular rings of different diameter. These rings were cut up
and welded into the sprawling legs.

7 Detail from a Greek vase dating from the transitional period between pre-classical geometry and classical realism. The distortion is the result of a free linear rhythm prevailing over precise volume.

8 Detail from an Egyptian relief representing the heretic pharaoh Akhnaton caressing his child. The linear distortions are extreme, elongated in the father, squashed in the child; obviously no caricature was intended.

9 William Pitt the Younger seen in three cartoons of 1805, by James Gillray (*left*), an anonymous French artist (*top right*) and George Cruikshank (*bottom right*). It is remarkable how we can recognize effortlessly the same face whether the features are oblong or squashed.

10 Paul Klee, *Ein neues Gesicht* (A New Face). Klee's images of humanity often seem near to caricature or playful joking; but in this water colour the rhythmical flow of a single line creates the likeness of a very real 'new' face.

12 Alberto Giacometti, *Standing Woman*.
Giacometti strained towards absolute truth. His
extremely elongated sculptures come true if one
accepts that vertical scanning can be done
quickly, while traversing the figure's thickness is
slow.

11 (*opposite*) Alberto Giacometti, *Seated Man*. In
terms of abstract appearance Giacometti's
paintings seem quite unlike his rod sculptures.
Yet they are equivalent likenesses of the same
kind of people. Realism does not depend on
matching abstract patterns.

13 (*opposite*) Detail from Rembrandt's self-portrait at Kenwood House, showing a hand holding brushes and a palette. In isolation the brush marks appear not unlike the excited handwriting of Tachism.

14 (*top left*) Rembrandt's self-portrait (whole picture). The same brush marks as part of a 'syncretistic' total object appear as a highly disciplined representation of a figure. But they may have lost some of their emotional meaning.

15 (*top right*) Dürer, drawing of Vilana Windisch. Compared with Rembrandt's handwriting. Dürer's drawing technique appears controlled and deliberate.

16 (*right*) Isolated, the micro-forms of Dürer's technique reveal their independent formal and emotional meaning.

Congolese soldiers & officers

FeliksTopolski

17 Feliks Topolski, *Congolese Soldiers and Officers*. Modern art (Kandinsky, Pollock) sometimes enlarged the abstract micro-forms of handwriting into the main composition. Topolski's generous handwriting almost disrupts the realism of the drawing. If we do not look too hard we seem to make out the fingers, hands, arms, equipment of the soldiers.

18 Jackson Pollock, *Drawing*. If we do not focus too hard, and take in the total rhythm, the brush marks will acquire an intense plastic life of their own, superior to Topolski's realism.

19 Braque, *Glass and Pitcher*. The work has the artist's characteristic simplicity; it represents just a jug and a glass. If we relax, the handle may suddenly be transformed into a classical profile, the ground behind the profile becomes another head or even two heads above one another, enclosed by a white bulging shape that overflows the rim of the jug. It could be a figure holding a palette and brushes. Is it a self-portrait? Was Braque aware of these complexities?

20 (*opposite*) Bridget Riley, *Straight Curve* (detail of upper section). The detail affords a simplified example of Bridget Riley's handling of a mobile pictorial space. The triangles on the edge of the design are comparatively stable and flat; the central (dazzling) area is stirred into perceptual stress, resists focusing and produces plastic oscillations.

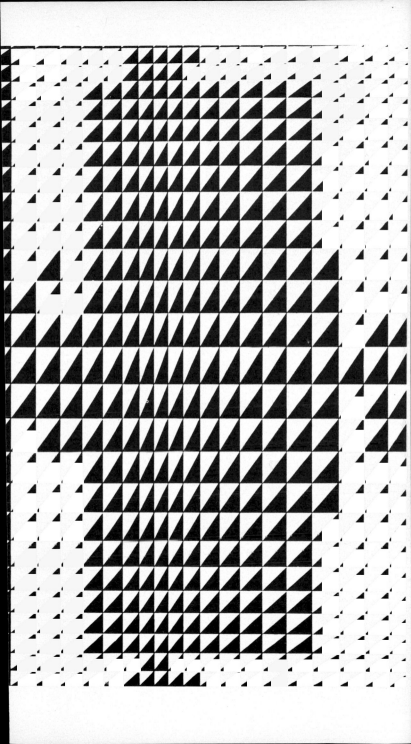

21–23 Maurice Agis and Peter Jones, *Enclosing and Opening Space*. Selection of diagrams from a note book on developing a spatial language in 'three directions' (limited to lines, rectangles and rectangular movements) for constructing active spacial areas related to the human scale. The formal language illustrated here is derived from practical experiments done in coloured panels and rods within a given architectural space. The dynamic effect of colour on active space is the main subject of the experiments, but unfortunately does not lend itself to photographic reproduction.

1 *Three directions* of space defined by three squares of equal size with a single common axis. Diagrams 2 to 6 are developed from this basic position (many intermediate developments are omitted).

2 One square moves in one direction from axis (sideways).

3 One square moves in two directions from axis (sideways and upwards).

4 Two squares move apart (sideways) from a single axis; the third remains static.

5 One square moves upwards, another sideways, the third remains static.

6 All squares move equally from common axis in three directions making two rectangular movements within their own plane.

7 *Three directions* of space defined by three rectangles of equal size relating to two axes.

8 Two rectangles move sideways, breaking their axis by a further move inwards.

9 *Three directions* of space defined by three rectangles of equal size with a single common axis, as in position one. Diagrams 10 to 15 are developed from this basic position.

10 As before; but two rectangles change direction; one remains static.

11 One rectangle moves backwards, another sideways; the third remains static.

12 As before; but the left rectangle changes direction.

13 As position 9; one rectangle moves sideways from axis (corresponding to position 2).

14 Corresponds to position 5.

15 Corresponds to position 6.

16 *Three directions* of space developed from the human figure as an axis.

17 Defined by three lines (closed space); one line has to be seen vertical.

18 Defined by three lines (open space).

19 Two squares symmetrically relating at right angles with two lines penetrating them symmetrically at right angles.

20 The same with lines penetrating them asymmetrically.

21 Two squares relating asymmetrically with two lines penetrating them symmetrically.

22 The same with lines penetrating them asymmetrically.

23 Two squares relating asymmetrically with two parallel lines free in open space.

24 As position 22, introducing a third free line to complete *Three directions*; the penetration of the squares is now felt as enclosing space.

25 Two rectangles relating asymmetrically at right angles with two lines penetrating them asymmetrically; here the penetration is felt as opening space.

26 As before, but rectangles change direction, thereby enclosing space (view from a different angle).

27 Closed space, as before, but one rectangle turned sideways (view from a different angle).

28 *Three directions* defined by three rectangles and three lines penetrating them and enclosing space.

29 *Three directions* defined by three rectangles and penetrating lines as before, but opening space.

30 *Three directions* defined as before, but with human figure as an axis.

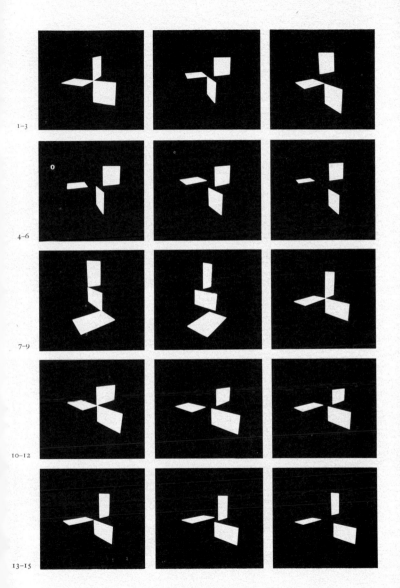

1-3

4-6

7-9

10-12

13-15

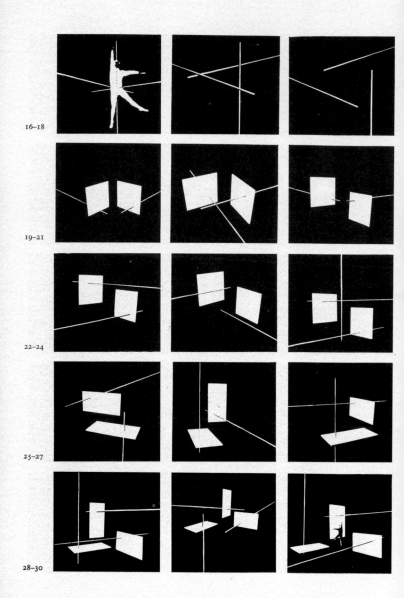

16–18

19–21

22–24

25–27

28–30

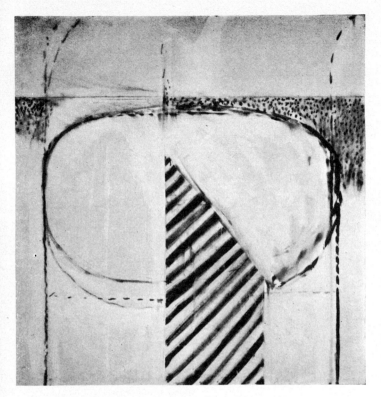

24 Peter Hobbs, *Form Space for Diogenes No.* 4 (approx. 6 feet high). This diagrammatic painting deals with a structural conflict between inside and outside space. A circular box contains an interior space, which for Hobbs can have a metaphysical quality; it is linked with the outside by a striped area of uncertain localization. The stripes are flat and emphasize the picture plane. But they also lead into the inside of the box and at the same time escape from it. Spatial conflicts of this kind belong to the subject matter of much modern art today.

26 Fritz Wotruba, *Figure of a Reclining Woman*. Though using cubistic elements, Wotruba has always worked in classical mediterranean tradition. The woman's limbs are scattered, but she also expresses wholeness and perhaps also the idea of rebirth. (Wotruba made the sculpture after the death of his first wife.)

25 (*opposite*) Picasso, *Portrait of Vollard*. Paradoxically, the peacefulness of the face is not disturbed but supported by the splintered cubistic space surrounding it. Cubist fragmentation dangerously approaches psychotic art. But while the splinters of psychotic art remain isolated. Cubist fragmentation is resolved by a 'depth coherence' belonging to a deeper level of experience.

27 (*left*) *Dormition of the Virgin*, detail from a Byzantine icon. This is the holiest of all icons: the son gives rebirth to his dead mother; Christ standing in majesty at his mother's deathbed cradles her childlike soul in his arms. The icon reverses the Western image of the *Pietà*, where the mother cradles her dead son in her arms.

28 (*right*) Michelangelo, *Rondanini Pietà*. Michelangelo comes near to reversing the traditional image. The dead Christ seems to carry his mother; she too hovers on the verge between life and death.

29 Henry Moore, *Helmet Head No. 5*. Moore, burrowing into his mother figures, created an inner space that appears bigger and stronger than the solid stone. His recent work has shifted to the male figure or head, but retains the same womb symbolism. The cavity in the phallic helmet is stronger than its outer shell.

30 Detail from Michelangelo's Sistine ceiling. Its subject matter is uncertain. We call it 'God dividing Light and Darkness'; Michelangelo's contemporaries gave it the heretical meaning of God creating himself, delivering himself as it were from his own womb. The same mixture of male and female power is repeated in the *ignudi* surrounding the panel.

there is any virtue in academic conventions it is their fitness for preventing a mess. But what we need today could be a mess. Perhaps it is because of the fear of making a mess that we shy away from content and subject matter and any direct reference to external reality. Nature is indeed disorderly and places next to each other forms, textures and colours that could not be tolerated by our refined abstract sensibilities. When abstraction first arrived it certainly brought a new freedom from narrowly naturalistic imitation. Conversely, could it not be that a renewed reference to nature and any other subject outside art could now help us to emancipate ourselves from the niceties of academic abstraction? Abstract art has helped us to experience the emotional power inherent in pure form. This capacity will not be lost so soon. If we now put together – by reference to external 'accidental' contexts – forms that we could never group together in a play with pure form, new emotional tensions can be set up in an intriguing counterpoint between the emotional meaning of pure form and the new intellectual context and subject matter.

Now that secondary processes have obliterated the sting of basic exercises in abstract form, it is important to put on record the heroic days of their first introduction. Then, it was only necessary to disrupt existing patterns and clichés in order to demonstrate the emotional and aesthetic power of simpler 'basic' structures. It came as a revelation that it was not necessary to compose complex pictures. Tearing them up and reassembling the fragments into seemingly accidental collages often produced better results. Inducing frustration in the students was part of the technique of disruption. Trying too hard to achieve some particular result was harmful. A modicum of despair at one's intellectual faculties was helpful in releasing more spontaneous impulses. Disrupting intellectual analysis, surprise, and baffling reason, seemed all that was then needed for enlightened teaching. But surprise soon wore off, new disruptive procedures had to be invented for every new course, an intolerable burden for the teacher's inventiveness. But worse was to come. As news spread about the rejuvenating effect of short courses in basic design or basic 'research' (as Harry Thubron, the most inventive teacher in Britain at the time, called it), professional teachers flocked to the courses fully prepared to be beneficially disrupted. In 1964 Harry Thubron rightly decided to discontinue such short courses. The time for disruption and quick results had passed.

A more constructive approach is now needed, a determined and sustained search for a really significant image and idea. I have tried this by means of syncretistic exercises where abstract form is transformed to retain the content. Let us remember how the caricature has to destroy and distort correct form in order to strengthen the subject matter. The British painter, Benjamin, teaching at Ravensbourne College of Art, imposed arbitrary rules for distorting conventional 'correct' life drawing. The students were not allowed to build up the body, limb by limb, part for part, but had to use a single outline ranging freely right across the picture plane. Benjamin prescribed that the outline had to touch the edge of the paper at least twice at points that were, say, at least six inches apart. To obey this condition the student would have to elongate a thigh in order to reach the edge. In most cases the result was immediately satisfying. The rule was far from arbitrary. The student was compelled to relate the shape of the body with the total shape of the picture plane. The shape of the body became wedged into and identified with the picture plane instead of being placed at some uncertain spot somewhere inside. What was missing, in my view, was the conviction that the distortion had helped the reality of the body. I mean the conviction on the part of the student that the distortion was justified from the viewpoint of a syncretistic whole, dependent more on the total rhythm of the line than on photographic correctness of detail. The exercise soon degenerated into decorative pattern making. Yet the principle of syncretistic distortion could have been right and a pointer to a better future. Even older disruptive techniques in life drawing retained their meaning only if they appealed to a syncretistic grasp of the total figure. Harry Thubron, for a while, successfully used a disruptive device that aimed at an overriding syncretistic grasp of the figure. When this syncretistic grasp was lost, the exercise too lost its meaning. Thubron surrounded his students by several models who moved in and out between the rows of students in an eternal dance. Much in the way in which Merce Cunningham manipulated his dancers, each model was given a different repertoire of movements among which they could choose so that a perpetual counterpoint was set up between their body rhythms. Thubron, at one time, exhorted the students to catch the fleeting posture of the models in a single unbroken line and to go on superimposing these lines until a new vision emerged. As in Picasso's composites, the more inspired drawings fused into new wholes that assumed the life of human beings. As long as the tension could be kept up, whether or not the discordant outlines would coalesce into a new whole, the exercise remained a sustained search for a new vision. But soon it too degenerated into a device for making textures possessing a fake liveliness. This is the reason why I think that any trace of disruption and wilful distortion must be eliminated from art teaching. All that matters is the reach for a syncretistic whole that can survive the disintegration, distortion or transformation of detail. The student must be taught to believe in his vision as he must be taught that content can be retained in formal transformation. Both beliefs run counter to the abstract formalism current in art teaching today (plate 10).

It is a sorry sign for our time that dead man-made objects rather than other human beings are more likely to involve students emotionally and produce ideas and themes that are strong enough to persist through a series of transformations. Harry Thubron sent his students on a search for interesting machine components. They had first to make dead-pan drawings, then select the most significant detail and study it in a series of freely drawn rhythmical diagrams. These diagrammatic drawings were further transformed into free brush drawings that ran counter to the metallic geometry of the original machine forms, yet preserved their essence. In the end these free painterly marks were turned back into three dimensions, this time made in wood. The graphic elements were turned into components that interlocked tightly like the original machine and – more important – like the limbs and organs of a human body. As Thubron remarked, not without irony, this machine sculpture looked more organic and alive than the usually stiff and dead life drawings. But in spite of this success there was still among the students a lack of conviction about the rightness of the transformations and the function of the underlying ideas. The underlying assumption was, of course, that the students were more likely to be interested in machine parts than in academically drawn life drawings; further, that this interest would be strong enough to survive the transformation of the original dead-pan drawing into a painterly sign language and its reconversion into three dimensions using a totally different medium, wood instead of metal. The students must be kept intellectually aware of their power to bring an idea unscathed and indeed fortified through such drastic transformation. The intellect must be enlisted as a potent helper of spontaneity. This is the essential point of which we must never lose sight. Still lives used to consist of fruit, game and other organic objects. One wonders whether machines would not do better altogether, or, better still, objects which the students themselves have manufactured, so that they were their own and could be sure of their emotional involvement. Pattern making and the flat vision it encourages would in this way be sufficiently balanced by such interest. Jon Thompson, who followed Thubron in teaching at Lancaster College, made his students make paper cubes which they covered with camouflaging patterns so that their shape became partly obliterated. Grouping them together again flattened out the cubes into striking all-over patterns. Yet as the students painted this still life the half-obliterated cubes pushed out into three dimensions here and there, and created a strangely animated ambiguous space. Obviously the original interest in reality aroused by actually making the cubes, was strong enough to survive the transformations into flat pattern.

I personally have preferred to tackle the intellectual challenge involved in these issues by a direct attack. I would explain to my students the need to find a theme that could survive any formal distortion, transformation, translation into other media. They were to start with any theme they thought significant (which in truth it rarely was) and to subject it to systematic transformation by what I called a series of 'tease-and-worry' exercises. The word sketch book has the wrong overtones just because in the nineteenth century a sketch book had a similar function, to collect motifs that mattered to the painter's imagination. But today's search for significant images or significant themes is too desperate and serious to be practised in the relaxed leisurely ways of the romantic artist of old. The image chosen is only a point of departure. If it is lost on the way it might prove that it was not strong enough to be treated as roughly as it must be treated. Any newly emerged image can serve as a new point of departure. My experience shows that sustained effort does pay off. The transformations can be very extreme. On my suggestion one of my students, David Barton, searched for words that would not just describe the image floating before his mind, but serve as a powerful verbal theme in its own right. He felt he was succeeding only too well and that the words that came to him were all too powerful and could never be matched in strength by any visual pattern he could envisage. But now the challenge had become really serious. He then developed a series of drawings which increasingly related to the eternal theme of the 'dying god' (plate 3). (I will discuss the 'dying god' motifs in the later chapters as external representations of the inner creative process.) This kind of theme sounds somewhat literary, and literary it was in the case of this particular student. What matters, however, in all these examples is the use of the intellect in order to challenge, assist and control spontaneous image making. The students gave themselves tasks that could not be solved by a purely intellectual analysis, again a case of the intellect obstructing its own way of functioning. But no disruption occurs.

The greatest need for intellectual control is found in the handling of colour. Most artists and art teachers consider colour as something that must be left entirely to spontaneous intuition or to an innate colour sense, that cannot be intellectually trained. Worse still, art teaching often begins with the training of draughtsmanship and introduces colour at a later stage in order to proceed from drawing to painting proper, an attempt that cannot succeed. Admittedly colour has its own emotional charge. In schizophrenic art the gaiety of colour is often contradicted by the agony of the draughtsmanship. For this reason alone it is quite inadmissible to separate colour and form without courting a schizoid split of sensibilities. Form cannot fail to affect colour and vice versa. The colour of a spot changes if its size is enlarged or reduced. As it approaches a small dot it tends towards blackness; if it is enlarged it tends to become more saturated, as every interior decorator knows to his detriment. When he chooses the colour from a small pattern, it may appear subtle and peaceful enough. As the same colour covers a whole wall it assumes a disturbing intensity, another reason why architects shy away from the use of colour, in spite of the unique power that colour has in creating and modulating space. This brings us to the main point. Colour seems intellectually unmanageable. A colour combination in a sketch book has to be changed somehow in a larger composition in order to retain the same effect. But is not such transformation the normal challenge of a spontaneous, yet disciplined practice of art? Most artists will simply ignore the extreme instability of colour because it is intellectually unmanageable. For instance, the colours of a picture will change with the changing light of the day; in twilight the colour balance becomes completely upset owing to the Purkinje effect which increases the intensity of blue at the expense of other colours. A good picture will stand this instability; so why bother to achieve full intellectual control? This is lazy thinking. Our intellectual defeatism makes us almost blind to colour. This blindness can be easily demonstrated. In lectures on colour we ought to protest vehemently against the use of coloured slides for illustrating great painting done in opaque pigments. Slides and transparencies can only approximate stained-glass paintings, which are also transparent in the original. Colour on stained glass and in colour slides looks entirely different from colour done in opaque pigments, so much so that stained-glass artists are gravely misled if they try to realize in glass coloured sketches done on paper. For instance, blue advances in stained glass while it recedes in pigment. But far more important, colour interaction (simultaneous colour contrast) is grossly exaggerated in the transition from pigment to transparency. It totally changes the appearance of colours, and appearance is all that matters in art. It would be silly to say that a colour only 'looks' different when it is enlarged or reduced in size; it 'is' different. Equally, colour interaction, where the juxtaposition of several colours mutually induces changes in the appearance of the colours, produces a real, not merely an illusionary change. Induced colours do not differ in any way from colours that retain their original values as pigments. Josef Albers has rightly devoted his life work to the exploration of induced colours. He retains a measure of control largely by forsaking the mixing of pigments and applying most of them straight from the tubes. Long familiarity with a particular pigment allows us at least to see its enormous instability, owing to interaction with other colours. The complexity of colour interaction must be intellectually controlled to the limit to which it is at all possible. It is comparatively useless, as most books on colour do, to devote all too much attention to the consonance and dissonance between two or three colours. Whatever precise inter-action is achieved is thrown out of balance as soon as another colour is added. The student wedded to the study of consonances and dissonances will refuse to go further and see this crudely learned discipline upset by further complication. He will become blind to colour interaction. The distinction between consonances and dissonances in colour has become as pointless in modern painting as it has in modern music. Modern music avoids consonances and explores the tensions between dissonances. So in a way does modern painting.

There is, of course, a tenuous physiological basis for singling out certain chords and colour combinations as consonant. Over-tones play a part in musical consonance, and in painting the colour receptors in the retina respond to complementaries in a particular way. In juxtaposition they tend to sizzle and dazzle; after-images tend towards the complementary colour. Colour interaction will also turn colours towards the complementary colour. For instance, a grey square in a green area will be (appear) a complementary pink and so on. But it is difficult to understand why colour books pronounce them as consonances for this reason alone. Owing to the trend to 'complement' each other they tend to be rather boring in close juxtaposition.

Certain colours are undoubtedly felt as more consonant than others, but this feeling is subject to changes in taste. In my youth, during the First World War and immediately after, red and blue were rejected as incompatible. Without much warning the French dress trade imposed the tricolour red-blue-white on popular taste and held it there for many years. Orange combined with pink was considered tasteless in the manner of tooth-paste colours until not so long ago. Now we already have a surfeit of them. When I worked as a colourist in the textile trade, blue and green were thought too much like landscape colours. Today this is no longer so. Dissonances are thus constantly transmuted into consonances. The same holds true for the history of consonances in music. I have mentioned that, according to Schoenberg, new consonances begin their life as 'accidental' combinations; later they are picked out as dissonances that have still to be explained away by due preparation and resolution, until in the end they can stand alone without inner tension. This means that they have at last become fully consonant. The real distinction between consonance and dissonance is their relative dynamic and static quality. Harsh dissonant combinations have to be justified by adding further matter. They are dynamic, therefore, and push on towards justification. Consonances are static and self-sufficient. It would be better to speak of static and dynamic colour combinations. This would expose the intellectual problem involved. Complementaries act like consonances because they are self-sufficient and seal themselves off from other colours. But it would be wrong to call them, for this reason alone, more 'beautiful' than more dynamic and restless colour combinations. As modern painting prefers dynamism it also prefers dissonant colour, much in the way in which modern music has rejected consonances.

The more general concept of colour interaction (or colour 'induction' as I prefer to call it) comprehends the static and dynamic use of colour within a wider framework, which also includes the all-important relationship between form and colour. This relationship is usually neglected in writing about colour; even by Josef Albers who, as an artist, was only too well aware of the problem. This neglect is all the more surprising because the relationship between form and colour, for once, is open to precise intellectual formulation.

Broadly speaking, a strong composition inhibits the mutual enhancement of colour surfaces (simultaneous colour contrast, colour interaction); conversely the mutual enhancement of colours tends to weaken form and tonal contrasts, the relationship between figure and ground and illusions of depth produced by perspective. Form and colour belong to different levels of the aesthetic experience. As Gombrich has pointed out, the experience of colour stimulates deeper levels of the mind. This is demonstrated by experiments with mescalin, under the influence of which the precise outlines of objects become uncertain and ready to intermingle freely with little regard to formal appearances; on the other hand colour becomes greatly enhanced, tends to detach itself from the solid objects and assumes an independent existence of its own.

Form is altogether more rational. In teaching draughtsmanship the control of line is more amenable to intellectual mastery. In accordance with the more intellectual climate now obtaining in art schools some intellectual control of colour is taught, but no systematic study of the fundamental conflict between form and colour is attempted. This is partly due to the dearth of good books on the artist's use of colour. For instance, there is a wide intellectual gap between the practical work of J. Albers and his theoretical writing on colour. His magnificent book on the interaction of colour has rapidly become a standard work. Yet in it he hardly mentions how much colour interaction depends on a comparative weakness of form, though his own painting is perhaps the best example of this law. His mature life's work is dedicated to the *Homage to the Square*. He experimented with a simple design constantly repeated in which a large square contains smaller squares of decreasing size. Now the weakest shape one can put into a square is another smaller square. It merely echoes the stronger outline of the larger square. (Equally weak is a circle within a bigger circle in the manner of fashionable 'target' pictures.) Because of the extreme weakness of such a design, colour interaction is greatly enhanced. Albers first thought that in his *Homage to the Square* (figure 10) he was really paying homage to a particularly simple strong design. Only gradually did he begin to realize that he had in fact dedicated himself, not to the study of form, but to the study of colour. He found that strong colour interaction could create its own spatial illusion. His three superimposed squares could represent now a long corridor leading into the depth, now a telescope protruding towards the spectator. There was no intellectual rule that could predict the exact spatial effects of different colour combinations. This was probably the reason why Albers failed to comment on his life's work in his book. Yet his work is the best possible documentation about the relationship between strong colour and an extremely weak form.

The British painter, Patrick Heron, once proclaimed in a talk that his work was solely dedicated to colour and that he had therefore 'abolished' line as well as the 'figure-ground' relationship. A strong shape will tend to stand out as a figure against an indistinct ground. The stronger the figure effect the weaker will be the colour interaction between figure and ground. For the same reason a strong space illusion created by perspective and other formal means, such as the overlapping of shapes, will also diminish the colour interaction within the picture. Subject matter will also play its part. If the interest of the subject matter makes us focus with greater intensity on a particular shape, this shape, though objectively weak in its formal structure, will also become separated from the rest of the painting; hence its colour will become isolated. All this could be read in books on experimental psychology, but rarely if at all finds its way into books on the aesthetic use of colour. One wonders why.

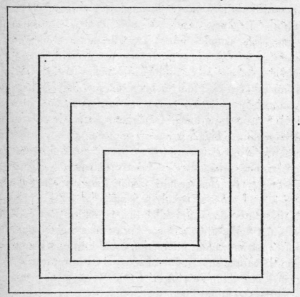

Figure 10. Diagram of a variant of Josef Albers's *Homage to the Square*. Of all the shapes that can be put into a square, another parallel shape is the weakest; colour interaction is therefore at a maximum. Similarly the weakest shape in a circle is another circle; hence the high colour interaction in 'target' paintings.

When Chevreuil, in the early nineteenth century, made artists familiar with colour induction, he did not touch directly on the problem of form and colour. The experiment which demonstrated interaction most clearly was to place a small grey square on a large ground of colour. On a green ground the grey square would turn a distinct pink. Obviously the more saturated the surrounding green ground, the stronger was the induced pink in the square. A few years later a most paradoxical phenomenon was observed; when a sheet of semi-transparent tissue paper was placed over the whole area the saturation of the green ground was of course severely diminished. One would have expected that the colour induction in the grey would be reduced to the same extent, that is to say that the induced pink of the grey square would also become much paler. But the opposite happened: the pinkness of the grey square became more pronounced. Many years passed until no less a man than the great Helmholtz gave the trite explanation of the paradox. The tissue paper made the outline of the grey square fuzzier and this weakening of its form increased colour interaction. A more impressive documentation for the overriding importance of line and form could scarcely be imagined. A comparatively crude weakening of the line was sufficient to compensate – indeed more than compensate – for the enormous loss in the saturation of the colours. Rothko, in carefully smudging his colour slabs, greatly increased their power to interact and mutually enhance each other. I doubt whether he was intellectually fully aware of what he was doing. As in all relationships between form and colour the reverse effect can also happen. Strong colour interaction tends to make sharp outlines seem much softer than they are; it levels down differences in tone. Colour slides of famous paintings show exaggerated colour interaction, so that the familiar shapes often seem curiously bleached out and obscured. Yet hardly anybody objects to the misleading effect of using colour slides for illustrating talks on art. This meek acceptance only tends to demoralize our already weak sensitivity to colour.

The excessive brilliance of colour transparencies teaches us another lesson. Maximum interaction is no virtue as such. It must be poised against the equal strength of form and space. The art of stained glass has not been made more easy by doing away with the heavy lead contours of medieval glass. If the glass panels are directly cemented together, as can be done with modern adhesive, the linear composition has to be exceedingly strong to contain and inhibit the colours, as it is for instance in Chagall's stained-glass designs. The heavy outlines of old glass were an immense help in bringing out the beauty of transparent colour. With pigments we may be seduced to heighten colour interaction at any price, but we have to eschew this fashion in stained glass and reverse it by favouring strong line and composition. I am convinced that the beauty of medieval glass has little to do with lost recipes for fabricating coloured glass and much more with the power of the lead contours that ate into and imprisoned the transparent colours. No wonder stained glass is a lost art.

We have to understand that in the conflict between strong colour and strong form each adversary grows in stature and power through their mutual confrontation. Patrick Heron began like Albers or Rothko with the use of the weakest possible forms, such as insubstantial circles and quadrangles insecurely suspended against a more solid ground. The lack of spatial depth suggested a mystic-oceanic feeling, of individual existence lost in the universe. The annihilation of space indicated a dreamlike level of experience where our commonsense concepts of space and time have no meaning. Since then Heron has rightly strengthened his shapes and toughened his pictorial space. Strong overlaps occur and the picture plane is dissected into definite levels in depth. His colour has accordingly gained in strength and decisiveness.

The incisiveness of form, such as the comparative sharpness of its outline, or its pregnant shape, or the conflict or parallelism between superimposed or juxtaposed forms and so on, can be summed up as qualities of a 'good' gestalt. We can summarize therefore that colour interaction between figure and ground stands in inverse proportion to the good gestalt of the figure. Hence also – as Albers implicitly demonstrated in his late work – the ambiguity of a weak figure on a strong ground immensely increases colour interaction. Gestalt psychology, without help from Helmholtz's discovery, stated independently that colour interaction increases within the boundaries of a good gestalt while it is inhibited across its borders. Again this simple law goes unmentioned in aesthetic writings on colour.

The inhibition of colour in painting has the same role that good counterpoint has in (polyphonic) music. In music too there is conflict between colour and form. We have seen how 'vertical' hearing of harmony fuses the single tones into a chord possessing either consonant or dissonant (tone) colour. The same tones are also fitted 'horizontally' into the coherent melodic lines of counterpoint. In polyphony melodic 'line' feeds on (harmonic) 'colour' and vice versa. The composer instinctively weakens the dissonant (harmonic) colour of a certain note by fitting it into a stronger polyphonic context. The preparation and subsequent resolution of a dissonant tone is a weakening device of this kind. To put it differently: to the extent to which a musical note is fitted into a clean melodic 'line' it is prevented from fusing into harmonic tone 'colour'; conversely a strong chord will temporarily fuse the loose strands of polyphony into solid tone colour so that the separate melodic lines disappear altogether. I have mentioned that the ear constantly oscillates between the harmonic fusion and polyphonic separation of the melodic lines; this conflict between 'form' and 'colour' belongs to the very life of music. A harmonically too luscious piece will soon lose its impact if it is not poised against a tough polyphonic structure.

The conflict between form and colour has the same role in painting. Strong form and space inhibit colour interaction while strong colour interaction obliterates form and space. This beneficial conflict ought to be intellectually grasped by the student. A too strident interaction between colours has to be counteracted by creating a strongly inhibiting form and space. The rather obvious interaction between complementaries or near-complementaries invites this inhibition. For instance, grouping complementaries together heightens colour interaction merely in a very local sizzle. The complementaries will embrace each other in a firm clasp and, like a secretive couple of lovers, refuse to take notice of their environment. The local enhancement of colour is achieved at the expense of total colour interaction. To the surprise of the student who has put together as many complementaries as he can, the total effect is rather dull. Generally it is better to separate complementaries or near-complementaries. Albers would often interpose between such colours a separating band of a neutral greyish or brownish colour. Each saturated colour will fight for the soul of the neutral colour, trying to tinge it with its specific interaction. As we focus first on one colour and then on the other, the induced colour in the neutral band will change accordingly.

Van Gogh did not rely on the open clash between complementary or near-complementary colours, like a blue-violet sky against warm yellow fields. He was more concerned to seal them off from each other and so heighten the dramatic tension between them. Harry Thubron liked to say that Van Gogh's imitators simply went for his blue sky and yellow fields, and neglected his subtler colours in fences, paths, houses, etc., that kept the sky and the fields apart, paradoxically increasing their dynamic pull on each other.

Van Gogh was a past master in sealing off and imprisoning over-strong colours. Sometimes he put the most active colours into contours. Of all surfaces the narrow ribbon of an outline is perhaps the most confining prison in which a colour can be held. We hardly consent to treat a line as a surface at all. In his *Sun Flowers* in the National Gallery, Van Gogh does not heighten the colour interaction by putting the dirty yellows of the flower heads against a complementary ground such as a bluish violet. In fact the ground is a rather weak unsaturated yellow-green which fails to set off the flowers. But help is close by. The missing bluish violet can be discovered hidden in the outlines of the table top and the vase. Imprisoned there it sends a harsh sheen into the green ground and gives it the edge that it needs to enhance the flowers.

Colour inhibition by imprisoning colours generally leads to their spreading. I once observed a strange phenomenon that points in this direction. A student painted a series of streamlined shapes in orange moving across a ground of a near-complementary ultramarine blue. The vehement colour interaction produced thick light-blue rims round the orange shapes. These rims were largely in the exact complementary, a turquoise blue slightly lighter than the ground. But where the streamline round the droplet forms twisted into a more incisive curve – usually opposite a neighbouring droplet – the turquoise rim turned into a definite mauve approximating the hue that in the colour circle would lie half-way between orange and blue. Was the mauve due to colour spreading rather than to interaction? Did the sharp turn of the streamline content 'imprison' the colour inside and so inhibit interaction, inducing spreading of the two colours instead?

This 'spreading' of an imprisoned colour is part of a more general phenomenon that is as little understood as the mutual enhancement of colour. The spreading effect is the very opposite of colour interaction. Colour interaction heightens the difference between two colours and pushes them towards the complementaries. In our example the green ground did not turn the central grey square greenish (that would be a 'spreading' effect) but towards a complementary pink. The spreading effect appropriately belongs to imprisoned, contained colours which fail to interact. Gombrich, in *Art and Illusion*, reproduces the classic examples of a spreading effect. If we look more closely we recognize that all of them contain linear patterns rather than broad surfaces. For instance, a line creeps in a meander pattern across a uniformly blue ground. As the line changes from black to white and then to red, the ground underneath turns from a greyish colour to a luminous blue and finally into a mauve. This spreading effect is due to the confinement (inhibition) of colour interaction through a linear (compositional) device. As such it turns out to be part of a more general phenomenon of colour inhibition which so far has been given little attention by artists. Ultimately it is an aspect of the basic conflict between form and colour. If a colour is inhibited by a strong composition (line, tonal contrast, etc.) it will instead tend to spread. Instead of enhancing colour contrast – as in colour interaction – it will tinge any suitable area with its own hue. Spreading seems to be capable of affecting an area wider than that usually affected by colour interaction, as though a colour which was able to break out from its prison had the strength to spread almost over the entire picture plane, checked only by the opposing action of colour interaction. The British painters, Maurice Agis and Peter Jones, built an architectural structure of coloured panels and rods. This was part of their study of colour in space, a study from which professional architects have largely shied away. The artists explain the use of rods rather formally. They need the rods protruding from the panels as a logical extension of their formal language. Just as painting needs line as well as two-dimensional surfaces so their space constructions need rods in addition to panels. The influence of the coloured rods is startling. They demonstrate the spreading effect of imprisoned colour in the most spectacular way. There seems to issue from the rods an invisible film of colour suspended freely in front of the panels.

Bridget Riley conducted experiments by adding colour to her dazzling optical painting. In one of her studies alternative bands of orange and blue gradually contract towards a critical area where the surfaces shrink into thin lines and assume a dazzling effect. Bridget Riley commented that it seemed difficult to judge which of the two colours – orange and blue – was deeper in tone.

This was indeed so in the area of the broader bands. The vehement colour interaction between these bands done in complementary colours of almost equal tone prevented the onlooker from making a proper comparison. But in the critical area where the surface contracted to thin dazzling lines it became quite clear that the orange was in fact darker than the blue. The linear shape of the coloured surfaces had destroyed colour interaction and replaced it by a 'spreading' effect. The orange and blue tended to spread into each other and to mix into a green. According to the theory proposed here this spreading is only another particular case of imprisoned (confined, inhibited) colour. The lack of colour interaction made it possible to see that the orange was much darker than the blue, a rather neat demonstration of the paradoxical fact that the inhibition of colour produces spreading and isolation (as far as colour interaction is concerned) at the same time. Seurat's scintillating dots are another example of excessive spreading as well as of extreme isolation. Apart from the line there is no more effective prison for a colour than a dot (apart from more complex forms which catch our attention owing to their formal, intellectual or emotional interest).

I have said that as yet no deliberate attempt has been made to explore the fundamental conflict between form and colour in painting, apart from extreme attempts, such as those undertaken by Albers and Heron, at eliminating the conflict between colour and form altogether. Colour interaction is always so strong anyway that it needs to be balanced by judicious inhibition. Even purely graphic (colourless) forms interact dynamically, though this may be less evident. I have spoken of the distortions of a good caricature, which somehow interact and balance each other. Undistorted geometric shapes demonstrate the same interaction if only we make ourselves sensitive enough. If we place a circle in one corner of the picture and then place a square in another corner, the square has somehow changed the shape of the circle. The circle now not merely looks different, it *is* different. Colour interaction is perhaps more violent. A new speck of colour in one corner will act right across the picture plane and affect any other colour within the entire field. Colour exercises should manipulate the total field of colours instead of being concerned with single colours added one by one. Here music can show the way. Through serializing musical elements it can manipulate the distribution of these elements throughout a whole series (field).

In an experimental course for art teachers I experimented with 'serializing' colour. I was tempted to try the experiment because I had become convinced that the relationship between the structure of musical colour and the structure of visual colour was more profound than the usual reference to the synaesthetic identity of our sense impressions, such as the vacuous statement that the trumpet sounds 'red'. No, there is a profound structural identity, which we can formulate by a precise mathematical proportion in the relationship between form and colour. Serialization in music can be interpreted in many ways. Classical harmony was based on a linear relationship between *single* keys. Atonal music establishes a balance between *all* elements of a series, such as the twelve semitones of the chromatic scale. A linear one-to-one relationship between keys is replaced by interaction within a total field which establishes cross ties between all its elements. A serial composer has to think in terms of the total series and not in terms of linear relationships between single elements. Hence the concept of consonance and dissonance, which is based on the relationship between single tones (e.g. a fifth is a consonance while a seventh is not, etc.), has lost its validity. In this way, serialization groups together dissonant sounds which a composer would not ordinarily combine; but through being justified as elements within the total field of the series they will sound right in the end.

Surprisingly the serialization of colours done by our students led to the same results. However arbitrary and even unpleasant the chosen colours in terms of traditional consonance and dissonance, they looked right if distributed over a field according to the rigour of a mathematical (numerical) series. In a way, Albers serialized a limited range of ready-made colours in the endless permutations of his *Homage to the Square*. These permutations look lost if they are not exhibited together; they lose much of their meaning if seen in isolation. This might prove that their effect is incumbent on demonstrating the underlying serialization. In my experiment the students began to fill in 'chessboard' designs according to permutations of a short series of colours (1–8, later only 1–4) (figure 11). It was not an entirely welcome result that these chessboards made almost any colour look pleasing, since, like optical art, serialization could easily be degraded into a commercial recipe for pleasant textile design and would cease to be the study in total fields of colour. Unfortunately, almost any exercise can be emptied of its relevance. The serial elements are represented by numbers. If numbers remain empty symbols this may be dangerous and lead to an empty

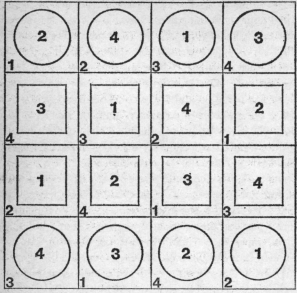

Figure 11. Diagram of colour serialization. The numbers represent: 1, say, green; 2, say, brown; 3, say, red; 4, say, blue (all near in tone). In music, serialization serves to produce a 'field' in which a series of elements can be arranged in serial permutations without affecting the identity of the field. Colours too ought not to be related in one-to-one relationships of consonances and dissonances, but also as components of a total field. The smallest modifications in the distribution will throw the colours off balance. Replacing circles by squares will greatly increase interaction.

juggling with numbers unrelated to artistic needs. But numbers need not be empty in this way. The child during the age of syncretism (before the age of seven or eight) treats numbers as real. Mathematical symbols generally can retain the same mysterious link with reality on a higher level. For instance, the physicist manipulates them according to their own (purely mathematical) laws, yet in the end they can be directly related to reality and give a new explanation of the physical world. So can numbers in art. Kenneth Martin, a British constructivist artist who is much in love with numbers, once assured me that he was not a mathematician, but manipulated numerical relationships just as he manipulated other tools like brush or chisel. If we serialize colour relationships we have to do the same and use numbers as a tool for controlling colour interaction through a total field.

A serialized arrangement of colours has to serve as a precision instrument for the study of colour interaction. For instance, I said earlier that a square was the weakest form within another bigger square, while a circle within a square was the strongest of all. Though this is undoubtedly so, not everybody will actually recognize this, owing to our general obtuseness to colour. But if we produce a serialized field of colours and combine a number of colours in diverse numerical arrangements, our sensitivity to colour interaction within the total field is immeasurably sharpened. Let us assume we have made a series of small squares within bigger squares in a chess-board-like field and colour them with four colours in a series of permutations. The strong interaction between certain colours may produce a local dazzling effect in some part of the chess-board. If we now convert the small squares into circles of the same size, the dazzle will be noticeably reduced owing to the inhibiting action of circles inside squares. That we recognize this so readily is solely due to the disturbed balance within the total field. If we cover up the rest of the field and compare only the isolated areas where the dazzle first occurred, the change from square to circular pattern will not produce so obvious an effect. The point is that only the balance due to serialization by number shows up those small differences in colour interaction that would otherwise escape us. Serialization exercises should use small modifications progressing step by step; otherwise such exercises, like the basic design exercises of old, can quickly degenerate into gimmicks for producing decorative patterns. Properly used serialization, at least for the time being, can afford us the much-needed intellectual control of a field of colour.

Of course, even a balanced numerical relationship cannot overcome the imbalance built into colour. Yellow can never become as dark as violet, grey will always be more sensitive to colour interaction than other colours and so on. The inner logic of serialization can overcome these natural imbalances. In music too the introduction of equal temperament upset the physical and physiological relationships between the overtones and the scale tones; yet it worked because it conformed with the technical requirements of musical craftsmanship. Schoenberg, in my view rightly, insists that the composer is still led by his unconscious search for remote overtones. These are practically inaudible to conscious hearing. As I have already indicated, their structure has been completely mauled by the artificiality of equal temperament. Moreover, every instrument produces different overtones to the same chord so that the unconscious overtone structure of music changes with the slightest change in instrumentation. Yet the conscious musical schema still prevails according to its own laws of craftsmanship.

Overtones are not consciously heard as tones, though physically they differ in no way from other natural sounds. Consciously they are fused into the diverse tone colours of different objects and instruments. Without overtone fusion all instruments would sound like bundles of insubstantial tinkles like the chirpings of a tuning fork and the disembodied piping of a piccolo flute. Through fusion the instruments acquire the solid tone colour associated with various objects, glassy, metallic or wooden. The thick and furry sound of a drum corresponds to a rich overtone chord transmuted into a particularly solid tone colour. The discovery of the inaudible overtones was not so much an advance in physics or acoustics as the psychological discovery that the brain fuses the multiple sounds emitted by most objects into solid bundles of tone colours, such as glass, metallic, wooden sounds, which help us to identify the sounding objects quickly and reliably.

Something very similar applies to Newton's discovery that white daylight is not a simple physical phenomenon but a bundle of complex spectral colours. Different objects reflect different segments of the spectrum which the brain promptly fuses into simple colour impressions characteristic of those objects. We see that Newton discovered a psychological faculty of the brain and not a physical quality of light. The analogy between overtone and spectral fusion is complete. It emphasizes another more fundamental relationship between musical tone 'colour' (based on overtone fusion) and visual colour (based on spectral fusion);

both turn out to be arbitrary products of the brain. Is it conceivable that the artist is aware of the suppressed spectral components of his pigments in the way in which the composer – according to Schoenberg – is aware of the faint overtones tinkling behind the consciously heard tone colours? It is possible that it is so. It would explain why whites and greys can be so different in their emotional qualities though to superficial inspection they appear practically the same. To unconscious vision they may appear to consist of very different components. The painter may unconsciously tease the various components out from various colour bundles, for instance interpret different whites by explicitly stating their suppressed unconscious components in some other part of the painting. These interactions may well be beyond the reach of intellectual analysis, even if some electronic colour organ were invented that would allow the painter to fuse and decompose spectral colours at will. I do not think that the painter needs to know the unconscious physiological basis of his colour sensations any more than the musician needs to know the overtone components of his music. We must fall back on intuition to control these regions of the deep. We may proceed with our intellectual analysis of our conscious colour perceptions and explore the dynamic laws governing them, without paying undue heed to their unconscious complexity.

Book Two
Stirring the Imagination

Part Four
The Theme of the Dying God

It is a commonplace to say that while traditional realism depicted outer reality, modern art turns inward to record the inner process of creating itself. But in a way the process of creating is always reflected in the work of art and to my mind represents its minimum content. Certainly, in much modern art the rational superstructure is torn away and the ordinarily hidden substructure exposed. This substructure clearly depicts various phases of creativity as I have described them. The modicum of fragmentation left in a modern work of art can be felt as a residue of the initial projection and fragmentation that signifies the first schizoid phase of creativity. To this extent a modicum of persecutory (paranoid-schizoid) anxieties still adheres to the work. I have shown how this residual fragmentation is counterbalanced by unconscious dedifferentiation on a deeper level. Modern art also demonstrates in its structure a modicum of this manic undifferentiation. To this extent the work mirrors the second manic phase of creativity when dedifferentiation leads to unconscious scanning and reintegration. As a conscious signal of unconscious integration a strong pictorial space emerges. Insofar as a good pictorial space – as distinct from a mere spatial illusion in the manner of Renaissance painting – is inherent in any painting, one could say that it represents the minimum content of art, an enriching experience of envelopment and unconscious integration. I have said that the work of art acts as a containing 'womb' which receives the fragmented projections of the artist's self. A mighty pulse issues from it which ripples through the painting and sucks the spectator into its embrace.

It is another commonplace to say that while traditional realism burrowed into the picture plane and, like a window, revealed a hidden space beyond, modern art builds space into the space in front of the picture trying as it were to occupy the room in which the painting hangs. In the desperate quest for conquering this frontal space, the modern painter has often turned to actual three-dimensional extensions. Rauschenberg's famous chair attached to a painting serves as a provocative manifesto for the new humorous 'space programme'. In our subjective vision, we have to knead that protruding and intrusive piece of furniture back into the flat picture plane and allow its bulging pictorial space to swallow and digest it. In witty despair some American pop-artists mocked up parts of a bathroom and bedroom. Are the drain pipes of the bathroom supposed to 'suck' us into the work, and the mock bed to 'envelop' us in its womb-like embrace? I think that the most consistent answer to this witty yet serious problem has been given by Maurice Agis and Peter Jones whose work I have already mentioned. They decided to drop painting and sculpture and re-build a whole room instead. They spent a year in rebuilding a slum basement. They divided it by severe intersections of plastic panels, floor coverings and also protruding rods that hindered or directed the progress of the itinerant intruder. Most surprising and impressive was the impact of these insubstantial coloured rods. I have mentioned how the colour imprisoned in these rods tends to spread. Moreover, they stirred the static architectural space into life. They would hold apart two walls that would otherwise close in too much on the visitor. They could make him go round them or step over them. Their colour was decisive. It made panels and rods recede or advance, or rather, most mysteriously make them do both at the same time (plates 21–23). These artists have reacted against the claustrophobia and fragmentation of modern architecture. It is either too expansive or too restrictive and fails to create a space in which we can really live. A claustrophobic room closing in on us may stir up deeply repressed fears of being trapped, fears that are ultimately connected with half-forgotten womb fantasies. Good architectural space must have the properties of good pictorial space; it must be capable of enveloping us and also putting us at a distance. The dynamic interior space as articulated by Maurice Agis and Peter Jones grapples explicitly, perhaps for the first time, with the problem of enclosing and opening up architectural space mainly by making use of colour. 'Basic' design exercises like these are badly needed in our over-professionalized schools of architecture and could make the students sensitive to the potentially life-enhancing qualities of interior space.

The theme of containment (trapping) and expansion (liberation) as the minimum content of art crops up in many different forms (plate 24). A potter once told me that he wanted to make pots the inside of which was to be felt bigger than the pots themselves. He mentioned that Indian caves had the same paradoxical feeling. In the Stone Age caves the Paleolithic artists treated inaccessible passages in a way that to us would be appropriate only in more expansive architectural settings. The freely scattered wall paintings may have counteracted the claustrophobia of the closed-in caves and given a feeling of limitless oceanic expansion. In psycho-analytical terms the feeling of limitless expansion is closely associated with womb fantasies. The womb taken in itself is perhaps the most cogent symbol of claustrophobic containment. Yet in the child's fantasies the mother's womb expands to contain the entire world. In creative imagery a fantasy of returning to the womb is well nigh ubiquitous. Otto Rank, in my view rightly, interpreted a vast quantity of mythological and artistic material as fantasies of undoing birth and returning to the womb. Where he failed in my view was in his attempt at interpreting this vast material as actual memories of and wishes for intra-uterine existence. His fellow-psychologists were unable to accept this interpretation and Rank's thinking gradually lost contact with the main body of psycho-analytic theory. Yet his challenge is still there and the ubiquity and insistence of the womb fantasy still remains largely unexplained. I have mentioned its obscure meaning in schizophrenic illness. Could it not be that the fantasy is not so much an expression of memories or id fantasy, as a direct reflection of the process of containment and expansion inherent in all creative work? If we look more closely we find that all three phases of creativity including projection, fragmentation, dedifferentiation, integration and re-introjection are associated with the basic theme of trapping and liberation. The minimum content of art, then, may be the representation of the creative process in the ego.

Rank's far-ranging material tends to cover the same ground which Frazer surveyed in his investigation of the 'dying god' theme. He too failed to account for its ubiquity. When Frazer began to collect his material, he was unable to limit it. It proliferated under his searching eyes, he had to fill volume after volume to add further to his magnum opus, *The Golden Bough*. It is said that he died a disappointed man feeling that he had not found the key to its proper understanding. One of his rationalizations was that the god-king had to die in order that a younger, more vigorous man could govern instead and ensure the fertility of the land. There is also a close connexion of the theme with the invention of agriculture, perhaps the most important advance in human history. Like the dying god the seed of the corn was killed, buried in the womb of the earth, to be reborn in the spring of the new year. But one cannot interpret the vast material in either terms. The compulsion to multiply the symbolizations of the same basic theme must be rooted in a need more profound than the magic rituals of agriculture and the provision of efficient government. The motif of the dying god re-emerges in the minds of modern poets and artists whose material interests are far removed from the fears and hopes of an ancient agricultural community. Weisinger [33] showed that the Classical Greek tragedy descends directly from the Neolithic ritual of the dying god. The hero of tragedy has to perish in order to triumph. Weisinger himself offers another rationalistic interpretation of the theme which he calls the 'fortunate fall'. He feels it rests on a need to maintain man's free will and self-determination in the face of overwhelming external forces. Psycho-analysis knows well enough how poignant our narcissistic mortification can become if our unconscious wish for omnipotence and immortality is thwarted by the limitations of reality. All wisdom we can muster is needed to accept the fact of our personal death. Indeed Freud himself, in his early mythological paper on the motif of the three caskets in Shakespeare's *Merchant of Venice*, suggests that the 'dying god' theme could be explained by a piece of wise philosophizing on the necessity of facing death as a fact. But this explanation is perhaps too restricted for so universal a motif of the creative imagination. As far as I know, it was left to Marion Milner, a psycho-analyst with unusual artistic sensitivity, to explore the motif through her own artistic sensibilities and to interpret it as a reflection of the creative process itself, an approach which I have adopted and expanded.

After Marion Milner became a psycho-analyst she continued her life-long search for increased creativeness. She felt that her self-exploration as an artist was something apart from her growing understanding of her id fantasies. We know how artists have to scan the world for potent imagery that could give a new edge to the quality of their imagination. These images need not serve them as picturesque motifs, i.e. as substitutes for free form inventions, but help them to keep their eyes fresh and their sensibilities alerted. Unlike motifs, creative images need not become part of the actual work. They act as catalysts for releasing the flow of the imagination and may ultimately lead to the invention of quite different concepts and shapes.

Marion Milner, in her book *An Experiment in Leisure*, written under the pseudonym Joanna Field [21], soon gave up her search for motifs and instead scanned the world, her memory, and her imagination for incisive images in a sustained effort to enhance her general receptiveness for the real and beautiful. It was then that she recognized that the strength of these images could not be explained by ordinary psycho-analytic interpretations in terms of id fantasies. They were, as I have said, in the main images of suffering, destruction and death centred round Frazer's theme of the 'dying god'. For their role as creative catalysts their sado-masochistic content mattered but little. As they stirred into motion the creative process they lost their burden of anxiety and guilt. Marion Milner [21] says:

> The still glow that surrounded some of these images in my mind, images of the burning god, of Adonis and Osiris, did it come because they satisfied surreptitiously some crude infantile desire that I ought to have left behind long ago? I could not believe that it was so, for I had enough psycho-analytical experience to recognize the feeling of disreputable desires ... the kind of thinking that brought these other images was of a quite different quality, it had the feeling of greatest stillness and austerity.

Of course, this does not exclude that the ever-present id fantasies may seize on these images for their own guilty purpose. Marion Milner admits that the image of killing a human substitute for the god can arouse pleasure in the infliction of pain, but at the same time the same image could point to the 'truth of a purely psychic process for which no more direct language is available'. Today we can name the process and speak of creative changes in the ego or, more specifically, of self-destructive processes that are inherent in all creative work. Long ago Silberer described a similar double aspect of imagery that accompanies and induces the act of falling asleep. These reveries in the twilight between waking and sleeping may already express, like the deep dream, forbidden id fantasies, but at the same time they reflect, in the directest possible manner, the changes in the ego in its transition from waking to sleeping. They may have a self-destructive character when the semi-paralysis of rational thought during sleep is experienced as self-destruction and even death. Silberer wrote about the images that induce and describe the coming of sleep. It is Marion Milner's achievement to have recognized the same functional character in the ubiquitous material of the White Goddess and her dead son-lover. I have coined the term 'poemagogic' to describe its special function of inducing and symbolizing the ego's creativity. (The Greek word *poema* means all kinds of creative making, not only the making of poems.)

Poemagogic images, in their enormous variety, reflect the various phases and aspects of creativity in a very direct manner, though the central theme of death and rebirth, of trapping and liberation, seems to overshadow the others. Death and rebirth mirror the ego's dedifferentiation and re-differentiation. This double rhythm can be seen as an interaction between basic life and death instincts active within the creative ego. Such an interpretation cuts directly into a critical controversy in current psycho-analytic writing, which is now divided between a literal acceptance of the death instinct (Thanatos) and its outright rejection as a faintly irrelevant biological speculation.*

Obviously the division of opinion is not a matter of rational argument, but – as so often in scientific thinking at the border of the unknown – a matter of emotional attitude. This attitude itself may one day become a legitimate subject for psycho-analytic interpretation. Perhaps the crude idea of an outright suicidal death 'wish' spoils the quality of the controversy. If we are talking about basic instincts we are talking about very abstract explanatory concepts and not about conscious attitudes and concrete wishes by which we conduct our practical life. If Eros (life) and Thanatos (death) correspond to a basic dualism of instincts

* See Appendix, p. 305.

it is clear that life as such would be impossible without the death instinct. The dualism of differentiation and dedifferentiation inherent in ego functioning brings this out very clearly. Temporary dedifferentiation if it is extreme, as in oceanic states, implies a paralysis of surface functions and so can act very disruptively. But the ego could not function at all without its rhythm oscillating between its different levels. The disruptive action of the death instinct in the phase of dedifferentiation is part of a healthy ego rhythm. Impeding the rhythm spells insanity and even physical death.

Marion Milner, commenting on my evaluation of the death instinct in the context of creativity, said in a lecture that real self-destruction and psychosis may perhaps be a distorted, because frustrated, form of the creative process. Jackson Pollock's creativity may have depended on his violent attacks on his own surface sensibilities. Is it a coincidence that his death in a car accident has been interpreted widely as a near-suicide occurring at a time when his creativity had become nearly exhausted? Had he been able to continue his attacks on his surface ego his physical self-destruction could have been beneficially absorbed and neutralized into the silent working of the death instinct within the ego. The example is, of course, almost entirely speculative. We would need more corroborative evidence to sustain it as a serious hypothesis. In this context it merely helps to illustrate in more concrete terms a possible relationship between psychosis, suicide and ego rigidity on the one hand and a creative flexible ego on the other. The schizophrenic stands in fear of undifferentiated fantasies which in sane people would act poemagogically. In him they merely lead to ego disruption. The London psychiatrists, Ida Macalpine and R. A. Hunter [20], speak of typical fantasies of bisexual procreation where the differentiation of the sexes is suspended and the schizophrenic assumes the role of the 'dying god'. They argue that the famous schizophrenic, Schreber, defended himself not so much against his unconscious homosexuality, as Freud thought, as against an undifferentiated fantasy where he was to be neither man nor woman, but some sort of primeval hermaphroditic being destined to give rebirth to mankind. Such a vision normally resists verbalization on a conscious level. It proves Schreber's not inconsiderable gifts as a writer that he was in fact capable of putting his frightening fantasies into coherent language. He called his account 'approximately' correct. He had to subject his memories to a secondary revision such as we have to do with all low-level memories, whether they are dreams, reveries, mystic experiences, or the evasive poemagogic images in creative work.

Schreber must have surrendered his healing surface ego to renewed disruption in trying to re-live his past illness. He must have faced very severe anxieties. His achievement is not diminished by the fact that his continuing illness forced him to act out his dying god fantasies. He reconciled himself to being emasculated in order to assume the role of mankind's recreator. This fantasy comes perilously near to poemagogic imagery of voluntary self-destruction in the manner of the 'dying god'.

Eric Simenauer [29] reports that Rilke struggled against similar bisexual fantasies of a messianic character before he became a true poet. He met Lou Andreas-Salomé, the cherished friend of Nietzsche and Freud. She encouraged him to surrender to the disruptive fantasies and the severe anxieties engendered by them. Simenauer claims that only after this creative surrender and symbolic self-destruction did Rilke come into his own as a poet, shedding all preciousness and cliché. (This loss of defensive surface imagery is, of course, an immediate gain of self-surrender.) He was then capable of verbalizing unspeakable bisexual fantasies without disguise and, more important, without any attempt at acting them out. His *Book of Hours* contains a prayer for the appearance of the bisexual Messiah in the image of Thanatos. Rilke addresses his godhead fervently: 'give the last proof to us, make the crown of your strength appear and give us man's real motherhood.' Anatomical details of this strange bisexual mother are not omitted. Yet there is no crudeness, because the poet still retains much of the undifferentiated structure of underlying poemagogic fantasy. Unlike Schreber, Rilke does not articulate his fantasy into precise and therefore obscene imagery; by holding on to the twilight of undifferentiation, he is able to express the poet's longing for death and creativity which is felt as man's real motherhood. This means that like so many examples of 'modern art', the poem describes the ego process of creativity itself.

Robert Graves gives us what almost amounts to a recipe for poetic creativeness. According to him the poet's worship of

Apollo belongs to a more superficial near-homosexual level of poetic imagination. The Apollonian poet shies away from the dangers of the deep where the true Muse, the dangerous White Goddess, awaits him. Her real threat lies in her triple aspect, the undifferentiation between life, love and death. In loving the poet she will also kill him. The poet, in worshipping her, invites his own death in exchange for love and rebirth, or (to put it the other way round as is always possible in such undifferentiated fantasies) he longs for life in death. Graves's eternal poetic theme is not masochistic fantasy – this is the salient point – but a poemagogic incantation for the gift of creative power. The poemagogic image of the goddess, through its extreme undifferentiation fusing life and death, killing and loving, brings poetic inspiration by shifting the poet's imagination to dreamlike levels. Graves has an intuitive grasp of the vast stratification in poemagogic imagery cutting through many levels of image-making, and suggests several levels of the dying god theme that make good psychological sense. His depth-psychological analysis of Greek myths has, much to my surprise, become a standard work in libraries all over the world. Yet his implicitly depth-psychological approach ought to be highly suspect to academic learning. He extracts the ubiquitous theme of the White Goddess from almost any myth by removing the top layers of late versions. In a way his work emulates Frazer's and Rank's methods; all of them searched for a basic theme in a vast amount of cultural material. Even the Oedipus myth, so dear to psycho-analysis, is not safe from Graves's analysis. The sphinx slain by Oedipus was the moon goddess of Thebes, Jocasta was her priestess whom a new king had to marry according to the laws of a matriarchal society. Oedipus in vanquishing the sphinx represents the patriarchal conqueror of the old society. Similarly in other Greek myths the patriarchal Olympian religion supersedes the older mother religion. Old elements of the myths are preserved in a disguised form. According to the old law the new king had to become a 'son' of the old king by marrying his widow. This holy custom is perverted into the crime of parricide and incest by the patriarchal revision of the myth. Graves would never have been able to link scattered clues in so bold a manner, had not psycho-analysis shown the way to such techniques of re-interpretation. Psychologically, it makes sense that ancient myths concerned with pre-oedipal material, such as a husbandless mother, should become later revised by an oedipal version where the father takes over some of the terrifying aspects of the primitive mother figure. But Graves falls into the trap into which Frazer fell before him. He tries to use a psychologically determined revision as a means to reconstruct prehistoric events. Internal psychological processes of repression are externalized into military feats of oppression, sadism and self-destruction, a misuse to which internal poemagogic imagery is liable. In particular, the internal censorship of the superego is externalized (projected) into political causes for the revision of ritual and myth, such as conquest and invasion or the replacement of matriarchy by patriarchy. It is, of course, quite possible that external and internal processes overlap as they continually do in creative work. But internal necessities must not be ignored in favour of purely external historical incidents.

When Frazer, half a century ago, put forward the archetypal image of the dying god, he too hoped that he had found a means for reconstructing prehistoric events. At that time social anthropology was still dominated by Darwin's reconstruction of human evolution. Physical anthropology was able to trace back the pre-history of the human body. Social anthropologists, like Frazer, hoped to reconstruct the origins of human culture from surviving traces. Today the search for 'origins' is discredited and Frazer's many volumes on a single theme are often left to collect dust on the top shelves of college libraries. But his standing is un-diminished with poets and artists. They share Frazer's intuitive understanding of the (poemagogic) power of the material and his sensitivity to its underlying unity, as yet imperfectly understood.

We may have to accept that Frazer's reconstructions of pre-history are as untenable as Graves's reconstructions of pre-historic battles between patriarchal invaders and matriarchal settlers. But it is still true that Greek myths share with other cultural material the same basic imagery. This unity need not point to a common root in prehistory; rather does it point to a common root in the human mind where eternal conflicts of a very different kind are fought out.

Before Marion Milner it was perhaps only Jung who grasped the poemagogic quality of Frazer's material. In this theory the images become 'archetypes' watching over certain creative processes of integration. Jung also anticipated Melanie Klein's findings about the pre-oedipal mother. But the ordered progress of a complex science like psycho-analysis is not helped by boldly anticipating leaps. I myself was not really helped by Rank, Graves or Jung. The stratification of poemagogic imagery is too complex for that.

What has been recognized long ago by writers like Turel [36], Grotjahn [14], Bienenfeld [2] and others is the fact that the transition from matriarchy to patriarchy reflects the child's development towards the genital Oedipus stage. In this final stage of infantile sexuality the father has attracted all aggressive, sadistic traits that until then tainted the image of the (pre-oedipal) mother. The very young child was faced with the terrifying image of the Great Mother who unites in her undifferentiated image both male and female attributes. The love of this mother indeed involves danger and possible destruction in the manner of the White Goddess who inflicts death through her love. In the genital Oedipus stage the double role of the Great Mother is split up; the father takes over her terrifying aspects (though already attenuated owing to the child's better understanding of human relationships) while the mother's love remains untainted by fear and aggression. It may well be that any social authority accorded to the women of a given society plays on the pre-oedipal fears of the mother. It is a fact acknowledged by anthropology that matrilinear societies tend to transform themselves into patrilinear societies while the reverse process hardly ever occurs. The relative instability of matrilinear societies may be due to unconscious fears. But matriarchy as reconstructed by Bachofen or Graves may have never existed.

In creative work we are constantly delving back into lower levels of mental imagery. There, the triangular Oedipus situation of father, mother and child which evolves during infancy is again dissolved. The father figure recedes behind the mother, who as the White Goddess unites in her undifferentiated image both male and female powers, love and hate, life and death. I have said that it is this structural undifferentiation alone that matters as a creative catalyst. It stands poemagogically for the ego's disintegration during creativity. I will show that the ego's partial fragmentation during the first phase of creativity can be experienced unconsciously as an oral attack of the superego on the ego. The superego is externalized as an image of the 'devouring, searing' mother. It is in this stage that the artist feels persecutory fears as he is faced with the fragmentation of his first projections. I will discuss the oral level of the burned, devoured god in a later chapter. For some reason its imagery seems to play a more important part in scientific creativity than in art. The scientist projects the superego's oral aggression and compulsion (gnawing guilt) into incoherent events in a fragmented external reality and perceives them there as the compelling law of causality which keeps the world on its course. The scientists' voyeurism and oral curiosity will be shown as being closely connected with the comparatively late (near-oedipal) phallic stage when the differentiation between the sexes is already achieved in a primitive form; the mother is fantasied as a castrated male. In art we are more concerned with a deeper level of imagery on which the distinction between the sexes does not yet exist and the mother is fantasied as the phallic woman equipped with the attributes of both sexes. Her aggression acquires an anal character. The burned, devoured god becomes the scattered, gathered and buried god. His image reflects the phase of creativity when the work functions as the womb which collects and buries the scattered projections of the artist. Through dedifferentiation creativity succeeds in joining the fragmented material and makes it suitable for later re-introjection. The torn god whose fragmented limbs are gathered and buried by the mother to ensure rebirth mirrors this second phase of creativity. In Frazer's material he appears as the corn spirit of Neolithic agricultural rites. Human or semi-divine sacrifices are torn limb from limb and scattered over the corn fields like the seed of the corn. There the scattered seed lies buried (trapped) in the womb of the earth to be revived the next spring. Osiris and Dionysus are corn spirits. Osiris too is torn limb from limb. In the most frequent version of the myth his evil brother, Set, is responsible for his murder; in Robert Graves's terms this could be due to a later oedipal revision of the myth. The male figure has still to take over the aggressive aspects of the mother figure. Isis does not appear as the tearing, scattering mother, but only in her loving integrating aspect. She collects and buries Osiris's torn body to ensure his revival in the netherworld. The tearing mother appears in the Dionysus myth as Agave, the mad mother of Pentheus. She tears her own son alive; after recovering from her madness she assumes the role of the burying mother and lovingly gathers her son's shattered body for proper burial. The priestesses of Dionysus, the raving Maenads, tear the sacrificial bull alive in the god's honour. But here a complication arises that points to a still deeper near-oceanic level of undifferentiation. The bull signifies Dionysus himself. Dionysus, as it were, sacrifices 'himself to himself'. On this level the mother too recedes and the child remains alone, being both subject and object of self-destruction. Strangely enough this deepest level of undifferentiation is often clearly expressed in poemagogic imagery particularly in works of art dealing with human creativeness (Michelangelo's Sistine ceiling, Goethe's *Faust*). We shall start a more detailed analysis of poemagogic imagery with this deepest oceanic level and work our way upwards to the near-oedipal oral level of the devoured, burning god. I first tried to proceed in the other direction, from the oral top level to deeper levels. But in the end this proved too difficult and I postponed publication of my findings for a long time. The top level of the devoured, burning god is accessible enough and many years ago (1949) I published a tentative account of it in a paper 'The Origin of the Scientific and Heroic Urge (The Guilt of Prometheus)' in the *International Journal of Psychoanalysis* [4]. It so happened that my findings showed a happy parallelism with Melanie Klein's work, of which I knew hardly anything at the time. John Rickman, then co-editor of the journal, pointed out to me the correspondence between my own findings and Melanie Klein's work and ensured the publication of my article. But the correspondence did not reach far enough to encourage me to publish my other findings about still lower and less differentiated levels of poemagogic imagery. I therefore postponed publication, apart from a lecture on the anal level of poemagogic imagery given to the London Imago Group. Moreover for a long time I did not feel entirely sure about the full implication of the dying god imagery in its various levels. Melanie Klein pointed to the oral origin of gnawing guilt feelings and remorse. But what about the superego's anal attacks on the ego? The quite unmistakable anal tinge of repression has so far gone practically unnoticed. This is surprising, because accepting the anal character of repression would have led to a perfect parallelism in the superego's two main functions of inducing guilt and repression in the ego. Oral gnawing and anal scattering represent primitive attacks of the superego. The ego reacts with gnawing pangs of guilt to the superego's oral attacks, with repression to its anal scattering. Anal self-scattering may be an accentuated form of earlier splitting and self-projection during the oral stage. Scattering is contained by the ego's new capacity for dedifferentiating and thereby repressing (burying) the split-off parts of the self. Without repression the split-off parts were freely projected (anally expelled) into a void. A permanent impoverishment is prevented by the good nursing mother who willingly receives, retains (buries) and finally hands back the expelled substance. Repression duplicates this process in the inner world, and so makes the child independent from his mother. Creative work immediately externalizes this process and replaces the mother by the external product of creative work (the work of art, etc.). I have emphasized throughout that it is impossible to separate the internal and external processes of creativity. A receiving (burying) 'womb' is prepared simultaneously internally by repression and externally in the creative work. Internal repression by scattering and burying parts of the self is duplicated step by step by the first two phases of creative work (projection and dedifferentiation). The same structural process of dedifferentiation shapes the vast buried substructure of the work of art and at the same time enriches and orders the artist's unconscious (repressed) fantasy life.

The capacity for containment (burying) as opposed to free scattering is connected with the child's learning of cleanliness and disgust, a still unexplained, possibly biological effect of maturation. In the first anal stage the child scatters his excrements freely and expects his environment to receive (contain) them as valuable gifts. In the second stage disgust arises that inhibits their free expulsion. He learns to contain them for a while and their eventual expulsion is no longer free, but directed towards a container. There is a definite rhythm of retention (containment) and directed expulsion that is closely allied to the basic metabolic rhythm of life itself. In creativity and internal repression the metabolic rhythm is reversed; directed expulsion comes before, not after, retention and containment, much in the way in which the male sperm is first ejected and then contained by the egg. I will discuss later in more detail the anal and genital aspects of the metabolic rhythm.

That the anal aspect of the superego's aggression against the ego has so far been ignored may have something to do with scientific fashion. Today anal material is neglected in favour of oral material. Oral material is considered more fundamental and primitive because it is shaped in an earlier phase of the child's development. This may explain why the anal aspect of the superego still awaits further elucidation.

Below the anal level of poemagogic imagery there is the still lower oceanic level. For some reason it is more accessible. Only its place within psycho-analytic theory has remained very uncertain. I have spoken of our failure to accommodate and explain the ubiquity of manic womb fantasies. It seems that in the final manic phase of creativity the ego at last breaks free from the superego's relentless attacks. Then, the boundary between the internal and external world gives way. The child's self merges with the mother and incorporates her generative powers. The mother figure disappears as an individual entity, absorbed by the self-creating and self-scattering child who remains alone. He identifies himself with the womb that bears him. This poemagogic fantasy dramatizes the momentous development when the child, by learning repression, makes himself independent from a benevolent mother figure acting as a receptacle (womb) for projected parts of the child's self. The child incorporates the mother's womb. This oceanic form of the familiar womb fantasies is largely neglected in psycho-analytic writing. But it is evident enough in the poemagogic imagery of art. There is Michelangelo's self-creating godhead on the Sistine ceiling. We find the fantasy in Goethe's figure of the man-made manikin, Homunculus, who is still unborn and encased in the glass womb which he carries about. He delivers himself from his own womb by scattering his substance at the feet of the sea goddess: birth, love and death in a single action. I will discuss the theme in more detail in the next chapter. In mythology, the figure of the self-scattering and self-creating god Dionysus represents the self-destruction and rebirth of the creative mind in the most poignant form.

Let me sum up once again our tentative gradual descent into the oceanic depth. The Oedipus level at the top is fully differentiated and shows the triangular confrontation of father-mother-child. As the father figure recedes the child has to face the mother in her increasingly terrifying aggressive aspects. On the phallic-oral level she appears as the devouring, burning mother who – as we will see – inflicts oral castration and is herself still felt as a castrated male, a remnant of the waning sexual differentiation. On the lower anal level the White Goddess assumes the full powers of both parents. Her aggression too mounts. The threat of castration is replaced by the threat of death, of tearing or burying alive. Ultimately the divine child himself absorbs the creative powers of both parents. He incorporates the mother's womb. He bears, expels and buries himself in a single act, an oceanic-manic image that can hardly be visualized in its extreme undifferentiation. It is important to ascertain the degree of de-differentiation achieved in a particular version of the dying god theme. There are many transitional states which still belong to a more superficial level, yet bear certain traits characteristic of greater depth.

Freud intuitively resolved the disguises of the dying god theme. He dealt with it in his only purely mythological investigation, his paper *The Theme of the Three Caskets*, which I have already mentioned. Freud admired Frazer and his work, but he did not try to evaluate the dying god theme in its universal significance, perhaps because he himself believed that the universal roots of human civilization were found in the Oedipus complex. Nevertheless, he had no difficulty in penetrating the many disguises of the death goddess. Like Graves he recognized that she is a triple goddess best represented by three women. Cinderella and her two sisters, Psyche and her two sisters, the three Graces, Parcae, or perhaps Wagner's Rhinemaidens, all these triple figures hide underneath their innocuous appearance the threefold aspect of the great goddess as the giver of birth, love and death. I mentioned earlier how Freud rationalized the dying god's ready submission to the goddess of death as a philosophical acceptance of human mortality, hardly an improvement on Frazer's rationalization of the theme. But he was not deceived by the near-oceanic undifferentiation of its representation in certain material. This allowed him to recognize the death goddess in a completely inverted situation. For him, the deeply moving scene in *King Lear* in which the shattered king carries his dead daughter Cordelia in his arms derives its immense emotional power from the unconscious reversal of the situation, the perennial image of the *Pietà*: the death goddess mourning over her dead son, Aphrodite mourning over Adonis, Isis over Osiris. Such complete reversals are not merely a play of a chaotic process condoned by irresponsible unconscious fantasy. They are structurally highly significant. They point to that deepest oceanic level where the child arrogates the role of the mother (so that in the end she disappears altogether). The reversal of roles allows us to locate Shakespeare's imagery precisely near the oceanic limit of poemagogic image making. Other examples come readily to mind. Eurydice is another death goddess comparable in her status to Persephone as the goddess of the underworld. But it is not she who conducts Orpheus to the underworld; she herself is guided by him from the underworld. The son gives life to the mother. The same total reversal of the life-giving role is depicted in the holiest of Greek icons, the *Dormition of the Virgin* (plate 27). The Virgin lies dying on her bed. Her divine son, proudly erect in his majesty, cradles in his arms the girl-like soul of his mother giving her rebirth and eternal life. As I have said, the child in his life-giving role in the end does away with the mother altogether, and in an image of extreme de-differentiation gives life and death to himself. On the manic-oceanic level death is not fully distinguishable from birth. The triple roles of the mother figure merge, the giving of birth, love and death, become a single act. Michelangelo's 'self-creating' godhead, Goethe's funny conception in his *Faust* of a man-made Homunculus who achieves birth, love and death in a single act of self-scattering at the feet of the goddess, have this manic aspect. Classical psycho-analysis may consider such fantasies simply as narcissistic and would not be wrong in doing so. There is the same withdrawal from external reality, the same limitless expansion of the self to embrace the whole world. What is missed is the significant structural aspect of oceanic dedifferentiation which places the fantasy firmly within the context of outward-going creative work. As this manic phase of creativity is approached the image of the White Goddess recedes and with her the terrors of a savage superego. The moment of the ego's rebound is near. It is then too that in Marion Milner's words the sadistic-masochistic tinge of the dying god theme disappears and is replaced by stillness and serenity. But this serenity is preceded by a genuine experience of death which we re-live in poemagogic imagery. In this respect the manic-oceanic experience of death and rebirth differs from pathological mania, which simply denies death.* It is difficult to disentangle the depressive and manic aspects of self-destruction in poemagogic imagery. A feeling of oceanic, cosmic bliss strangely contrasts with the imagery of inexorable suffering and death. What seems to matter is that death has first to be faced and the experience of dying worked through before the oceanic-manic level of liberation and rebirth is reached fruitfully. The uncreative, sterile mind shies at death and the fact of human mortality. For this reason uncreative man cannot tolerate the genuine emotional experience of self-destruction which accompanies the creative ego rhythm on its swing downwards, and desperately clings to his surface functions. The ego rhythm is always there in a shallow form. Its potential experience of self-destruction is hardly noticed as long as the death instinct is 'mute' and the self-destructive phase of de-differention is smoothly absorbed into a flexible oscillation of the ego between different levels. The ego rhythm of creativity tests the ego's flexibility severely. If a modicum of ego rigidity has dissociated the ego functions and impeded the more profound shifts of consciousness in creative work the forcible fragmenta-tion of surface imagery preceding dedifferentiation is emotionally experienced as total self-annihilation. As all of us suffer from a measure of schizoid dissociation (I have described intermediate cases bordering on creative sterility in the preceding chapters), we have to face the anxieties and fears of self-destruction. Marion Milner maintains that the facing of this experience is also a test for the full emotional (not purely intellectual) acceptance of death as part of reality. She recalls that in Spanish bullfights the killing of the bull is called 'the moment of truth'. The ritual of the bullfight is emotionally highly undifferentiated. Is the bull the aggressor, or an animal representative of the dying god, a symbol of our fantasies of self-destruction? In Picasso's *Guernica* the bull was first planned as the victim, but in the finished ver-sion became the pitiless aggressor, with the dying horse playing the role of the victim. The confusion of roles must be part of the emotional excitement experienced in these fights. The moment of truth in death finally determines the victim. The poemagogic imagery of the dying god certainly helps to confirm the psychic

* See Appendix, p. 304.

reality of death. There can be no emotional cheating in the ritual of mourning the dead god. His resurrection is never entirely assured. I was brought up in a Roman Catholic country and I remember how unrelieved by any hope of resurrection the mourning on Good Friday was. Yet the Friday of despair was 'good', death was accepted emotionally as part of reality.

It may seem strange that we should have to surrender our surface functions, the very seat of our rationality, in order to deepen our sense of reality and truth. Is it not held that only our rational mind, not our unconscious, acknowledges death and mortality? But it is only the unconscious id which ignores death and time. The unconscious part of the ego constantly experiences self-destruction in its basic rhythm of dedifferentiation, if only in the slow alternation between waking and sleeping, or in the more pronounced rhythm of creative work. Most likely it is this rhythm inside the ego which gives us the sense of time as well as of death. We can thus substantiate Freud's speculation that time could be the mode in which the ego works. The uncreative man flattens or resists the ego rhythm owing to his fear of dedifferentiation; he also denies thereby the flow of time and the existence of death as an emotional fact. (Another reason why the rational surface functions alone could not afford us a true sense of reality was adduced earlier. I showed how the liveliness of our conscious experience depends on a vast unconscious substructure.)

The second feature of dedifferentiation seems to contradict its value as reality experience. This is its distinct manic quality. The killing of the bull, the sacrifice of the dying god no longer have a truly depressive feeling about them; death once accepted becomes a feast of cosmic bliss, a liberation from human bondage. Bach's *St Matthew Passion* is perhaps the most heart-rending mourning for the dying Christ in our art. There is no hint of the coming resurrection, no hope of rebirth; it is indeed the true emotional acceptance of death. Yet once the supreme sacrifice has been offered up, a deep inexplicable peace quells all lament. A serene melody speaks of the coolness of the evening after the work is done. The work of mourning was indeed done as never before. The ultimate manic experience of death is consistent with the extreme dedifferentiation when death and birth, love and hatred have no separate meaning. This fusion (part of unconscious scanning) sets the scene for the reintegration of the fragmented self and later rebirth. This important constructive role of manic fusion in creative work has not yet obtained a secure place in psychoanalytic literature, though there are signs that it is beginning to.

Creativity is usually treated as a faculty for successful symbol formation, which indeed it is. Marion Milner enters the general discussion about the psychological conditions for effective symbol formation by saying that oceanic fusion and dedifferentiation are prerequisite for it. She speaks of a child patient who re-enacted in his play the old ritual of the dying god [22]. She watched the child solemnly burning the effigy of a toy soldier. There was a deep sense of mystery and involvement. She saw the sacrifice as meaning the creative surrender of the common sense (surface) ego that watches over the boundaries between things and between the outer and inner world. Here is the very opposite of a pathological denial of reality. A communion is enacted between the surface ego and its undifferentiated matrix in the unconscious from where all new symbols and ideas must grow.

Melanie Klein has much stressed the depressive aspect of creativity. The child realizes the harm his aggressions have perpetrated and feels committed to reparation. Depressive anxieties are certainly part and parcel of creativity. I have suggested that the first phase of free projection and fragmentation is beset by schizoid-paranoid persecutory anxieties. The scientist, in particular, seeks out parts of physical reality that are still seen as incoherent or fragmented. He almost provokes schizoid anxieties as he contemplates this fragmentation. This is why, in my view, the image of the burned, devoured god is characteristic of scientific work. In the second phase of creativity creative man prepares, as it were, in his work a receiving 'womb', the image of a benevolent mother figure, to contain and integrate the fragmented material. Insofar as integration succeeds, persecutory anxieties are replaced by depressive anxieties. The progression from schizoid projection to depressive containment repeats the momentous crisis in the child's development which I have mentioned. At first, paranoid-schizoid anxieties lead to excessive splintering of the self and to massive and undirected projections (projective identifications) into the void. This squandering of the ego's substance may lead to its permanent impoverishment.

Later on the child learns to deal with his anxieties in a different way. I have suggested how instead of projecting split-off parts of the self into a void he prepares a 'womb' in his unconscious into which the split-off material is repressed. After due transformation into symbolic representations the repressed material can gain re-entry into the surface ego.

I have said that creative work in the external world contains and integrates the projections, while at the same time another womb is prepared in the undifferentiated matrix of the unconscious to carry on the work of integration within the ego. On this secret stage occur fruitful dedifferentiations and oceanic fusions which are essentially manic in character. Perfect integration is possible because of the unlimited mutual interpenetration of oceanic imagery. All opposites merge, death and birth become one, the difference between the sexes, the differentiation of parent and child disappear. Temporarily, all splitting is undone.

In the third phase of creativity a partial re-introjection of the oceanic imagery into consciousness occurs. Because it is only partial, the rest remains repressed and forms art's unconscious substructure. Also, as we have seen, the re-entry into the surface ego involves a secondary revision. Narrowly focused surface perception cannot comprehend the wider sweep of undifferentiated imagery. This explains why the final result of creative work can never achieve the full integration that is possible in the second oceanic-manic phase of creativity. Depressive anxiety is the inevitable consequence. The creative mind must be capable of tolerating imperfection. Creative man awakens from his oceanic experience to find that the result of his work does not match his initial inspiration. Unconscious linkages established on the manic-oceanic level have not been fully translated into surface coherence. But the incoherence need not cause persecutory anxieties, because unconscious linkages still persist in the undifferentiated matrix (substructure) of his work. The depressive anxieties may lead to renewed immersion of the result into the unconscious matrix in order to create further linkages. In this manner the ego rhythm of periodic dedifferentiation and re-differentiation will be accompanied by alternating manic and depressive feelings. However perfect the unconscious linkages, their re-introjection into consciousness will still lead to depressive anxiety.

I know of an artist who puts his finished picture next to his bedside so that he can see it as he wakens in the morning. Possibly in the twilight state between sleeping and waking his still weak self-critical faculties will make it easier for him to introject what he had done half blindly and spontaneously the day before. But the grey light of the morning is not always as gentle. Part of the training we can give a young artist is to stiffen his resistance against an anal impulse of casting away the imperfect achievements of the previous day, in order to start again with a clean sheet. Partial fragmentation has to be tolerated. I will discuss in the next chapter how in their maturity great masters of the past learned to ignore the fragmented surface appearance and to retain their trust in the unconscious logic of spontaneity. Maybe, a manic element belonging to deeper near-oceanic levels of dedifferentiation (where unconscious scanning is carried on) must persist to sustain the artist against the onslaught of depression at the sight of persisting surface fragmentation.

The process of (creative) symbol formation obeys the same rhythm. In order to symbolize another object, the symbolic image must interpenetrate with it in the undifferentiated matrix of image making. On being re-introjected into consciousness, the undifferentiated linkages will contract. The symbolic image alone catches the narrow focus of secondary revision and the other symbolized object remains repressed. But as long as unconscious linkage persists the symbolizing image will not be dissociated and remain imbued with unconscious meaning and reference. Its symbolic power wanes as soon as its unconscious linkage is severed. This will inevitably occur owing to secondary processes that tend to dissociate surface imagery from its undifferentiated matrix. Ernest Jones, in his classic paper on symbol formation, quite rightly excluded the age-old artifacts of civilization from his discourse. We use a plough, knife, or house without necessarily reacting to their powerful phallic or womb symbolisms. This dissociation does not serve the surface ego's 'autonomy' as is sometimes assumed. It is a definite loss. Our daily life has lost some of its vividness, which is dependent on its contact with the unconscious matrix of image making in which the old symbolism is still active. The artist's main social function may well be to regain for us the lost vividness of our experiences by re-activating their deeper symbolic linkages that alone give them plastic life.

The schizophrenic, as I have shown, fears dedifferentiation because he equates it with death. He has failed to create a 'womb' in his unconscious that could serve as a matrix for establishing unconscious linkages (I will later discuss the failure of repression in psychotic illness). All he can do is to copy the process of de-differentiation on a conscious level which is impossible. He merely splinters his rigid imagery. Owing to their incompatibility the fragments become telescoped into 'bizarre' (Bion) mixture forms. Symbol formation becomes impossible. What ought to have been conscious symbol and unconsciously symbolized object violently collide on the same conscious level. One of them must give way. Hanna Segal speaks of a psychotic patient who refused to play the violin because, as he said, he did not want to masturbate in public. Here the symbolized object usurps the place of the symbolizing object. The violin no longer symbolizes the genital, it has been pushed out by the concrete genital object. Hanna Segal proposed the term 'symbolic equation' for this violent displacement [27]. This is not a very happy choice. What happens is neither symbolic nor an equation. One thing has pushed itself into the place of another because it refused to be equated with it. The term fits better the unconscious substructure of creative work where symbol and symbolized object freely interpenetrate without doing each other violence. What the uncreative psychotic does is a horrible attempt at doing in the conscious world of hard unyielding objects what is only possible in the undifferentiated unconscious matrix of image making.

An undue emphasis on the role of depression in creativity at the expense of mania neglects the polarity of mania and depression. They are fundamental human attitudes, perhaps representative of the two basic instincts, Eros and Thanatos. Once we accept the equal status of the two polar positions, we can discern their cooperation rather than antagonism in the work of creative integration. Creative depression allows the ego nuclei which are split apart on a conscious level to be contained and held together, while creative mania swings down to an undifferentiated level of awareness and resolves the sterilizing dissociation between the many levels of the ego. Depression achieves the ego's *horizontal* integration (occurring on the same level), while mania leads to *vertical* integration by joining surface imagery to its unconscious matrix. Together they bring about the basic rhythm on which the ego's health depends.

As creativity is apt to link the extreme bottom and top levels of image making, it is often difficult to distinguish the initial fragmentation, due to near-schizoid splitting from the final manic self-scattering (dedifferentiation) which contains the seed of integration. In the oceanic state the superego's aggression against the ego is at last neutralized. The surface ego no longer resists the pull of the deep. Dedifferentiation is no longer felt as a danger. Reason has learned to accept gestalt-free 'open' structures. The final solution of a problem can be kept open-ended and retains variables (serial structures) that will only be filled in by future usage. For instance, the ambiguities of abstract art may be filled by the more concrete interpretation on the part of the spectator, indeterminate musical pieces are fitted into definite sequences, buildings are used and transformed for unorthodox uses, the wording of legal statutes is redefined by the changing needs of society. In order to be able to accept such open solutions the superego's aggression must be greatly weakened. The surface ego has become suffused with undifferentiated structures which must be tolerated and welcomed in spite of their apparent fragmentation and chaos. A measure of manic well-being, the gift of a benevolent superego, is needed for this final re-introjection of imagery that is still partly undifferentiated and vulnerable to secondary revision by the rational gestalt principle. When the residue of manic dedifferentiation is massive, the misleading appearance of fragmentation, gaps, sudden transitions becomes unavoidable. This is a source of recurrent doubt for the artists themselves as they consider their manic work in the grey depressive light of the next day. Fortunately for us they are usually able to resist their self-doubt with the help of a pacified superego. Up to a point they are able to resurrect the old oceanic fusion. It is then that the poemagogic images of the self-creating and self-destroying god or of the Muse as the loving and killing goddess help the artist to retain his hold on the manic level of creativity. Their images come triumphantly through the rude cracks of the surface and justify conscious chaos by the extreme un-differentiation of their contradictory aspects that reconcile the incompatibles of birth, love, death and transcend the limits of individual existence.

I have mentioned the figure of Homunculus in Goethe's *Faust* as perhaps the most extreme embodiment of the self-creating god. It so happens that the Homunculus episode in the second part of the tragedy also creates the most notorious rupture in the plot, which tends to incoherence anyway. This is no coincidence. Goethe, for one, had come to trust his manic inspiration. He had composed his *Faust* in bits and pieces from the outset, much to the sceptical amusement of his princely patron, the Duke of Weimar, who reproached Goethe for leaving everything in 'shambles'; and in shambles *Faust* still appears today, at least to the over-rational reader who is offended by a lack of surface coherence. Goethe was attracted by manic fragmentation, that is to say, that kind of fragmentation that reinforces depth coherence at the expense of surface coherence. This is documented by Goethe's seemingly preposterous interest in Mozart's *The Magic Flute*, another work of notorious incoherence, but of much lighter weight. The libretto of *The Magic Flute* was concocted by Schikaneder, a suburban actor-manager, who was out to write a good role for himself and to incorporate effects that were good box-office. Musically, too, *The Magic Flute* is a rag-bag of dis-parate musical styles which Mozart borrowed left and right with little apparent originality. In the case of *The Magic Flute* the result was most profound. The mystery of the opera has not ceased to provoke new attempts at interpretation. The most imaginative, but on the surface least successful, interpretation was attempted by Goethe himself. He wrote a sequel to the opera in which he hoped to clear up some of its obscurities, but suc-ceeded only in adding a few more. Yet the joint effort of Goethe and Schikaneder became perhaps the most profound conden-sation of the dying god theme, cutting through to the deepest level of the self-creating, self-scattering womb, the parentless divine child. Goethe, after abandoning his operatic sequel, transplanted its imagery bodily into his *Faust* where it led, as we would now expect, to new inconsistencies and gaps. It is worthwhile tracing the whole history of the theme through all its seemingly light-hearted vicissitudes.

The beginning of Mozart's opera is conventional. It follows the cliché of the 'rescue' opera which was very common at the time. Prince Tamino is saved from a giant snake by the three ladies in the service of the Queen of Night. He is shown a picture of the Queen's daughter, Pamina, and is told that she has been abducted by the wicked magician Sarastro. Tamino promises to help the hapless mother and to rescue her daughter from Sarastro's power. He is given a magic flute to protect him from danger. Three boy genii conduct him to Sarastro's temple. If the conventional plot had been pursued he should have battled against the wicked magician and rescued his princess in order to marry her. Psycho-analytically speaking, this plot would have moved exclusively on the genital Oedipus level; the son takes the side of the wronged mother, defies his father and wins his mother's love. Nothing of the kind happens. It appears that Sarastro has abducted Pamina for her own good. He is the priest of the sun poised against the Queen of Night as the evil goddess of darkness. Tamino undergoes the trials imposed on him for his purification so that he can become a worthy member of Sarastro's secret male society. It has been suggested that Mozart as a freemason changed his (and Schikaneder's) mind half-way through the plot in order to incorporate masonic teaching. We are back, as it were, at the secret rituals of the Holy Grail. This may be so; but it seems more likely that it was a hotchpotch from the start. However, last-minute changes by great artists usually turn out also to be dictated by overwhelming inner necessity; in this case, deeper pre-oedipal levels of poemagogic imagery. The changeover, in addition, is not quite so abrupt as it first appears. The Queen's three ladies, like all triple female figures, point to the status of the Queen as the dread triple goddess. When the Queen herself appears to the sound of thunder, she does so in the role of Ceres, the mournful and revengeful mother. Her stabbing *coloratura* recalls the equally dark figure of Donna Anna in Mozart's *Don Giovanni*, whose sole aim, too, is to take revenge and who rejects love and life until the criminal is brought to justice. The disguise of the remorseless White Goddess is quite transparent and so is the disguise of the dying god. Don Giovanni certainly provokes his own destruction and sacrifices himself. Goethe was ready to acknowledge him as a precursor of his *Faust*, and his admiration for the opera *Don Giovanni* made him hope that Mozart would also set his own *Faust* to music. I have already indicated how the dying god motif can also be felt in *The Magic Flute*. The castration symbolism in the killing of the snake is reflected in the scene of restitution in which Tamino is given his magic flute, a curious bisexual symbol. Tamino becomes Orpheus who has to descend into the subterranean caves filled with fire and water in order to gain spiritual rebirth. The concept of male society giving rebirth to young males is at the core of the ubiquitous rites of passage and puberty ceremonies in primitive societies. The community of the males appropriate for themselves the female powers of the womb, as Margaret Mead has pointed out. The boy to be initiated is hidden from the women and received into the 'womb' of the body social represented by the community of men.

But on a still deeper level, as Bettelheim has shown in his book *Symbolic Wounds* [1], it is the initiated boy himself who creates the female powers in himself in the figure of the self-creating dying god. The youth creates the female organs within his own body, e.g. by subincising his genitals. He achieves rebirth with neither his mother's help, nor that of the body social represented by the fathers. Prince Tamino in *The Magic Flute* appropriates the bisexual flute as his own means of salvation. It has been noted that the power of the magic flute is curiously independent of the struggle between the father and mother figures; and so also are the three boy genii who at first accompany and guide Tamino to Sarastro at the behest of the Queen, but later intervene quite autonomously. This independent role of the three genii is perhaps the most recalcitrant feature in a plot replete with obscurities. From the three boy genii issues the long trail which Goethe took up. Their detachment from the struggle between patriarchy and matriarchy points to the lowest level of poemagogic imagery when the self-creating child assumes the generating powers of his parents. Very perceptively, a recent discussion of Goethe's indebtedness to Mozart (Joseph Müller-Blattau, 'Der Zauberflöte zweiter Teil', *Jahrbuch der Goethegesellschaft*, Neue Folge,

18, 1956) follows the trail that leads from the unattached three genii in *The Magic Flute* to Tamino's child in Goethe's sequel to the libretto and from there to the boy charioteer in *Faust*, Part Two. I would add as further multiplications of the theme the figures of Homunculus, Euphorion and the blessed boys in the final apotheosis of Faust. These figures too behave with disruptive independence and produce unbridgeable inconsistencies that have defied all literal interpretation. I hope it will be understood by now that these inconsistencies cannot be considered as undigested remnants of some primary-process fantasies that were left untouched through accident or negligence. They are of eminent structural significance through their origin in the deepest oceanic level of poemagogic imagery. These fissures and cracks in the surface lead right down into the undifferentiated depth where the poemagogic image of the divine child begins to make sense. Without the rupture we would fail to experience its potency and be misled by the divine boy's unconcerned light-heartedness. The surface has to be blown to bits as a tribute to his divinity, a shattering salute to his creative potency.

In Goethe's sequel to *The Magic Flute* the Queen of Night is transformed into a true earth goddess without ado and is so addressed by her followers. She is a chthonic goddess who dwells – true to her character – self-secluded in subterranean caves. She at once acts in her true role as the 'burying goddess' ruling over death and rebirth. She revenges herself on Tamino and Pamina, now married and just blessed with a baby son, by burying the child alive in a golden casket. Moreover this coffin sinks into the womb of the earth guarded by wild animals and by barriers of fire and water. Goethe could not have made the true womb symbolism of Mozart's fire and water caves more explicit. The reaction of the father principle – embodied by Sarastro – is true to form. Sarastro in turn tries to act as a male god of birth. Papageno and Papagena are childless and yearn for children. Sarastro advises them to place some magic eggs in a cave – yet another womb symbol, this time arrogated by the oedipal father figure.

In the end it is the child himself who usurps the powers of the parents. Tamino and Pamina penetrate through fire and water to the coffin containing their child; they are helped by the magic flute (Goethe prescribes explicitly that the same decor should be used in this scene as for the corresponding scene in *The Magic Flute*). But the ending is most unexpected, a spontaneous twist which brings the plot to an abrupt end. Goethe never went on to finish the libretto. The casket turns incandescent and transparent. Within it the baby turns into a powerful spirit and gives birth to himself by bursting out from the coffin and throwing himself into the air where he is lost in infinite space. It stands to reason why Goethe could not go on. He meant to continue the plot and to bring it back to a contest between the father and mother figures. The only possible way out is to subdue the power of the child by undoing his manic suicide-birth. Goethe's tentative sketches for the last act try precisely this. The genius is 're-captured' during a battle between the two hostile powers and restored to firm earth. The power to give rebirth is thus once again shifted to the parents. This may make sense logically, but never from the viewpoint of poemagogic truth as a depiction of the creative process. There the self-creating, self-destroying child (identified with his own womb) must emerge victorious. The violent disruption of the surface plot is only another logical result of his manic triumph.

This is also what happens in Goethe's *Faust*. Goethe as a young man is said to have been inspired by a casual newspaper notice reporting the trial of a child murderess. In *Faust*, Part One, she became Margarete, the distraught and abandoned mother who kills her illegitimate child, but is saved by the grace of heaven. She represents a still very superficial image of the killing White Goddess of death and rebirth. In the second part of the play, Faust assumes the role of the mother giving rebirth. He attempts to bring Helen of Troy back to life. This is a neat reversion of roles characteristic of a high degree of dedifferentiation; the mother killing her son is replaced by the son (Faust) giving rebirth to his mother. I have mentioned how, in the classical form of the myth, Orpheus conducts Eurydice from the underworld, instead of being taken away to the underworld by the death goddess. Faust is explicitly compared with Orpheus. The priestess Manto, who once smuggled Orpheus into the underworld, promises to do the same for Faust, so that he can plead with Persephone for Helen's release. But the decisive confrontation between Faust and Persephone never came off. A last-minute change of mind, typical of a manic intrusion from below, substituted a quite different story of rebirth, which remains quite unconnected. It completely disrupts the continuity of the story. The chemical manikin, Homunculus, achieves his own suicidal rebirth in love. I have already mentioned the extreme oceanic undifferentiation of the episode. Homunculus is still unborn, enclosed in a glass phial which can become incandescent and lift itself into the air (this is an additional phallic symbolism). The manikin achieves rebirth by shattering his glass in a fiery explosion at the feet of the sea goddess, Galatea, amidst a general scene of orgiastic self-abandon.

Nowhere in literature is there a more condensed image of the self-creating and self-scattering womb, or rather the divine parentless child identified with the womb from which he delivers himself in a threefold act of birth, love and death. The haunting image of the boy genii in *The Magic Flute* has at last found its true mould. Faust, the embodiment of the creative quest for self-realization, has not really yearned to give rebirth to the mother figure; although the artist does resurrect in his work the dead or wounded mother and offers restitution by integrating the fabric of art, at the same time he also descends into the underworld of his own unconscious and reshapes in its womb his own fragmented ego. But – and this is the point I want to make in this context – the intrusion of the poemagogic image, while standing for integration in the matrix of the womb, also disrupts surface coherence and creates an almost intolerable impression of fragmentation. It is completely left in the air whether Faust has in fact penetrated into Persephone's presence and succeeded in his pleading. The birth–love–death of Homunculus ends the scene. As the curtain lifts again, Helen is already reborn; she, like Homunculus, seems to have achieved rebirth by her own power. Of her own accord too she visits Faust in his medieval castle. This irrational confusion of space and time retains some manic element. But otherwise the tragedy of Helen is severely classical, emphasizing the contrast with the free verse and manic licence that characterized Homunculus's self-sacrifice. The manic element re-emerges in Euphorion, the fruit of Helen's and Faust's union. Like Dionysus he grows to full maturity in a few days, an allusion to the self-creating powers of the divine boy. As soon as he has brought himself to maturity he achieves his self-realization by scattering his substance into the air. He immediately calls from the underworld below. Self-scattering meant self-burial in the womb of the earth, a neat reversal of the temporal sequence found in the sequel of *The Magic Flute* and in the Homunculus episode, where self-scattering follows burial alive. After Euphorion's death the plot takes a new turn. But this lack of cohesion is not as disturbing as the break after the death of Homunculus. Goethe meant to tie up a few loose threads and give greater emphasis to a few points. But he died before he could do so. One feels that he did not mind too much. As I have said, he had worked on his *Faust* in bits and pieces all his life. He had published parts of it as a 'Fragment'. It starts quite abruptly in the middle of a verse with the word 'and'. He did not care all that much about niceties of surface coherence and allowed himself to be led by the needs of a more profound logic. In his last years when he became anxious to bring the work to completion, he rationalized his instinctive disregard for superficial logic as a conscious principle of poetic composition. In a letter to his friend, W. von Humboldt, he reported a 'secret psychological development' which deserved 'scientific investigation'; possibly he thought that Humboldt could help him to understand what had happened to him. He had, so he wrote, lifted himself to a kind of poetic creativity that, in the full light of consciousness, brought results that could stand up to later self-criticism, but 'he could never swim in the same river again'. Though he himself accepted his spontaneity and appreciated its 'fully conscious' logic, he was in no doubt, as he wrote, that Aristotle and other 'prosaists' would have ascribed his state to some kind of madness. He foresaw his failure to make his poetic logic understood by his prosaic audience. Though he was at the height of international fame he knew that his late work would be driven like a wreck to some distant shore to be scattered and buried by 'the dunes of time' ('Dünenschutt der Stunden'). This was indeed to come true. Only twentieth-century commentators, like Helen Herrmann, M. Kommerell and Stuart Atkins at Harvard, have begun to draw to the surface the hidden order of *Faust*. The early commentators, in spite of the general exaggerated reverence for Goethe, saw only the superficial fragmentation, and criticized it as being chaotic much in the way in which classical psycho-analytic theory described the superficial chaos of the primary process. O. Pniower, one of the most respected interpreters of Goethe's work (in *Dichtungen und Dichter*, Berlin, 1912) censures Goethe's indifference to essentials which he hid in 'insignificant details'. (The primary process displays the same indifference and displaces emphasis on essentials in this way.) Goethe was also blamed for treating major themes laconically, for stifling them by wilful retardations, sudden transitions and gaps. Serious themes are treated lightheartedly when Faust's yearning for self-realization is parodied by Homunculus, the synthetic manikin. This, we are told, deprives the theme of the solemnity which is its due. We may again have to blame the irresponsible pranks of the primary process. In dreams it expresses terrifying fantasies in sweet images, and transforms reassuring ideas into fear and horror. This, of course, is not chaos but simply another instance of our unconscious capacity for dedifferentiation which reconciles opposites and other more complex serial structures. Goethe's disregard for surface coherence appeals to the same unconscious faculty in us. Incidentally, the Homunculus episode was originally to be fashioned as light relief in imitation of *The Magic Flute*. There, Papageno apes his master's quest for self-realization by his search for a half-human bird girl like himself. In the first sketches, Homunculus was to look out for a chemical maiden of his own cast. But light relief turned into earnest. What was to be only a comical mirror plot interrupted the principal action of the play.

Goethe's 'secret development' led him to accept the constructive function of the primary process. Not being a 'prosaist', he was able to penetrate through the misleading surface of fragmentation, frivolity, manic abandon and obscurity to feel the submerged logic of his poemagogic fantasies. Expressed in poemagogic terms, his initial vision of the White Goddess as the child murderess, Margarete, a particularly aggressive projection of the superego, gradually gave way to the image of the manic ego reigning supreme, the self-creating, self-scattering boy called Homunculus or Euphorion or boy charioteer, etc.

The artist has to learn to trust his unconscious and its hidden logic and coherence. He may have to suffer much pain, anxiety and doubt in order to complete his secret development. The ego has first to submit to the superego's attack. In Robert Graves's terms, the poet has to submit to the killing love of the White

Goddess. The ego learns to neutralize this attack by turning it to a power of active dedifferentiation and increased control over the primary process. This dedifferentiation is not merely a 'controlled regression' (E. Kris) to more primitive forms of ego functioning. The point is precisely that the artist transforms passive primitive undifferentiation into an active faculty for moulding images of extreme dedifferentiation never achieved before. The contemplation of poemagogic imagery speeds the ego on its way and at the same time indicates the degree of dedifferentiation achieved at any time. This is why it is so important to distinguish the various structural levels of poemagogic imagery. Once the ego has achieved full control over the dedifferentiation of images inherent in the primary process it is ready for the manic overthrow of the superego, symbolized by the self-creating womb and the divine boy. Then, the surface and depth of the ego merge and the super-ego fuses with the ego, until the cycle of creativity pushes on to the third depressive phase of creativity.

The temporary fusion of the surface and depth functions implies a manic scattering and elimination of all existing clichés and mannerisms. The ego can afford to shed this lumber because the loss will be more than made good by the re-introjection into consciousness of repressed material waiting in the unconscious matrix below (the third phase of creativity). Of course, the secondary revision incumbent on conscious re-introjection will soon tend to debase the newly created symbols into another set of rigid and defensive clichés. For a while, as we have seen, these will retain their generating power and fertility, as long as their link with the undifferentiated matrix below still holds. But as the new images cut themselves loose, as they inevitably will, the scene is set for a new enactment of the ritual of self-destruction and rebirth in the sacrifice of the dying god.

The rejection of pre-existing solutions, the acceptance of disruption and manic self-abandon is perhaps most clearly stated in the choral movement of Beethoven's *Ninth Symphony*. Beethoven had by then entered his late period, when he abandoned strict form and relied increasingly on intuitive depth coherence. He had to pay the same price which Goethe so willingly paid; in spite of his growing fame his late works went unperformed for a long time. Richard Wagner in his teens discovered the late quartets and, although he probably never had a chance to hear them, they may have helped him to bring about the greatest revolution in music almost by accident. I have spoken of the rhythmic incoherence in the first movement of the *Ninth Symphony* where the cosmic weaving of the first bars does not tally with the thunder claps following them. I said that unity of rhythm can only be achieved by actually changing the speed, an old paradox of unconscious logic with which we have become familiar. The symphony, considering the rigid standards of concert performances, is rarely performed satisfactorily even today.

In the last choral movement Beethoven explicitly rejects all antecedents. The resources of the orchestra no longer suffice for him, he needs the human voice to explain the deeper meaning of his music. The rejection of antecedent was contained in the strange recitative of the double-basses that answer and reject – imitating a full-throated human voice – the quotations from the earlier movements. In the first sketches these answers were actually sung by the human voice, which repudiated the quotations as insufficient for expressing what had to be expressed. Making the double-basses 'sing' instead is a more subtle idea. It demonstrates the intolerable muteness of a purely instrumental music; he tries to make the instruments sing in a human way, but fails. In the end the human voice itself must break in as a symbol of extreme disruption in order to obey a more profound logic.

At the same time the final intervention of the human voice also rejects chaos and destruction. It does not, as the double-bass recitatives do, reject the melodious memories from the earlier movements; it answers the shattering thunder of chaos with which the movement begins and which is finally repeated to sweep aside the orchestral quotations for good. The singing voice rejects the thunder of destruction and demands more friendly music. The ecstatic hymn to the spirit of joy follows. Manic self-surrender comes after aggressive self-destruction according to the logic of poemagogic imagery. Beethoven remained in painful doubt whether the choral movement was the right solution. He had not, as Goethe did, learned to accept superficial disruption for the sake of a deeper logic. Incidentally, it brings out the full irony of our persistent misunderstanding of what poemagogic imagery is about that Beethoven's fragmentation device was soon turned into an intellectual assembly device. Quoting from preceding movements was welcomed as a good gimmick for producing a superficial unity between the movements of the symphony.

The symphonic form is not teachable because it is a supreme example of the poemagogic need for fragmenting surface coherence. While each movement on its own possesses a shape that can be comprehended analytically, the breaks between mean more than pleasant contrast in key, rhythm and mood. An underlying unity can only be sensed by accepting and emphasizing the superficial ruptures. The interval of silence between the movements cannot be measured, but is of immense structural significance. The brief flowering of the classical symphonic form institutionalized, as it were, surface fragmentation and therefore only remained viable as long as composers were able to rely on their low-level sensitivities for structuring the gaps in surface continuity. Beethoven, in breaking traditional forms, showed that already by his time, breaks and contrasts between symphonic movements had become a matter of mechanical habit and lacked a deeper unity. The *Ninth Symphony* parallels Goethe's *Faust* by taking as its principal theme the working of the creative mind itself. His self-doubt, tentative rejection of precedent, the several attempts at solving a new formal problem and their rejection, the overcoming of the ensuing chaos by manic self-surrender are all incorporated into the fabric of the work itself. I have said that modern art cannot claim to have abandoned objective subject matter and to be the first to have represented the subjective creative process. We have now seen that the greatest works of the past were poemagogic in exactly the same way. It seems that once greater depths are reached in the image making of art, the structure of the work of art must reflect this perilous descent.

Michelangelo depicted on the Sistine ceiling the creation of the world. He ended up by depicting poemagogically his own creativity in the biblical panel closest to the mural of the *Last Judgement* on the altar wall, which he painted last when he was at the peak of his powers (plate 30). This small panel is usually ignored and seems curiously vague and hazy. This too seems part of the poemagogic subject matter. Before creating the world, the great creator had to create himself. Far from being the potent virile father figure of the creation scenes, a feeble old man tries to emerge from the womb of a whirling cloud which envelops him like a chrysalis; his one arm gropes upwards to disentangle himself from the envelopment. The upward groping movement was due to a last-minute decision suggesting the sudden disruptive effect of spontaneity. We have come to appreciate such late changes of mind in our discussion of the disruptive effect of the Homunculus episode. As happened in *Faust*, the poemagogic theme of the self-creating womb intruded into an otherwise quite orthodox biblical story. Michelangelo himself never gave an interpretation; nor is this necessary if one accepts my hypothesis of an inner need intruding into orderly planning. His contemporaries soon jumped to the interpretation of the panel in this heretical manner and no other satisfactory explanation has been offered since. To describe it as 'God dividing light and darkness' ignores the weakness of the gesture and may have contributed to its neglect by the general public.

A friend of mine once ventured a somewhat profane explanation why the godhead in this panel so little resembles the powerful father figure creating the universe. The weak and ugly man lifting his weary arm upwards also represents the old master Michelangelo himself in the act of painting the ceiling. Often enough light-hearted jokes on depth-psychological matters happen to hit the mark. The figure's attitude and the awkward movement of his right arm is not at all unlike the tortuous attitude of a painter who paints a ceiling. There is some doubt as to whether Michelangelo painted the Sistine ceiling lying on his back or standing up. He may have done both, nor is it material to know this exactly. We have a small sketch by Michelangelo (figure 12) which represents a painter standing up and painting a ceiling in the unavoidably tortuous stance. This amply demonstrates how Michelangelo pictured to himself the act of painting a ceiling and he could have had such a vision of himself in his unconscious mind. The joke would explain both the astonishing frailty of the divine figure and also the tolerance of both the master and his public to a patently heretical treatment of the biblical creation. On the deepest poemagogic level any true artist identifies himself and his work with the generating powers of the womb. He feels at the same time inside and outside the enveloping womb and in the last resort represents the womb itself. The story of divine creation turns into the story of human creativity.

To my mind, the glorious and equally incongruent naked youths could intrude into the ceiling with impunity for the same poemagogic reasons. Even today their provoking muscularity

Figure 12. Marginal sketch by Michelangelo on the manuscript of a sonnet in which he describes his physical difficulties in painting the Sistine ceiling frescoes. Could the image of the 'self-creating god' on the ceiling (plate 30) represent Michelangelo in the act of painting the ceiling?

and nudity antagonizes a pious public. But admirers of Michelangelo's work acclaim them as the highest achievement of the ceiling. I would add that they also depict directly the main theme of creativity. They are close relatives of the impudent three genii in *The Magic Flute* who scamper through the opera owing allegiance to no one, and to the many self-creating divine boys who arrogate the authority and power of the parents. They certainly also bring about formal disruption and fragmentation as far as the architectural articulation of the ceiling is concerned. In an early sketch their place is still taken by conventional architectural ornaments which brought out the curvature of the vault. Without these the rising curve of the ceiling cannot be read properly and must confuse and disturb the spectator. All architectural clarity was abandoned once the *ignudi* had invaded these architectural key points. Their inordinate size upsets the balance of the composition and produces a feeling of overcrowding. Their enormous bodies form preposterous frames around the comparatively small biblical panels inside. On each corner of each panel one of the naked giants has seated himself. With divine self-sufficiency and indifference they seem to sweep aside the biblical scenes within and dwarf the biblical figures depicted in them. Their pagan nudity goes ill with the holy stories and impresses many as wholly sacrilegious. Yet to the properly attuned spectator there is neither confusion of space nor of meaning. I am inclined to accept A. Stokes's interpretation of Michelangloe's nudes. Their objectively gross distortions symbolize, on an undifferentiated level of vision, the properties of a mighty ambisexual being. The quilted squareness of their torsoes is not so much a sign of male strength as of their female fecundity. Because this undifferentiated fusion cannot be analysed on a conscious level, it evokes anxiety. Stokes says [31]: 'virile creatures such as ... Sebastian (in the *Last Judgement*) are superhuman: without a trace of effeminacy they incorporate the female powers: hence their *terribilità*.' This accords with my interpretation that the *ignudi* represent the self-creating genie identified with the womb. Like the biblical scenes from Genesis they tell the story of divine and human creativity; they could not but intrude and upset all aesthetic and iconographic considerations. They succeed in triumph just by their power of violent disruption, which is part of their most profound symbolism. Their aloofness and unconcern for the pictures they are supposed to frame sustains the basic theme of divine self-sufficiency. They echo throughout the ceiling the mystery of creativity and by disrupting its superficial continuity link it into a more profound unity.

Because this disruption was part of the poemagogic fantasy it was never imitated successfully. Baroque painters copied all of Michelangelo's innovations and naturally they also tried to produce their own *ignudi*. At best, some powerful youth dutifully holds up a frame containing the panel, a rather tame affair. Never again was the mutual interpenetration and confusion between panel and *ignudi* attempted, nor would it have been successful without the prompting of a deeper logic.

13 The Scattered and Buried God

The exact role of the superego's aggression in creative work will probably be fully understood only when we have found out more about its role in causing mental illness. In many ways creativity and mental illness are opposite sides of the same coin. The blocking of creativity through ego rigidity is apt to unleash the self-destructive fury of the superego, which is otherwise absorbed and neutralized by the periodic decomposition of the ego during creativity. An increased measure of the superego's oral and anal aggression against the ego is utilized for deepening the normally shallow oscillation of the ego as it swings down to less differentiated levels. The superego's anal scattering attacks drive the ego inexorably towards an extreme oceanic depth until the process of dedifferentiation even suspends the distinction between ego and superego. Then the ego can shake itself free from the superego's aggression. It was easier for me to start describing poemagogic imagery on its deepest oceanic level, on which the superego's aggression is spent and the ego prepares for its manic rebound and rebirth. The cruel White Goddess who represents the superego's anal and oral aggression has disappeared and the divine child (representing the self-destroying and self-creating ego) usurps the creative function of the womb. Space and time no longer count. Containment (burial) may come before scattering and expulsion into the void, or just as easily in the reverse order. Death may come before birth and love. The phallus, normally the instrument of penetration and ejection, turns into a containing womb. The glass case of Homunculus certainly stands for both. In his recent work Henry Moore seems to have abandoned his life-long theme of the Great Mother and the cavity of her womb. His new sculptures often look like giant phalli. Yet these phallic shapes express the old theme on a deeper level where the male child has incorporated the powers of the womb. They too are hollowed out like the cavernous bellies of the Great Mother. Child and mother have become one (plate 29). Michelangelo developed in the opposite direction. His mature work was dedicated to the autonomous self-creating god who had no need of his mother. But in his last work, the *Rondanini Pietà* (plate 28), he returned to the mother mourning over her dead son as had Aphrodite and Kybele before her. The work seems unfinished as though death had prevented Michelangelo from bringing it to completion. A hefty athletic arm that belonged to an earlier abandoned version stands free like an amputated limb, quite unconnected with the rest of the work. Yet it is an integral part of the whole, as Henry Moore once insisted in an interview. Moore spoke of the deep impression the work made on him. Fragmentation, as so often in great works of late maturity, is fully overcome on a manic level. The rest of the sculpture is anything but unfinished. Michelangelo increasingly pared down the originally athletic body of Christ into an almost transparent fragility. His mother hovers above the body caressing it with a paper-thin hand, enveloping it with infinite tenderness. Strangely enough, the dead, limp body of the son seems to carry his mother as though her womb-like embrace had become part of his own body. We are reminded of the icon of the Dormition where the divine son carries the soul of his mother. This reversal points back to the manic level of poemagogic imagery symbolized by the self-sufficient child. Both figures tremble on the threshold between life, death and possible rebirth through love. Manic bliss denying death is mixed with a sense of deep mourning, which belongs to a higher depressive level of poemagogic imagery. The power of the work may be bound up with its capacity for conveying both levels of experience. Nevertheless the mother figure has emerged!

There is also some differentiation of time and space. On the oceanic level the child's self contains the whole world; on the depressive level mother and child, the outer and inner world, are already discerned as separate. Time has also returned. Birth, love, death are not a single act, but are extended in time. The dual rhythm alternating between mania and depression and the equivalent rhythm alternating between dedifferentiation and differentiation already makes itself felt, however dimly. The depressive-anal level is not far off. The mourning on 'Good' Friday may be good and even sweet, yet death is acknowledged without certainty of later resurrection. Dionysus, the self-creating god, is also the dying god rent limb from limb by his priestesses. In the image of Pentheus he is torn alive by the mother figure, Agave. But Agave also recovers from her madness and assumes the role of the burying mother who gathers the torn body for proper burial, to ensure his survival in the underworld.

I have already alluded to another near-oceanic trait in the imagery of the torn and buried (scattered and contained) god, namely the easy reversal of the roles of mother and son. According to Freud, King Lear carrying his dead daughter Cordelia represents the reverse situation of the death goddess carrying off her dead son lover. The mother of Dionysus, Semele, also has to take over the role of the dying god. In one of the many versions of the myth, Semele, like Cordelia, is cast out by her father. She is enclosed in a casket which is allowed to drift out into the sea, an image which has traits both of expulsion and containment. But ultimately Dionysus remains the motherless self-creating god. Like Macduff in *Macbeth* he is not 'of woman born' because he was 'from his mother's womb untimely ripp'd'. Birth by Caesarean operation makes both Macduff and Dionysus into self-created beings. Dionysus repeats the motif of self-creation in the way already discussed. Through his own powers he grows to manly maturity in a few weeks. Freud came very near to interpreting *Macbeth* in this way. He considered as its unconscious theme the failure of Macbeth and his wife to produce children. But it is more important that they are defeated by Macduff who has no parent. We have again to reverse the situation on this near-oceanic level. The motif of childlessness has to be read as the motif of parentlessness, that is to say, the most profound poemagogic theme of the self-creating child. Dionysus, on the same level, becomes Dionysus Zagreus. He was torn limb from limb as a child, but could be reconstituted from his still beating heart. When the figure of the White Goddess emerges, the child maintains his superiority by the already familiar mechanism of reversing their roles. The mother figure shares the fate of the dying god. Not only his mother Semele, but also his wife Ariadne has to take over the passive role of being expelled and contained. Ariadne is the containing mother as the goddess of the labyrinth, possibly the most potent symbol of the containing (trapping) womb which devours the intruder. But she is also the castaway on Naxos rescued by Dionysus. As the god Iacchus, Dionysus is also allied to the great goddess of agriculture, Demeter, and her mysteries. There Demeter's daughter, Persephone, takes over the role of the dying god. The seed of the corn shares the fate of the scattered and buried god. The corn is symbolized by Persephone, who is buried and trapped in the womb of the earth. In revenge, Demeter turns into the trapping, burying mother. In order to achieve the release of her daughter, Demeter makes the earth infertile. The buried seed, like Persephone, remains trapped underground and fails to grow in spring. In normal creativity, containment (burial alive) of the scattered material leads to integration and re-introjection into the self. The fantasy of being trapped in a dead or empty inner world is more characteristic of psychotic fantasy. As such it represents the arch-crime of Greek mythology, which set into motion a never-ending chain of guilt. Hesiod's cosmogony ascribes this crime to the All-Father, Uranus. He outrages the fertility of the earth goddess, Gaea, by constraining her unborn progeny in her womb. (I understand that this incident has an exact parallel in the cosmogony of the Maori.) Both the trapping of the seed by Demeter, and the trapping of Gaea's progeny, have an immediate reference to agricultural rites and the ever-present persecutory fear of the primitive peasant that the seed buried in the earth may not come to life in spring. This very real danger does not detract from the ultimately poemagogic meaning of the theme. All creative work and inventions, however important in objective reality, will take their first and most significant meaning from their subjective poemagogic role in the creative process. Being trapped in a dead inner world signifies creative sterility and even death. Of this fate the psychotic stands in fear. Projection (expulsion, scattering, casting-out) and containment (burial alive, trapping) are two poles in the creative rhythm of the ego.

This dual rhythm is much protracted during a severe crisis in the young child's development. I am referring to the emergence of anal disgust at the age of about eighteen months, when the first anal stage yields to the second stage. Before the child has learned anal disgust he will freely scatter his excrements as part of his own valuable substance and expects his environment to receive them as precious gifts. This is important to him also because in the highly undifferentiated anal fantasies of this stage the child equates all products of the mother's body; he himself as the product of his mother's body is not distinguished from her excrements. In other respects too, anal fantasy is near-oceanic in its lack of differentiation. The male genitals too are treated like excremental extrusions of the body. All body openings and cavities are treated alike.

The emergence of disgust serves to re-differentiate the body zones. The anal zone becomes debased. The genital zone retains and increases its value. The oral and anal openings are once again sharply differentiated and so are their functions of eating (containment, trapping) and excretion (expulsion, scattering). The origin of anal disgust has never been satisfactorily explained. It is most certainly not just imposed on the child by toilet training. It is too fundamental for that. Disgust greatly reinforces the ego's tendencies towards containment. The heedless projections of the first anal stage are contained and excrements deposited with discretion. As the child still equates himself unconsciously with his mother's body products it becomes essential for him to be reassured that he himself is not devalued, cast out and abandoned like an unclean excrement. His ever-present fear of being abandoned is greatly sharpened. We know that separation from his mother, however short, is particularly harmful at this critical age. It is likely to lead to delinquency, the forceful stealing of love. The child, feeling like a valueless, dead excrement, accepts the role of the criminal outlaw, cast out from the womb of the society. Even more important, anal containment at this stage also teaches the ego to contain the wasteful self-projections (projective identifications) and resort to repression instead. In the first anal stage the child tended to eject freely split-off parts of his self without caring sufficiently whether they were accepted and safeguarded by his environment. It was up to the good nursing mother to entertain her child's projections, to tolerate the anxieties attendant on them and to allow her child to re-introject his lost substance enriched by her own elaborations. I have shown how, through learning repression, the child creates a receiving womb in his own unconscious. There the split-off material is 'buried alive' like the seed of the corn in the womb of the earth.

Unconscious dedifferentiation will transform the material and make it acceptable for later introjection – in unrecognizable symbolic form – into consciousness. If the transformation does not occur and repressed material returns unchanged, the conscious reaction is most revealing. The reaction points decisively to the anal origin of repression. Freud has shown that an untoward 'return of the repressed' is apt to evoke a mixture of feelings, anxieties mixed with disgust and feelings of uncanniness. He pointed out that the German word *grauen* (feelings of uncanniness) is sometimes rendered as *grausen* (disgust). If anal disgust is one of the means by which the superego compels the ego to repress split-off material, it is natural that feelings of disgust recur if the repression proves unsuccessful.

The ego uses structural dedifferentiation as a technique of repression. Through being dedifferentiated the repressed material becomes inaccessible to conscious experience. We begin to understand why dedifferentiation is so easily experienced as (anal) scattering, followed by burial alive. All the fears of death and abandonment which once accompanied the rise of disgust and the learning of repression will penetrate into the poemagogic process of creativity. The failure of repression may be the cause of psychosis and its torments. The psychotic ego has not learned to neutralize the superego's attack by using it for its repressive mechanism. For instance, the manic depressive patient acts out the child's self-identification with excrements. In his manic phase (corresponding to the first anal stage) he hurls himself against his fellow beings with little regard for their willingness to entertain his advances; in his depressive phase (corresponding to the second anal stage) he buries himself away from decent society like an unclean, dead excrement. He has not yet prepared in his unconscious the containing womb which would be ready to receive the split-off parts of his self and so absorb the superego's anal aggression. The psychotic too seems to have failed in the learning of repression. I have spoken of his hostile womb fantasies of being trapped alive. He fears to be caught in an inner void, buried alive in a dead object. His fears conform to his psychic reality of inner emptiness. I have suggested that there is no need for interpreting psychotic womb fantasies as a defence against other (possibly oral) anxieties. If my interpretation is correct the psychotic womb fantasies emphasize the trapping labyrinth-like character of a hostile and empty inner world unnourished by repression. Because they are real they are bound to arouse acute anxieties bordering on fears of total self-annihilation.

From the viewpoint of a healthy ego, repression serves to uphold the ego's richness and differentiation. Splitting no longer leads to a lowering of internal tensions and differentiation; through the repression internal tension and conflict is tolerated and built up. The ego splits into conscious and unconscious parts united by what W. R. Bion has called a 'contact barrier', a barrier that keeps conscious and unconscious apart and at the same time allows an easy crossing of the barrier.

The concept of structural dedifferentiation can explain this double aspect of the barrier which at first sight might seem contradictory. Dedifferentiation makes mental imagery inaccessible to conscious gestalt perception. Hence, as I have suggested, the ego makes use of dedifferentiation to carry out the superego's demand for repression. At the same time dedifferentiation prepares the way for the later re-introjection into consciousness. It eliminates the obnoxious anal (disgusting) traits of the material which had offended the superego and substitutes instead symbolic equivalents that fall within the wider sweep of its serial structure.

In spite of its close relationship with anal containment (repression) and expulsion (scattering) it would be wrong to consider the creative ego rhythm in any way 'anal'. Rather both phenomena have their common source in a more fundamental rhythm that may be associated with the interaction of the life instincts, Eros and Thanatos. The London psycho-analyst, L. Rubinstein, pointed out to me that it would in any case be appropriate to call the anal rhythm of retention and expulsion 'or-anal'. For it combines oral internalization and retention with the originally uninhibited anal expulsion. Abraham rightly pointed out that the anal rhythm alternating between temporary retention and expulsion was utterly primitive. It belongs phylogenetically to an animal lacking all internal differentiation, possessing a single body cavity and body opening that had to serve all the main biological functions of eating, excreting and propagating. The single cavity and opening would operate the basic or-anal rhythm of life regulating internalization and externalization, eating and excreting. In psychic life – and such a primitive organism would not lack mental life – the rhythm would alternate between the or-anal experiences of retention and expulsion, introjection and projection, differentiation and dedifferentiation.

In the last resort the interaction between the two poles of the rhythm can be meaningfully construed as such an interaction between the two life instincts. In my earlier writings I followed the physicist, Schroedinger, in assuming that life (Eros) tends towards ever enriching internal differentiation through eating (internalization, retention), while death (Thanatos) tends towards entropy, a levelling down of the difference between inside and outside and a diminution of internal tension through externalization (excreting, expelling). Freud, too, identified the death instinct with the nirvana principle of entropy, a complete running down of tension within the psychic organism. Freud has been criticized on the ground that recent experiments with states of boredom show that the living organism aims at a certain optimum level of stimulation rather than a complete nirvana of nothingness. This truism does not invalidate the concept of Thanatos as entropy. But it forces us to reformulate the opposition between the two instincts in terms of an optimal threshold for further increases in differentiation. Life can only prosper by a balance between differentiation and dedifferentiation. Both instincts are needed. The power of the organism to contain the tension caused by rising internal differentiation without resorting to splitting and expulsion is a measure of its vitality. In a more complex psychological life the rise of anxiety would signal the approaching threshold of tolerance and the impending rebound of the or-anal rhythm. When the limit of tolerance is reached, splitting, projection and repression reduce internal tensions.

On the level of the lowest organism, cell-division could be described as a splitting process that gets rid of excessive internal differentiation within the cell. On this level the basic metabolism is both anal excretion and pre-sexual propagation. The splitting halves of the cell expel each other as it were to the enrichment of organic life in general. As always Thanatos is linked with Eros. While differentiation is lowered within the new cells, life at large has gained in its differentiation by increasing the number of organisms. Sexuality, the next and yet wholly unexplained step in the evolution of propagation, has to be seen in this double aspect. While the male sperm expels itself into the void, as it were, there is the egg waiting to introject and contain it. The act of expulsion (dedifferentiation) in the service of Thanatos is linked with containment (re-differentiation) in the service of Eros. But the metabolic rhythm is distributed between two separate individuals, a momentous mysterious change. It is prepared by what I have called 'directed' expulsion which already has an element of containment. There are degrees in the directedness of the expulsion. Herrings, both male and female, simply expel sperms and eggs freely, though in close proximity. The developments of male genitals and of the womb are an advance in directedness. In the mental sphere the primitive form of projective identification hurls parts of the self on to other objects with little regard for their willingness to receive and nurture them. In creativity this process becomes more 'directed'. In repression the mind prepares a womb-like receptacle in the inner world into which it can deposit split-off parts of the self. What I have called anal fantasies resemble in their fundamental character closely the basic metabolism of life. The dying god theme on this level is much concerned with expulsion, free scattering and the directed projection ('burying') in a womb-like receptacle. Anal disgust certainly plays its part in inhibiting and 'directing' the free expulsion of the first anal stage. We now see that far from being purely anal in origin this development fits into the mysterious interaction between Eros and Thanatos which also caused the advance in the propagation of the species from asexual cell division and free self-scattering to the more directed expulsion and containment of sexual propagation. Both developments in 'directedness' are equally mysterious in their origin and for the time being have to remain quite unexplained.

In terms of poemagogic imagery this development is clearly discerned in the imagery of Dionysus, the torn god. The self-creating god freely scatters his substance. At best the fragments themselves reconstitute themselves into new individuals by their own effort. Dionysus Zagreus is resurrected from its still beating heart. Here scattering and reconstitution still occur within the single individual. On a higher depressive level, however, another individual, the figure of the burying mother (Isis, Agave, etc.), checks free scattering by gathering up and containing the torn body of the god. She thus assures his rebirth in her womb. The supra-individual distribution of the basic metabolic rhythm then transcends the boundaries of individual existence through the emergence of sexuality. We understand now why it would be misleading to call the creative rhythm of expulsion and containment anal or even or-anal. It is also eminently genital. It seems to occur on every level perhaps because it repeats ever and ever again the metabolic interaction between the two basic instincts.

The first anal stage represents a crisis. The two instincts threaten to become defused during what Melanie Klein in her early writings called the maximum of sadism and self-destruction ('Blüte des Sadismus'). It fits well with my own interpretation of the death instinct (Thanatos) as the principle of entropy and dedifferentiation, that the ascendancy of Thanatos during the anal stage coincides with a maximum of dedifferentiation in anal fantasy. Expulsion and projection become heavily invested with anal aggression. Excrements are felt to be dangerous weapons that inflict heavy damage on the object into which they are projected. At the height of the crisis Eros intervenes to turn the tide. We have seen how anal disgust becomes his first helper. It redifferentiates oral and genital body zones as distinct from the new debased anal zone and its products. It also checks the indiscriminate expulsions and projections of excrements by the new need for cleanliness, and so prepares the way for 'directed' projections. This kind of anal containment or continence still occurs only within the single individual organism. As genital sexuality develops further, the momentous change occurs. Another individual takes over the function of containment and so defeats the expelling tendencies of the death instinct. In poemagogic imagery the changes mainly affect the character of womb fantasies. On the manic-oceanic level the self is identified with the womb. As projections become 'directed' and seek a receptacle in the outside world the miracle happens. The mother figure and her womb are found and felt to be ready to receive and contain the child's projections.* This supra-individual process cannot be explained on the basis of individual or group

* During the earlier phase of undirected free projections the good nursing mother also contains and hands back the expelled fragments of the child's self. But she is as yet not fully felt as another individual who is willing to serve as a receptacle. Projections are not directed and only the accidental intervention of the good nursing mother prevents the child's self from squandering its substance.

psychology. Of course, the oceanic state was already supra-individual in another way. It simply denied the boundaries between the self and other individuals. But now the magic circle is closer and confined to two individuals only. Could this be another interaction and compromise between the two life instincts? I am putting this question only in order to demonstrate the unexplained mystery of the step from asexual to sexual projection (expulsion). Understanding seems a long way off and may require a degree of abstraction of which we are not yet capable. All that we can say now is that the mysteries of creation and of human creativity seem one.

I once gave a talk on scattering and containment in art and explained how the work of art functions as a 'womb' to receive and nurture projective identifications. One member of the audience criticized me by saying that I was not really talking about art, but about human relationships in general. This was quite true. One cannot separate creativity from its social basis. The child's creativity accompanies and sustains his developing human relationships. In order to enrich ourselves as individuals we have to re-shape and change our human relationships without respite by projection and introjection. A frequent failure in human relationships is due to the same ego rigidity that impedes creativity. We have to give our substance freely, project it into other people or creative work for further transformation. As in creative work we must be humble and grateful to receive back far more than we ourselves have put in. Our personality will grow through this creative interchange, which underlies the metabolism of our social life. This may be the moral of Ibsen's Faustian play *Peer Gynt* and his hero's quest for self-realization. Peer went round the world in order to find himself. His search ended in the lap of his mother-wife who had waited to receive and contain him all her life. Creativity, then, may be self-creation, but it is possible only through social intercourse, whether with other individuals as happens in social creativity in the narrower sense of the word, or through the medium of impersonal creative work. The work of art is certainly not merely a projection and direct reflection of our inner world through 'self-expression' as is often assumed. It receives the fragmented projections of our inner world only to nurture and transform them.

The social aspect of creativity cannot be over-emphasized.

Unfortunately, we know next to nothing about social creativity and its most potent impulse, our innate, deeply ingrained feeling of justice. There is a tendency in psycho-analytic writing to consider the sense of justice merely a projection of the superego. Social laws are considered externalized guilt compulsions. The punitive quality of penal laws is certainly characteristic of a severe superego. But somehow such a view completely discounts the importance of our more balanced sense of justice. I think it useful to consider the body social or the 'womb' of society in terms of the basic metabolism of expulsion and containment and examine social justice in terms of their balanced interaction. We are inclined to wonder at the senseless and compulsive cruelty of our penal systems. Admittedly we do no longer simply eject criminals from our society. We pay homage to the need for containing them in the body social by literally burying them alive in prisons and casting them out after a while with little direction into a hostile society unwilling to receive and nurture them. It is useful to measure the health of a society and its power of social cohesion by the strength of its resistance against fragmentation and expulsion of deviant and marginal members. Minorities, criminals, lunatics, old and dead people tend to be marginal and possibly alien elements that seem to provoke expelling and fragmentation tendencies in a given society. Rich internal differentiation and a variety of classes and 'institutions' (Malinowski) in a society indicate great strength of social cohesion, while envious egalitarianism and intolerance of social differentiation point to weak social health. The less the power of containment in a society, the more easily will a deviant member be treated as an 'alien' element that ought to be expelled. The excessive need for sameness and equality in modern society has led to the now all too frequent phenomenon of the 'displaced person', a sinister symptom of social illness. The criminal, by deliberately putting himself outside society, invites the role of the scapegoat, to be duly expelled, a willing target for the fragmentation tendencies active within a society. Frazer traced the institution of the scapegoat back to the universal theme of the dying god. In religious and social ritual only the high-born were eligible for voluntary sacrifice, in order to sustain the vigour of primitive society. As time went on such sacred rites were debased into purification rites bearing a distinct tinge of anal expulsion. At certain periods the township cleansed itself by casting out scapegoats laden with the sins and ills of the community. Marginal members of society, such as vagrants or criminals, would be kept ready for the occasion.

At no other time does a human body come nearer to being an excrement than after death, particularly after decomposition has set in. The social cohesion of a society could well be measured according to the treatment which it metes out to its dead. Fragmentation tendencies may express themselves in a hasty and undignified elimination of the dead. The bodies are hurriedly dug in or thrown into the bush. The unhappy island of Alor which Kardiner used as an example of social tension does little for preserving or containing the dead. At the other end of the scale are civilizations that use up a great deal of wealth and energy in order to contain and preserve their dead in their midst, possibly even in a grave within the homestead. Then, no trace of expulsion or anal elimination remains. It is a strange symptom of the compulsive behaviour in penal law that the bodies of executed criminals were not allowed proper burial in hallowed ground. They were buried in the prison grounds, immersed in quick-lime like rotting refuse.

The improper treatment of the dead and fugitives is apt to arouse our sense of justice. It seems that nowhere is the balance between expulsion and containment more delicate. For the Greeks it was the figure of Antigone who most deeply stirred their sense of justice. Antigone is perhaps the most sublime embodiment of the burying goddess, favouring containment and resisting expulsion. Her blind father, Oedipus, has cast himself out from decent society after having recognized his crime. He vainly roams the earth in search of redemption. Antigone guides him on his wanderings. Sophocles in his *Oedipus at Colonus* describes his final release. Antigone leads him to the chasm in the sacred grove of the Eumenides near Athens. (The Euminides are the Erinnyes in their benevolent aspect as earth deities.) She allows Oedipus to enter the sacred grove alone and to descend through the chasm into the underworld. He has buried himself alive in the womb of the earth. The scene has an air of solemn serenity which cannot quite be explained by the conscious action, particularly as it occurs off stage. We somehow feel that justice has been done. Why this should be so is difficult to say. What we are witnessing is the ritual of the dying god and its strange power to satisfy our sense of justice.

Antigone rises to the full status of the burying goddess in the play which Sophocles named after her. This tragedy became for the Greeks the supreme manifestation of a divine justice which overrides human reason and law-giving. We know from contemporary records how deeply the tragedy moved the Athenian audience, this in spite of some repulsive, distinctly anal traits. The plot is quite openly the treatment of a human body like anal dirt. Antigone's brothers were killed in fratricidal combat, one defending his native city, the other criminally attacking it. King Creon, their uncle, decreed that the good brother should be given a state funeral; the bad brother's corpse, however, was to be cast out from the city and lie unburied to rot. Antigone secretly attempted perfunctory burial rites in order to ensure her brother's survival in the underworld. Creon decreed that any further attempt at burying the corpse would be punished by burying the offender himself alive. The theme of casting out and burying alive could not be rendered more insistently. Nor are we spared anal disgust. The sublimity of the play is not marred, but heightened by emphasizing the relationship between the unburied body and excrements. The stench from the decomposing exposed body is said to waft into the city. Antigone feels that she must obey the divine law prescribing proper burial rites and defy human laws. She again dispenses the rites and is duly condemned to be buried alive. As so often on the near-oceanic level, the roles of mother and son are reversed. Hence Antigone, the burying goddess, must herself be buried alive. It may have now become clearer why our 'innate' sense of justice cannot simply be explained as a projection of our superego. The ego's sense of justice serves to modify the primitive superego's extreme, near-psychotic aggressions. Justice is done by assisting the ego in its struggle to sustain itself against an over-aggressive oral and anal superego. In short what is projected is not the superego alone, but its fruitful interaction with the ego. The ego must be able to modify and assuage the severity of the primitive superego, usually through its growing creativity. The drama of human justice guarantees the individual the due process of law so that he himself can play an active role in the administration of justice and modify its severity. Justice sustains the proper balance between superego and ego, controlled by the ever swaying battle between the forces of Thanatos and Eros. In a future society in which the containing tendencies of Eros are sufficient to counteract the expelling tendencies of Thanatos, no punishments by the law would be needed for containing the fragmentation tendencies within that society. As things are now it would be dangerous to tamper with the existing penal system. The criminal endangers social cohesion by triggering off its latent fragmentation tendencies. He offers himself as a scapegoat to be duly expelled or – as happens in our prison system – to be buried alive. All this is highly compulsive behaviour on our part. To inhibit it by premature reform might endanger the precarious cohesion of the social fabric.

One often speaks of the 'womb' of society which contains the individuals. The members of the society project parts of their selves into the womb and to this extent sacrifice their individual existence in the supra-individual process characteristic of creativity and of social creativity in particular. Society makes good this loss by receiving and containing safely the surrendered parts of the individual. The good mother first performs this role. When the child learns social adaptation, he too must give up part of his individual existence, this at a time when he becomes first poignantly aware of his own separate individuality. His surrender becomes a gesture fraught with anxiety, particularly also because of the simultaneous rise of anal disgust which makes the child unsure of his own value as a body product of his mother. It is crucial that the good mother should not reject the clinging child at this time, but fully entertain his advances and anxieties. To my mind the criminal was unable to perform the social self-surrender because he was too unsure whether his person was acceptable to his mother. So he removes himself voluntarily from the body social (the womb of society) and as an outlaw provokes the fragmenting and expelling tendencies active within that society.

14 The Devoured and Burned God

Freud trusted the poets. They more than others have an immediate understanding of unconscious fantasy. They also have a very direct understanding of poemagogic imagery and its function in creative work. In great works of art the stratification of poemagogic imagery into oedipal-genital, schizoid-oral, depressive-anal and manic-oceanic levels is usually clearly discernible.* Progress from the oedipal surface towards the oceanic depth follows the inner logic of the creative imagination and its structural laws of differentiation and dedifferentiation. We have seen how Sophocles handled the myth of Oedipus. It hardly matters for us that he made the freest possible use of the many popular variants of the myth, adding possibly a new freely invented detail here and there. We rightly treat his version as the most authentic; being a poet, he understood better than others the proper poemagogic meaning and function of myths. In *Oedipus Rex* he treated the genital 'oedipal' theme together with the oral-schizoid imagery immediately below it. The king's oral curiosity brings his downfall. He had met the devouring mother in the figure of the monstrous sphinx. The sphinx asked questions and devoured her victims if they could not answer them. In the play Oedipus takes over her role. He in turn asks the questions that lead to his own destruction. His self-punishment, putting out his eyes with a jewel from the dress of his mother, signifies his oral castration. This oral-schizoid symbolism of the question-asking scientist will occupy us in more detail presently. My preliminary interpretation of the play only serves to sketch broadly the complex stratification of the myth. In *Oedipus at Colonus* we descend into the anal–depressive level. The king, having cast himself out

* See Appendix, pp. 302ff.

from decent society, searches the world for an asylum to receive and contain him. Antigone, his faithful guide, plays the casting-out mother. In the end the king finds redemption through his own efforts. I have stressed the curiously manic-oceanic character of his self-immolation. He commits suicide by burying himself alive in the sacred chasm of the Eumenides in a scene that has no trace of depression or resignation. It was reserved for the tragedy of Antigone herself to unfold to the full the depressive aspect of burial alive as opposed to free casting out. A similar analysis of deeper levels of poemagogic fantasy is possible with almost all great works of art, such as the *Ring of the Nibelungs*, *Faust*, and the great tragedies of Shakespeare. A full-scale analysis will have to be left to another investigation. I am here concerned with establishing the broad structural framework.

The great poemagogic myths undergo constant transformation. Poemagogic themes are dissociated from their unconscious matrix and made to do work in the current iconography of popular art. The scholars of the London Warburg Institute have made it their special task to follow up the vicissitudes of a potent mythological theme through all its transformations. They have rightly stressed the need to interpret each new version against the background of its precise historical setting. We must know this setting in order to understand the external influences that pressed the theme into a particular mould. This constant use and abuse of a potent theme makes the testimony of the poets so indispensable. Poets, like Sophocles, Wagner or Shakespeare, can remove the accumulated lumber of secondary revisions and go back to the unconscious fantasies that gave them their tough-ness and endurance in the first place. Far from debunking a direct depth-psychological approach to old iconographic themes, the Warburg historians have helped to demonstrate its validity for understanding great art. In trusting the internal evidence of major works of art we will be less liable to error than if we try to sort out the welter of accumulated dross in more popular, minor versions of the same theme.

Poetic cosmogonies are an excellent source for studying the rigorous stratification of poemagogic fantasy. Michelangelo's treatment of the biblical cosmogony proves how the logic of creative fantasy forces the artist to interpret the outer creation of the universe also as a poemagogic representation of inner human creativity. Hesiod's great cosmogony is no exception. On the surface it seems an unending story of oedipal-genital crimes, fathers going in fear of their sons and sons overthrowing their fathers in due course. Uranus seals (traps) his dangerous progeny in Gaea's womb. His son Cronus duly overthrows him by castrating him during intercourse with his jagged sickle. Cronus in turn devours his own offspring, but is overcome by Zeus. Zeus himself sits uneasily on his throne waiting for his own conqueror. Even this brief description sketches in the more submerged traits of oral devouring and anal trapping which so far have received little attention. The deepest oceanic-manic level of the self-creating god is represented in a somewhat abstract manner by Eros, the god of love, who must exist before Uranus, to enable sexuality to work. The Orphic writings turn Eros into a truly self-creating god. He delivers himself from the cosmic egg and possesses the procreative powers of both sexes. The next higher anal-depressive level of burial alive I have already mentioned in a previous chapter. Uranus commits the arch-crime of trapping Gaea's unborn children in her womb. As Gaea represents the earth there is an immediate link with the agricultural rituals of the corn spirit who is trapped in the womb of the earth during winter. There is an element of genital-oedipal revision, which shifts aggression from the mother to the father figure. It is not the burying mother who traps her offspring in her womb. It is Uranus, the father, who appears as the arch-criminal and has to suffer Gaea's revenge. (Only Demeter, the most motherly and tender among the Olympian goddesses, can afford to assume openly the character of the trapping womb, when she prevents the seed from germinating. Even her aggression is rationalized as a 'revenge' for a crime committed by a male god. Her daughter, Persephone, representing the buried seed, was abducted by Hades into the underworld and remains trapped there. Demeter soon assumes her role as goddess of fertility and rebirth after her daughter is restored to her.)

When wronged Gaea seeks revenge on her husband Uranus she herself does not openly commit the retributory crime. She merely instigates her son Cronus. He castrates his father during intercourse with Gaea, a rather stark incident for our contemporary taste. It becomes clear from the instrument of castration, the famous jagged or toothed sickle, and also from the fact that the act is committed during intercourse, that it is Gaea's own *vagina dentata* which bites off her husband's genitals. Through the sickle she becomes the first incarnation of the devouring mother in her typical castrating aspect. As so often, the tale duplicates the theme of oral castration. From the blood dripping from the mutilated genitals arise the terrible Erinnyes, the symbol of the oral-sadistic (devouring) superego. Their main task is to revenge mothers wronged by their sons. They hunt the guilty son down and drive him to madness. Their favourite punishment is castration. Their most celebrated victim is the matricidal Orestes. They drive him to madness, but do not inflict castration on him themselves. According to Pausanias, Orestes recovers from his madness by voluntarily biting off one of his fingers. He thus inflicts (symbolically) the punishment of oral castration on himself. Orestes in mutilating himself sees the black Erinnyes transformed into the benign white Eumenides. This reinforces my argument that Orestes' self-inflicted punishment indeed represents the castration which the Erinnyes in their persecutory aspect would have imposed on him. Oedipus by gouging his own eyes out anticipates his castration and escapes the punishment of the Erinnyes. The eyes which are capable of 'devouring' objects visually stress the important oral character of his symbolic castration.

Myths, particularly cosmogonies, are pre-scientific attempts at explaining reality. It is perhaps for this reason that the oral-schizoid material is so abundant in them. The scientific explanation of the world, particularly through the myth of a compelling causality, is a very direct projection of oral-schizoid fantasy. According to Kelsen the law of causality is quite redundant for scientific explanation; it is a remnant of a more primitive explanation by guilt. The primitive explains natural events as being caused by crime and guilt. His curiosity is aroused by disasters and these he interprets as effects of guilt either committed by him or by his fellows. This type of pre-scientific curiosity also accompanied the rise of Western science after the Renaissance. Natural disasters were blamed on the witch and her help-mate, the devil. The tale of paradise was then revised to turn the cunning serpent into the medieval devil who persuaded Eve into her oral crime. In the Hebrew version the serpent was just an animal like any other in the paradise garden.

The libidinous id content of scientific curiosity is voyeurism, a development of a still more primitive wish to 'devour' something with one's eyes. Eve's and Adam's oral crime represents symbolically the devouring of breasts and genitals. Eve despoils the tree 'growing in the centre of the garden'. In Goethe's *Faust*, another tale of the witch and the devil, we find two dream interpretations that anticipate Freud. In the Walpurgis Night Faust tells a young witch a dream in which he saw an apple tree bearing two beautiful apples. The pretty witch promptly connects the dream with the tale of paradise and feels gratified that her own 'garden' bore such desirable fruits. Mephistopheles conversing with an old witch tells her of an anxiety dream about a cleft tree. The hole both repelled and attracted him. The symbol of a cleft tree recurs in fairy tales and has a definite castration symbolism. Devils and other demons have a fatal propensity for getting caught in cleft trees, bottles and similar symbols of the vagina as a dangerous trap (the anal equivalent of the oral *vagina dentata*). The tree which Eve despoils in Paradise represents Adam's genitals. Adam plays a curiously passive role. It is the phallic snake which tempts Eve into her oral crime. His punishment also symbolizes castration – Eve will bruise his head.

The oral crime of the witch and the devil was re-enacted in the medieval fantasies about the Black Mass. It culminated in an oral tribute to the devil: the witch kissed the devil goat under his tail and the devil retaliated by sucking the witch's blood. The marks on the witch's body where the devil had sucked her blood were held to be the most reliable proof of her guilt. In many other respects the learned witch-hunters showed great circumspection and even scepticism. The official handbook of the witch-hunters, the famous *Malleus Maleficarum* (*The Witches' Hammer*) makes disturbing reading. Once we have accepted its premises that there were dangerous people about with superhuman powers that threatened mankind with disaster, the learned discourse of *The Witches' Hammer* shows remarkable fairness and circumspection. The witches were sometimes asked to repeat their magic rites in the court room; the effects were closely watched, noted and evaluated. We shudder as we recognize in the witch trial the authentic precedent for modern scientific procedure in the laboratory. We may well wonder whether the modern scientist would be capable of equal detachment and painstaking observation if he were put under the same emotional stress, under which the witch trials were necessarily conducted. As the fears gradually subsided, acquittals were reasoned with the same subtlety that had gone into the previous, often cruel convictions. In this context of pre-scientific experimentation the uncritical acceptance of the marks produced by the devil's vampirism as convincing evidence points to a particularly strong unconscious motivation. The thorough and often indecent search for the hidden marks may have satisfied a primitive truly devouring voyeurism directed towards the results of oral aggression and self-destruction. This kind of pre-scientific voyeurism projected the superego's oral aggression very directly into the external world. Unlike Freud who had thought that the superego came about by internalizing the castrating oedipal father, Melanie Klein traced back the early beginnings of a primitive superego to the oral fantasies of infancy. The very young infant suffers from intense self-destructive fantasies which according to Melanie Klein are a very direct manifestation of the death instinct. The origin of the superego is still largely obscure. (My own speculations about the origins of the ego's repression in the superego's 'anal' scattering of the ego also bear this out.) In an earlier paper I have suggested that the superego neutralizes genuine self-destructive fantasies [4]. The ego instead of seeking or accepting physical destruction allows the superego to bite and gnaw it with cruel guilt feelings of remorse. But the old fantasies of physical destruction linger on in the poemagogic imagery of scientific curiosity.

The irrational beliefs of the witch-hunters come very near to paranoid schizophrenic fantasy. The schizophrenic may sometimes act out self-destructive fantasies by inflicting physical mutilation or castration on himself. He has not learned to absorb and neutralize self-destructive fantasies into the intra-psychic processes of creativity, where the ego submits to the attacks of the superego almost to the point of total annihilation. We have seen how the manic-depressive, too, treats his entire self in the way in which the scattering and burying anal superego treats his ego. He alternately projects his whole self freely during mania and traps and buries it during depression, while the sane creative mind merely submits his ego functions to anal scattering and burying by the superego. Some evidence in creative work and poemagogic fantasy points to incomplete superego maturation as an important source of mental illness. The ego has not absorbed the death instinct into the mute workings of the creative process so that self-destruction goes rampant to destroy the entire self.

Guilt feelings are closely allied to feelings of shame and cannot always be clearly distinguished from them. The tale of Paradise connects the learning of shame with the first guilt. Freud speculated whether the male sex had to learn shame after mankind had adopted an erect posture in order to protect the now exposed genitals. The danger threatening them may have been not so much an external enemy as the guilty wish for oral castration pressing from within. In the biblical tale shame also came from the crime of devouring, which in my interpretation was oral castration. Shame is opposed to exhibitionism. Language reveals the oral tinge of exhibitionism as a fantasy or wish to be devoured. American salesman's slang does not tire of extolling the virtues of successful self-advertisement, of a sales talk 'going down' well, of an applicant being 'lapped up' by an eager employer. Adam in developing shame did not protect himself so much from oral-sadistic voyeurism as from his own self-destructive wish to be devoured. We have to remember that it was the serpent himself who invited the act of oral castration. The self-destructive *passive* element of exhibitionism tends to be more repressed than the oral sadism underlying voyeurism. The male has never tired of accusing the witch of an *active* crime inflicted on the unwilling victim in order to repress the self-destructive element in his creative fantasies, the passive role which the ego has to play in relation to a cruel superego. Here the secondary revision does not shift aggression from the mother to the male. The son's self-destructive fantasies are shifted to a cruel image of the mother as the White Goddess. I feel that the enormous emotional resistance which the concept of an innate death instinct has aroused may have something to do with our unwillingness to accept the virulence of self-destructive tendencies within ourselves. One of the conditions for becoming creative, however, must be a modicum of insight into the ego's need for self-destructive passivity. In the world of science the myth of causality has injected a perhaps unnecessary fantasy of passivity and compulsion into our world view. We accept a passive role, a lack of 'free will', while we see our life determined and compelled by inexorable laws of causality. Yet this primitive fantasy of compulsion shows greater insight into psychic reality than the modern cheap view of the scientist as a powerful magician who has subjected the recalcitrant forces of nature to his will. Here passivity has been replaced by an equally excessive active control of reality that is nearer to infantile daydreams of omnipotence. They bolster up the dominant role of the male. They deny the creative need for passive submission to the superego and its oral attacks.

According to Frazer the biblical tale of the Fall of Man revises a more archaic rendering of the myth, that is akin to many other explanations of the primitive world about the way in which death and mortality came into the world. These primitive myths tell that mankind once had the choice between immortality and death; man chose death, sometimes because he was tricked, sometimes through negligence, rarely as an outright choice of self-destruction. The biblical tale as it now stands contains two contradictions that can be resolved by reference to the earlier, now suppressed version. There was another tree in the paradise garden apart from the tree of knowledge; it was the tree of life. Had the first human pair eaten from the tree of life they would have become immortal. It seems only logical that the second tree in the garden was the tree of death, the fruit of which would have given instant death. It was not a forbidden tree; the choice was voluntary. What God still says to Adam and Eve is: 'for on the day thou eatest thereof thou shalt surely die,' not as a punishment, but as the natural outcome of their ill-advised choice. In fact they do not die. This inconsistency gives away the urgency with which the secondary revision tried to destroy most if not all elements of a tale of open self-destruction. As usual, self-destruction is replaced by a punishment inflicted from outside. Instead of being killed the guilty pair lives to a ripe old age. But they are cast out from the womb of paradise into a hostile world. This motif of birth is equated with mortality and death, another instance of oceanic undifferentiation. Like most mythical material the tale of the Fall of Man thus contains at least three levels. The oedipal level speaks of the son rebelling against the father and winning the love of woman. We have discussed at length the next oral-schizoid level of oral castration inflicted by the devouring mother figure. Now we are given a glimpse of a still deeper anal-depressive level where Eve is cast into the role of the casting-out and killing mother. Mutilation is replaced by total annihilation and death. Man is cast out like an excrement from his womb-like existence in paradise, where he had lived in peaceful union with God and beasts.

Why a noble choice of voluntary death should have to be transformed into involuntary punishment is at first difficult to see. But I have already mentioned that, according to Frazer, voluntary human sacrifice, for which only princes were eligible, later became transformed into ignoble punishment inflicted on the low-born, or into periodical purification rites by which society rid itself of its internal tensions by casting out excrement-like vagrants and criminals. It seems that it is easier to bear punishment inflicted from outside than to face internal self-destructive tendencies. Possibly the origin of the superego also represents a similar attempt at externalization. The ego instead of being rent by internal tensions, or attacking the body ego, projects its self-destructive aggression on to a split-off part, the superego, and prefers to submit to its attacks, which now come to it from the outside, as it were. By projecting in turn the superego's aggression into the outside world on to the figures of the devouring and casting out mother, and into social institutions like sacrifice, purification and punishment, self-aggression is still further removed from its original source in the ego itself.

The scientist unconsciously connives in his castration by the devouring mother, who represents the externalized gnawing superego. In mythology we meet with an unending procession of blind or lame seers. Tiresias, the greatest among them, was 'punished' by Athene with blindness. Haephestus, who alone among the Olympian gods has the gift of prophecy, is lame. The Nordic god father Odin acquires wisdom by voluntarily sacrificing one eye.

Having accepted oral castration, the seer and scientist can identify himself with the devouring mother. He unconsciously equates her with a castrated man like himself and assimilates her oral sadism and insatiable curiosity. This identification makes him a seer and scientist. The first object of his curiosity is the devouring mother herself, the smiling sphinx whose secret he fails to unravel. Her smile threatening and promising mutilation becomes the mystery he never tires of exploring. The lure of

248

Mona Lisa's smile might rest on the same promise and threat. Freud explains it as the blissful smile of the breast-fed infant. He relates it to a childhood fantasy related by Leonardo da Vinci. A kite descended on the infant's mouth and beat it with its talons. Freud, in spite of his obviously incomplete knowledge of the historical facts now available, rightly interpreted the fantasy of the attacking kite as a fantasy of castration. It may still be legitimate to speculate that Leonardo's mother had smothered her child with excessive love and so intensified his oral wishes and fears. Not without reason Mona Lisa's smile is called sphinx-like. I have called the sphinx the supreme symbol of the mother's oral aggression and curiosity. The figure of Turandot, another incarnation of the oral-sadistic question-asking woman, seems to have attracted Puccini deeply. He was unable to finish his opera, probably because it was impossible to resolve the conflict of love and self-destruction. Turandot's ultimate submission to her suitor does not make sense. Lohengrin has to leave Elsa, his 'pure' wife when she succumbs to her question-asking curiosity, and he safely returns to the secret all-male society of the Holy Grail.

In Mozart's *The Magic Flute* the ability to keep silent is one of the first trials before gaining admission to the all-male community of Sarastro's secret society. The opera warns the guileless male against the unguarded tongues of women. The secrecy of such all-male societies stimulates curiosity and a somewhat tortuous exhibitionism. Their various messages of salvation and purification may be defences against the male's own un-acknowledged oral yearnings and fears. Wagner's treatment of the Holy Grail myth in his last opera *Parsifal* contains the whole arsenal of poemagogic images on the oral level in scarcely disguised form. There is Kundry, a dangerous witch in the service of the devil figure, Klingsor. Kundry sins and seduces the pure knights through her compulsive laughter. She once laughed at Christ on his way to Golgotha. Klingsor, like the lame devil, acquired his magic power through accepting voluntary castration. His vendetta against the knights of the Holy Grail is to inflict on them the same shameful mutilation, by using Kundry as the seducer. As Kundry embraces Amfortas, the king of the knights, she is compelled to laugh and (as she later tells Parsifal) 'a sinner falls upon her bosom'. It seems strange that compulsive laughter during intercourse should be sinful or even seductive. But the meaning and effect of her laughter is made abundantly clear by the injury Amfortas suffers as a consequence of his sin. He loses the holy spear to Klingsor and suffers an incurable wound in his side. The symbolism of castration inflicted by the laughing mouth could not be made clearer. As in Shylock's bargain and the torture of Prometheus, the castration wound is displaced upwards.

The whole arsenal of oral castration symbolism is again mobilized in the scene in which Kundry tries to seduce the 'pure' fool Parsifal. It is important that Parsifal is an ignorant fool; he does not share the devil's forbidden desire for knowledge which can only be bought by accepting oral castration. In his purity he can defy Kundry's laughing mouth and its seductive promise. Kundry openly represents the mother's oral aggression which Freud assumed as the basis of Leonardo's childhood fantasy. Kundry tries to seduce Parsifal by recalling his dead mother's passionate love for him and promises him that he will re-experience his mother's love in her arms. She asks him whether he had not as a child feared his mother's vehement kisses. As she kisses him in his mother's name, the boy starts up with terror as he feels King Amfortas's wound burn in his own side. The potentially mutilating effect of Kundry's mouth could have hardly been made more explicit. By rejecting her, Parsifal regains the holy spear, that is to say he retains his manhood.

On a deeper level Kundry appears in the double role of the casting out and cast-out mother. This level is only lightly but firmly sketched in. Kundry, like Persephone, leads a double life. As a beautiful witch she serves the devil to seduce the knights of the Grail; as an ugly hag of gypsy-like appearance, dark-brown complexion, fluttering hair, with snake skins as her girdle, she serves the knights like a slave. Whenever she escapes Klingsor's control, she casts herself out into the wilderness to die like a wild animal, to be discovered and saved by the knights. She then lives as a willing servant remaining on the fringe of the holy community. Casting out is never quite redeemed by containment. After Parsifal has resisted her in her role as the devouring mother he wants to return to the Grail in order to heal the wounded king. Then Kundry curses him to be lost in the wilderness, a cast-out like herself. The dual role of the casting out and cast-out mother is possible on a near-oceanic level.

The figure of the devil, the witch's companion, also demonstrates several levels of poemagogic imagery. His rebellion against the father figure of God may be oedipal. On the oral level we have described him as the devil serpent who tempts Eve into her crime of oral castration. On a lower anal level he is also the cast-out, scattered god. As a punishment for his rebellion he was cast out from heaven into the abyss of hell. There he lies eternally bound (trapped, contained). The devil has with other gods of fire, such as Logi and Hephaestus, several of these oral and anal features in common. Hephaestus, like the devil and Logi, was once cast from heaven. Logi lies bound in hell like the devil. Hephaestus, again like the devil, is lame. These fire gods also share a curious contradiction in their make-up. They are terrifying, cunning and in possession of magic knowledge, but at the same time they are clumsy, ridiculous and possibly mutilated. The reason for these contradictory aspects is the same: their castration. The terrible clever devil is also the poor silly devil who gets himself trapped in all sorts of castration symbols, such as bags and cleft trees. In fairy tales the holy virgin invariably gets the better of him. Hephaestus, the Greek god of fire, is terrible, spiteful as well as ridiculous and impotent. He has powerful shoulders, but withered legs. His statues invariably wear a loin cloth, an expression of shame that is unusual among Greek deities. But he is also cunning and spiteful, bent on trapping others in revenge. He traps his own mother, Hera, on a magic throne, and the adulterous Aphrodite and Ares in a hunting net. Yet his cuckoldry is also ridiculous and the gods laugh at his discomfiture. The deeper meaning of the ridicule is the same as that of Kundry's laughter: to be laughed at means to be orally castrated. This meaning is more openly revealed in a tale concerning his counterpart, the Nordic fire god Logi. When Logi tries to move a girl to laughter, he does so by a strangely self-destructive trick. He binds his testicles to a goat and suffers great pain as the goat tries to free itself. His contortions make the girl laugh. The laughter has the same oral-sadistic meaning as Kundry's laughter. The goat is very much the devil's animal. He too possesses powerful horns, but spindly legs. One cannot invalidate the image of the castrated devil by invoking his numerous phallic attributes, his horns, his tail and his protruding tongue. The castrating Erinnyes and the Gorgons, the acknowledged symbols of castration, also carry snakes in their hair. As castration means aggression against the phallus it seems consistent that a comprehensive symbolism of castration should condense both phallic power and its loss.

The combination of phallic attributes with castration is characteristic of the symbolism of fire itself, the dangerous element with which all these gods are associated. Fire is perhaps the most condensed symbol of oral self-castration. It seems most surprising to me that its oral meaning should have been ignored in favour of its phallic meaning. Superficially the oblong form of a steady flame may suggest a phallic shape, but it suggests even more a licking tongue. Untamed fire is perhaps nature's strongest manifestation of unbridled oral aggression. With myriads of greedily licking tongues fire devours man and all his goods. No apter symbol could be found to represent both the power of the phallus and the threat to its power by oral castration. The gods of fire had to connive at their emasculation by their all too close association with the self-consuming phallic flames.

At the same time the steady tamed flame has become the universal symbol for scientific curiosity, its quest for enlightenment and truth. The taming of fire reaches back to the very dawn of humanity. In archaeological excavations the discovery of a fireplace is taken as the best proof that some stones nearby owe their sharp edges and points not to a quirk of nature, but to deliberate selection or preparation by *homo faber*, man the toolmaker. One is inclined to think that like all basic inventions the taming of fire should not be explained primarily by human reason, but by a compulsive act obeying inner needs. Unconscious fantasy would not have differentiated between the burning pangs of the superego within and the raging fire without. In taming the self-consuming fire, man also assuaged fantasies of oral self-destruction and fears of submitting to the gnawing aggression of the superego. The ceremonial use of fire may not have served a truly rational purpose at all, but purified man of his self-destructive fantasies, which threatened his ego with annihilation. Before satisfying his own oral aggression, man had to purify his food by cooking. When the old fears welled up during the pre-scientific persecutions of witches and heretics, the fires burned lustily on the stakes to cleanse the victims of their forbidden magic and heretic knowledge. There is little doubt that medieval heretics only claimed the scepticism about orthodoxy which is the birthright of modern science. In this sense too they were true percursors of the modern scientist.

The various civilization myths that tell of knowledge bought at the price of guilt differ in their moral tinge. In the Greek civilization myth it was not the Olympian gods, but Prometheus, the Titan, who brought fire and civilization to mankind and had to suffer cruel punishment for his generosity. The equivalent Hebrew tale of the Fall of Man in paradise is even more heavily tinged with guilt. Not only is the origin of civilization guilt-laden, but the benefits of civilization are represented as punishments. The acquisition of moral knowledge to distinguish between good and evil, the learning of shame, the invention of clothing and of agriculture are not blessings, but are imposed on an unwilling mankind. Apart from this far-reaching difference the two civilization myths are fully analogous, once we have fully interpreted the oral symbolism of fire. The crime of Prometheus is Adam and Eve's crime, namely oral self-castration. Prometheus was an even older deity than the Olympian fire god, Hephaestus. They were in a way rival gods. A myth reports that the upstart, Hephaestus, approached Prometheus with awe. The most quoted version of the Promethean myth has it that Prometheus stole the heavenly fire from Hephaestus and brought it to mankind. As a punishment he was chained to a rock. Daily an eagle sent by Zeus descended on his body and tore out his liver which grew again by the following day. As almost always, the punishment expresses an underlying self-destructive fantasy more clearly. Self-destruction is presented as aggression inflicted from outside. The tearing beak of the eagle attacking his body represents the superego's biting attack by the pangs of guilt feelings. As in the case of Amfortas or Shylock the castration wound is displaced upwards. The eagle's beak is merely another variant of the theme which the motif of the fire on its own expresses in so condensed a manner. Moreover the fire is stolen from lame Hephaestus. The theft repeats symbolically the mutilation which the god has already suffered. Prometheus is also 'Lucifer', that is to say, the bringer or bearer of fire. Like the devil serpent in paradise, he brings civilization to mankind at the price of an oral crime against the phallus and turns his own body into a symbol of the phallic, self-consuming fire. If we were to choose a new term for the oral-masochistic fantasies underlying the guilt projection of science and technology, no more fitting name could be found than that of Prometheus, who brought knowledge and skill to mankind by offering his own body to the eagle's beak and so heroically defied the cruelty of the superego. (It may be useful to speak of an oral-schizoid Prometheus level as well as of an anal-depressive Antigone and oceanic-manic Dionysus level in poemagogic fantasy.)

Heroic defiance of oral aggression is very near to the scientist's meek submission to the compelling superego. Heroic self-exposure is allied to oral-masochistic exhibitionism in the way in which scientific curiosity is associated with oral-sadistic voyeurism. Voyeurism contains a fantasy of 'devouring' something with one's eyes. This is well recognized. Not so the equivalent fantasy 'to be devoured' as a correlate of exhibitionism. Had it been so acknowledged, my concept of oral-masochistic Prometheus fantasies, as I have described them, would have easily suggested itself.

The relationship between (phallic) exhibitionism and fire is well enough known. But usually the relationship is only explained on a genital oedipal level, and so succeeds in ignoring the oral symbolism of fire. For instance, Gulliver indulges in a feat of phallic exhibitionism which any small boy of four or five would love to emulate. He extinguishes the fire in the apartments of the empress of Lilliput by urinating on the flames. This casual deed has been duly interpreted on the oedipal level as the exhibitionism of the hero who defies the phallic fire by displaying the power of his own phallus. But the more significant pre-oedipal oral meaning cannot be discarded. The fire is also female, i.e. the burning vagina to which the phallus is exposed at grave risk. As is usual, the punishment of the crime exhibits the self-destructive elements of the fantasy more clearly. Gulliver is to be punished by the empress for defiling her imperial apartments. He is to be blinded; or else he is to perish trapped in a burning house, or more explicitly still, his servants are to pour poison on his shirt and sheets. The poison would sear his skin so that Gulliver was to tear his own flesh and die in utmost torture. Gulliver escapes from Lilliput to evade unjust punishment. Yet his punishment would have set him on equal footing with the greatest of Greek heroes, Heracles himself. The symbol of the burning vagina is unmistakably expressed in the searing garment given to Heracles by his wife. It clings to his body and sears his flesh. To escape from his agony Heracles allows himself to be burned alive on a funeral pyre. Either of these successive 'burnings' brings out an essential element missing in the other (a procedure also characteristic of dreams). The searing garment, being a gift from his wife, clearly represents the burning vagina. But the hero is tricked into wearing it. His willing self-destruction is expressed by his voluntary self-immolation on the pyre. The hero is not tricked into submitting to the burning vagina, he braves the devouring mother and provokes his destruction.

A Roman tale, meant to extol unflinching heroism, tells of Mucius Scaevola. In order to intimidate Rome's enemies he put his living hand into the fire and allowed it to burn slowly to a cinder. This revolting tale is paralleled by an equivalent Greek tale that was meant to instil self-destructive heroism into the youths of Sparta, that most 'Roman' of Greek city states. A Spartan youth was allowed and even encouraged to steal, but he was not expected to be caught. A boy stole a live fox. In order not to be detected, he hid the animal under his garment. He allowed the fox to bite him cruelly rather than give himself away. The Spartan tale is the heroic version of the scientific Prometheus myth. There is undoubtedly also a heroic tinge in Prometheus' defiance of his tormentors. But his sufferings are not openly self-inflicted, but disguised as involuntary punishment. The lack or the defiance of all guilt feelings characterizes the heroic attitude and distinguishes it from the scientist's meek submission to inner and outer compulsion. Perhaps guilt is attenuated because the ego's self-destruction is converted back into physical self-destruction of the body ego. Orestes escaped the persecution of the Erinnyes when he bit off his finger.

The link between mental self-destruction by guilt feelings and physical self-destruction can perhaps explain the still obscure origin of the profound guilt and shame feelings attaching to male masturbation. Masturbation is described as self-abuse, an attack against man's own body. Because it retains a residue of physical self-destruction, masturbation would call forth the irrational fury of the superego. Though we may feel tormented by burning guilt, we would still avoid the more dangerous physical self-destruction. The hero succeeds in withdrawing his self-destructive actions from the censorship of the superego. To this extent heroism represents a triumph of the ego over the superego. The hero challenges his own superego as much as he challenges external danger. Yet even the Greeks sensed the crime contained in the heroic defiance of the gods, which they called hubris.

Oral castration fantasies also have a definite homosexual tinge. Hero and scientist seek each other. Mythology abounds in strangely assorted friends who fight and love each other, heroic Thor and cunning Logi, the brave and naïve Achilles and wily Odysseus, the virile and stupid Ares and his crafty rival, Hephaestus. A closer study of voyeur and exhibitionist types among homosexuals would probably uncover the close connexion of the two polar types, who work out the same oral Prometheus fantasies in different ways. The threat of castration, however, is never absent. I have said that in the poemagogic fantasies about the burned god the devouring mother is imagined as a castrated male. But by submitting to castration, the male himself can identify himself with the devouring mother and appropriate her oral sadism and cunning. Rank pointed out that the devil was once female. The gaping mouth of hell still symbolizes the female genital (*vagina dentata*). It may be that defensive homosexual fantasy accepts the castrated male as a true equivalent of the devouring mother of whom he stands in excessive fear. The cunning unheroic companions of the hero also stand for the threat of oral castration. The heroic god Thor possesses the magic hammer Mioellnir, the symbol of lightning. Its handle is too short and was at one time stolen. Thor in order to regain it had to don female clothing. but almost gave himself away by his voracious appetite, that is to say, he had to accept the role of the castrated greedy woman. One of the goats pulling his war chariot limps owing to the greed of his despised, yet inseparable companion, Logi, the Nordic god of fire. (It makes sense that the god of thunder and lightning and the god of fire should be inseparable companions.) Thor was able to slaughter the goats pulling his chariot and eat their flesh as long as their bones were left intact. With his magic hammer he could call them back to life. Logi, himself a mighty eater, persuades one of the guests to devour a bone as well. So one of the goats limps as he is called back to life.

In Greek mythology Ares represents the heroic *alter ego* of the cunning, unheroic Hephaestus. It is he who is caught in the magic net, during intercourse with Aphrodite. But, as always, it is not the mother figure Aphrodite who brings him to harm, but her husband, the lame cuckold, Hephaestus. The aggression is shifted to a revengeful male. (The open female rival of Ares is the war goddess Athene. Ares is wounded twice by a mortal helped by Athene.) In the heroic set-up the castrating mother recedes behind another devil-like male who as a rule has accepted castration and so assumed the role of the castrated oral-sadistic female; this is the role of the other lame and cunning fire gods, the devil and Logi. As the divine smith, Hephaestus shows the way to restitution open to the castrated fire god. By taming the self-destructive fire he forges the sword that the hero will use. The figure of the magic smith combines the ridiculous and terrifying traits of the gods of fire. Anthropological study reveals that the status of the smith is highly ambivalent among primitive tribes. They are at once held in awe and despised with the same mixture of feelings which makes the terrifying devil also the poor limping devil. Accordingly the mythological figures of the smith combine the restitutive powers of the scientist with the spite of the castrated villain. The magic smith, Wieland, is lame too. He was mutilated on the advice of the king's wife. He takes his revenge, as Hephaestus likes to do, by a cunning trick of trapping. He invites the young princes to look into a chest and slams the lid on their necks to decapitate them. After his revenge he lifts himself into air with the help of magic wings. His magic has restored his manhood. This crude tale illustrates the destructive and restitutive power of science. It can tame the devouring fire in order to create phallic weapons and tools. But as long as the neutralization of oral self-destruction into creative work is not complete we find the unmanly mutilated fiends, Lucifer, Satan, Klingsor, Logi, Hephaestus, who avenge their lost manhood on other still happier men who, like the exhibitionist hero, can still boast their virility.

The paranoid fantasy that created the lame devil as the medieval god of fire and black magic, still survives today. In modern science fiction we find the sinister scientist bent on the estruction of the world. The fantasy also persists in the fear of the circumcized cunning Jew. The most compulsive belief of the Jew-baiters accuses the Jews of horrible oral crimes, such as the slaughter and devouring of children. Anti-Semites also overrate the intellectual cunning of Jews, which goes ill with their contempt. I have found it difficult to persuade Anti-Semites to accept that there were as many simpletons among Jews as there were among Gentiles. In this manner the Jews partake of the ambivalent image which the gods of fire display: ridicule and contempt side by side with awe and fear of their allegedly superior intellectual ability. The devouring Jew is castrated and threatens the naïve heroic Gentile with castration. The more strongly the Germans entertained heroic fantasies of self-destruction and a Wagnerian twilight of the gods, the more were they compelled to project their fears on devil-like figures, international conspiracies and cunning subversion, fears that at last concentrated on Jewish minorities, which somehow had always served as scapegoats to relieve internal social tensions within their host societies. As marginal members they had to be cast out or burned in order to save the body social. In this sense there is below the schizoid-oral level of Anti-Semitism also a depressive anal level of fantasy. There seems something in the Jewish fate which symbolizes an anal fantasy of voluntarily casting oneself out. It is sometimes forgotten that the Jewish dispersal all over the world was partly voluntary and antedates the destruction of the temple. Was not the supreme symbol of Jewish deliverance their success in casting themselves out from fertile Egypt into the desert? Is there something self-destructive in the Jewish fate that attracts the role of a scapegoat or displaced person who is driven into the desert to die in order to purify the community? Whatever the cause of these fantasies, they are of theoretical interest because they too show the complex stratification of anal, oral and oedipal levels that we can find in so much cultural material. The displaced person today is a pathetic image of the illness that has befallen our body social, namely its inability to tolerate diversity within without undue anxiety. The threshold up to which Eros can enrich internal social differentiation is greatly lowered today. Splitting tendencies will bring on a compulsive need for expelling alien elements who are felt to pollute the body social. The balance between Eros, the principle of differentiation, and Thanatos, the principle of entropy dangerously tilted towards entropy and death, towards the mutilation of an egalitarian society which cannot nourish inter wealth and diversity. The schizoid character of much moder art reflects the self-destructive tendencies at large in our civilization.

Poemagogic fantasies are constantly projected into outer reality and re-enact there the eternal struggle between ego and superego. The psychotic articulates these fantasies into crude concrete wishes. The schizophrenic Schreber involved himself in the task of cosmogony, of re-creating the world. His fantasies verged on the concrete wish for castration in order to be fertilized by god and to procreate a new mankind, a horrible parody of the creative process. Marion Milner [21] has commented on the perennial abuse of poemagogic imagery in organized religion and in social institutions. She says:

the whole history of popular religions could . . . be looked upon as a materialization of the image; once it was no longer looked upon as a truth of spirit (representing the inner creative process), but instead a truth of external fact, then it became the instrument of all kinds of exploitation, lustful, political, social, the instrument of crudest infantile desire . . .

This may be so. Yet the creative process works partly just through such a projection of inner processes into the manipulation of external reality. I have discussed the basic inventions of human civilization, the discovery of agriculture, of taming the fire, and the causal interpretation of reality as just such projections. It is only when the inner process of sublimation breaks down and the superego attacks the ego too cruelly, that the outer projections assume their over-concrete psychotic tinge. Our criminal law is certainly still dominated by psychotic mechanisms of this sort. The struggle of the criminal against society is experienced in terms of a cruel superego. Melanie Klein has suggested that the criminal, far from lacking a superego, has retained a useless and too cruel superego which forces his ego to project the same senseless cruelty into the behaviour of society. Unfortunately – and this is the psychotic part of social reaction – society accepts this role. Progress is possible by strengthening the role of the ego. Instead of being trapped and shut in, the criminal should be taught to use the process of law and to

ulate the reactions of society. Prison could be an excellent
ground for exercising his social skills. Malinowski has
erally attributed to a healthy society a multiplicity of semi-
dependent 'institutions' which allow and indeed invite the
itizen to manipulate social skills, instead of being the passive
subject of a central public administration. As it is, prisons do
develop criminal sub-administrations working under cover. It
would be essential to organize these sub-administrations as semi-
autonomous 'institutions' – in Malinowski's sense – which the
prisoner can manipulate with increasing skill for his own advantage. A London psychologist once talked about the wish of the
murderer to set into motion the process of law leading to his own
execution and about his disappointment if an enlightened process of law refuses to be used in a mechanical and predictable
fashion. His disappointment is understandable considering the
normal compulsive reaction of criminological procedure. What
is needed are subtler and more flexible reactions on the part of
society, suggesting – and this is the important point – a more
flexible superego that can be shifted by the no longer helpless
ego.

I am putting forward these suggestions not as a practical issue,
but as an illustration that the externalization of the internal processes of creative ego functioning need not be pathological; quite
the contrary. The main object of this book is to demonstrate that
creating a work of art means externalizing the inner workings of
the ego; its submission to the superego's fragmenting and scattering action is reflected in the fragmentation of art's conscious
superstructure and the scattering of its unconscious substructure.

The theatre supplies the external stage on which the internal
struggle of the ego is most readily projected. It is now considered
naïve and even wrong to attempt to interpret great plays piece-
meal and to treat single characters like Oedipus, Hamlet, Lear,
Faust as self-contained individuals acting out their personal problems. The play as a whole represents the author in his many
facets, or rather, the working of the creative process within his
creative mind. I have followed Weisinger's suggestion that
tragedy continues the age-old ritual of the dying god. If my
assumptions about the poemagogic significance of the dying god
theme are correct, then the tragic hero of the stage play also acts
out the poemagogic fantasies of the ego's struggle against a cruel

superego. Freud applied his interpretation of the triple .
of life, love and death (Robert Graves' White Goddess) .
Lear's three daughters. There is no need to rationalize L
insane submission to his daughters once their symbolism
recognized. (A recent production at London's Old Vic broug.
the difficult first scene off convincingly by emphasizing the old
man's bluff boastfulness and exhibitionism.) Freud recognized
that three sisters always stand for a powerful mother figure. We
can easily discern her in her oral aspect as the devouring and
castrating mother as well as in her anal role as the casting out
and containing mother. The play begins on the more superficial
oral level. The king indulges in his self-destructive exhibitionism,
which invites the oral sadism of the bad daughters (devouring
mother). They immediately inflict a sequence of castrations on
him. They hurt his boastful pride by 'cutting down' his train, a
figure of speech that comes very near to the real meaning of the
symbolism. They put his faithful servant, Kent, into the stocks
and pluck out the eyes of Lear's *alter ego*, Gloucester. (The
punishment of the stocks and the pillory relate to shame and
exhibitionism. Shame and guilt are never far apart. When we are
put to shame through no fault of our own, we may not only feel
ashamed of ourselves, but also inexplicably guilty. Medieval
punishments show good psychology. The criminal may lack
guilt feelings, but he will learn something very similar when he
is exposed to shame on the pillory or in the stocks. The stocks
trap his legs, the pillory his neck. This symbolic threat of castration would be apt to arouse unconscious fears of castration
and through them feelings of shame as well as of guilt.)

At last Lear is cast out into the wilderness. At this point the
play reaches the deeper anal level that was already expressed
earlier by the customary reversal of roles, when Lear cast out his
dutiful daughter Cordelia. Lear's *alter ego*, Gloucester, in whom
the motif of self-destruction is allowed to show itself more
openly, attempts to cast himself from the cliffs of Dover. He is
prevented from doing so by his dutiful son, Edgar, a male
counterpart of the dutiful Antigone who led Oedipus to his self-
chosen death at Colonus. I have mentioned several times how
Freud, with his acute intuition, looked through the disguise of
the crowning scene in which Lear cradles his dead daughter,
Cordelia, in his arms. The casting out is undone and atoned for

ersal of the image of the *Pietà*. Lear cast out into the
ness, castrated of his manhood (so that in the end he
ars garlanded and sweet like the mad Ophelia), is redeemed
the burying, containing mother.

The casting-out mother appears in her full horror in the figure
of Lady Macbeth, who forsakes her motherhood. I have mentioned how Freud, in another of his acute intuitive interpretations, sees the main theme of *Macbeth* as childlessness. Lady
Macbeth's rejection of children is matched by Macbeth's yearning to found a dynasty and his envy of Banquo's descendants.
The motif of childlessness has to be augmented by the hidden
motif of parentlessness of which it is a more superficial reversal.
The witches' prophecy goes that Macbeth can only be van-
quished by a man who was not born from woman. He succumbs
to Macduff who, like Dionysus, was 'untimely ripp'd' from his
mother's womb. The figure of Macduff sketches in vaguely the
deepest of all poemagogic motifs, the self-creating divine child.
But it is only a vague allusion. In fact Macduff reverses the
situation of the casting-out mother. Macbeth and his wife suffer
from increasing self-disgust, which at times becomes almost
physical. Lady Macbeth cannot wash her hands clean of blood
stains. While Duncan had marvelled at the purity of the air
around Macbeth's castle, we feel the foul air closing in. As the
self-creating son figure of Macduff appears the guilty couple are
ready to be cast out. Macbeth says: 'My way of life is fallen into
the sear, the yellow leaf.' Lady Macbeth obviously dies an untimely death of her own volition. The time is ripe. In the last
analysis Macbeth is a victim of the triple goddess, Hecate, who
drives him to madness through stirring up his heroic hubris and
over-ambition. He is an exact counterpart to Hamlet, who is
unable to act. Macbeth dies through heroic over-activity in vain
defiance of his superego. Hamlet dies from his depressive inability to act; while defying the superego figure of his father's
ghost, he submits to self-disgust, that is to say, to an ego ideal
that rejects his own weak ego. He cannot translate fantasy into
deeds because they would falsify his purpose. He says at the first
opportunity: 'I have that within that passeth show.' And he
despises himself for his inactivity. I have elsewhere described
the basically self-destructive attitude of Hamlet, which is openly
stated in his first soliloquy: 'that the Everlasting had not fix'd

his canon 'gainst self-slaughter!' He is replete with disgust the world and of himself, another embodiment of anal disgu. and self-rejection. In psycho-analytic theory the ego ideal plays a comparatively shadowy role compared with the superego. It might be better to call it the most destructive anal aspect of the superego which rejects, expels and buries parts of the self with the help of anal disgust. Through the usual reversal of roles on the anal level, the self-destructive psychotic theme is more openly revealed in Ophelia, who, unconsciously, is not so much the lover of Hamlet as his female duplicate. Like Hamlet, she cannot hate her father's murderer and rather seeks refuge in madness and suicide. Hamlet does little else but provoke his royal uncle into killing him and can only take his revenge when he himself is mortally slain. Even the theme of self-burial is sketched in the harrowing scene at Ophelia's open grave. He envies Laertes for his attempt to be buried alive in Ophelia's grave. R. Flatter, who acted as adviser to Laurence Olivier's film production of *Hamlet*, recognized, with commendable depth-psychological insight, that the cringeing Osric, who invites Hamlet on the king's behalf to the final duel, represents, on an unconscious level, the terrifying angel of death. Hamlet sees through the invitation with forebodings which, as he says, would only trouble a woman. 'The readiness is all.' Osric had to be a ridiculous figure to make Hamlet's suicidal submission more acceptable. Unfortunately Olivier made a wrong use of Flatter's psycho-analytic suggestion and gave Osric a sinister leer. But what has to be unconscious has to remain so to keep its full impact. Psycho-analytic interpretation of unconscious fantasies should never lead to making them explicit in a work of art. This would be a bad misunderstanding of the spontaneous role of unconscious fantasy in art. Psycho-analysis cannot help the artist in manipulating unconscious fantasy. There is no harm in know-ing about the depth of fantasy; but during creative work the artist must have the power to forget and to repress his intellectual knowing all the more securely. Hamlet's encounter with Osric is a moment of truth in other respects too. It is also an encounter with his *alter ego*, with what he holds most in contempt in him-self. Osric's words are empty and have no substance. 'Thus has he – and many more of the same breed that . . . the drossy age dotes on – only got the tune of the time and outward habit of counter; a kind of jesty collection . . .' Ironically, the whole the play is rather wordy and full of linguistic jokes, a formal play with the grammatical structure of language, which today Beckett uses to convey his own malaise about the emptiness of human relations, the imperfection or the danger of all attempts at communication, perhaps the imperfection also of precise words and images in shaping the fullness of creative vision.

Hamlet, then, may ultimately be a poemagogic self-portrait of the artist who despairs at fitting form to content, and who would rather shatter his work and himself than be unfaithful to his inner vision. This theme underlies the greatest dramatic work of the first half of this century, Schoenberg's opera *Moses and Aaron*. The opera deals directly with the depressive and manic attitudes to creative work. Art formulates what cannot be formulated. Consciously shaped gestalt on the depressive level cannot do justice to the fullness of a manic low-level vision. The secondary revision can only condense, simplify, solidify the scattered broad images into narrowly focused and tight patterns. As far as these new forms remain 'symbolic' of other suppressed images little is lost. I have tried to show how the wealth of the unconscious matrix adds to the new symbol plastic power and a feeling of intense concrete reality. This new illusionist reality, however crude, the artist has to accept gratefully as a sign of his success. Yet ultimately the initial creative vision has been falsified. In Schoenberg's opera, Moses stands for the ineffable oceanic-manic theme of creativity, the timeless and spaceless godhead of creation. He cannot sing, nor act decisively, immersed in his depressive impotence like another Hamlet. He can only speak. His manic *alter ego* is his brother Aaron, who can sing and shape the ineffable message of creativity into definite differentiated imagery, because he can sense the identity of vision behind a fragmented multiplicity of expressions. It makes sense that their dialogue is really a simultaneous duet; the creative process takes place on several levels at once. When Moses retreats to Mount Sinai, Aaron has no other choice than to make the divine message concrete in the image of the golden calf. Depression is overcome by manic orgies of self-abandon, self-destruction and love. Moses returns to destroy the golden calf. Yet Aaron wins; he argues rightly that the tablets on which God's commandments are engraved are also concrete falsifications of the message. Moses in despair breaks the tablets. He remains behind, cast out from all human communication, while Aaron leads the people away following the pillar of cloud, yet another concrete manifestation of divinity. The opera breaks off with Moses' spoken words of despair at not being able to give word to the unspeakable. The libretto, written by Schoenberg himself, provided for a third act in which Moses triumphs over Aaron. Aaron is led in as a helpless prisoner, possibly to be executed. Moses breaks off further argument and addresses the people. His message is topical and deals with the vain attempts of dispersed Jewry to find acceptance among other nations. This too, he says, falsifies their true creative task. Only by returning to the desert will they succeed. Moses dismisses Aaron. Aaron rises and collapses dead under the weight of Moses' disgust. Stravinsky has said that the unfinished opera is complete as it is and so also does Gertrud Schoenberg in her epilogue to the vocal score. If the opera is a poemagogic exposition of the creative process, as I believe it is, the third act adds nothing and perhaps weakens the beneficial fragmentation of the second act. To remain in the desert, never to reach the promised land, is the fate of Jewry as a whole – as expressed in the abandoned third act – and is the fate of Moses who stays behind in the desert, alone, at the end of the second act. Aaron's death as the dying god in the third act makes little sense. Poemagogically it can only mean the peremptory casting out of existing cliché and preconception that hinders the expression of creative truth. But in the second act Aaron means much more. In many ways he stands for the courage of the artist to attempt the impossible and to fail. Schoenberg gave the manic orgy the most poignant music, which by its compact shape seems to be destined to become a set concert piece. Such a fate would indeed be poetic justice and a vindication of Aaron's manic self-abandon. Aaron stands both for the deepest level of manic self-scattering as well as for the concretion of the oceanic vision in a new image. Human sacrifice and orgiastic love in front of the golden idol come very near to the fertility rites in honour of the dying and rising god, the most profound symbol of creativity. But ultimately creative man on the depressive level has to accept the imperfection of his work. This in a way Schoenberg has done. His failure to continue the work, of course, proves that he somehow knew that Moses and Aaron were only two sides of the same creative process. When Homunculus' orgiastic oceanic rites disrupt Faust's pleading with the gods of the underworld, Goethe has already become aware of what he called his own 'secret development', which allowed his logical discursive reasoning to accept the more profound logic of manic abandon. Depression and self-criticism, the Faustian self-disgust and dissatisfaction with human achievement, has to be tempered by manic ecstasy and its more profound insight. I have shown how any such incursion of manic thinking into surface thought leaves behind a measure of incoherence and fragmentation, a gap in the solid rocks of superficial logic that opens a secret access to the irrational underworld of fantasy. Accepting a partly incomplete and incoherent surface structure brings about a synthesis between the too precise gestalt of surface images and the infinitely richer matrix of undifferentiated fantasy from which the images have risen. Moses stands for the inexpressible, undifferentiated structure of primary-process fantasy. Aaron represents its necessarily incommensurate translation and revision in terms of the secondary process, but, and this is the important point, he also embodies the artist's ability to use the failure of complete translation as a residual manic link with the depth. It seems that Schoenberg, for personal reasons, identified himself too much with Moses. His own music had no singable melody that a popular concert audience was ready to understand. Moses triumphing over the popular singer Aaron smacks of wish-fulfilling daydreaming, always the wrong kind of inspiration for an artist; for it excludes the essence of tragedy. The score ends now on a spoken whisper of despair. The final silence is more shattering than all the trumpets of victory. We must be grateful to the unconscious logic of poemagogic fantasy and its disruptive effect on conscious planning which prevented a happy ending. In accepting his failure to translate his planning into music, Schoenberg also paid tribute to Aaron and his failure, and produced the greatest tragedy of the dying god in our century.

Part Five
Theoretical Conclusions

This preliminary analysis of poemagogic imagery has important theoretical aspects. Though much detail may be only vaguely sketched in, the rough outlines strongly suggest that we are dealing with material which psycho-analytical theory has as yet hardly touched. I have mentioned how my largely independent investigation into the oral (Prometheus) level of poemagogic imagery covered much the same ground which Melanie Klein had explored in her analysis of very early oral fantasies of devouring and being devoured. But in a way this far-reaching correspondence made me all the more hesitant in putting forward the deeper anal and oceanic (Antigone and Dionysus) levels of poemagogic imagery. It became more and more apparent that so-called 'applied' psycho-analysis promised to be a tool that for once would cut more deeply than clinical analysis. The reason for this is easy to see. Insanity may be creativity gone wrong. It is impossible to investigate deeply repressed creative fantasies without at the same time making assumptions about the origin and character of the equivalent psychotic fantasies, a field of clinical psychology which has so far resisted all attempts at fuller understanding. What seems to emerge without reasonable doubt is the fact that both kinds of fantasies arise from unconscious levels which we would ordinarily call deeply unconscious.

The poemagogic fantasies with their various degrees of de-differentiation testify to the deeply unconscious quality of dedifferentiation in general. Structural dedifferentiation, as discussed in the first part of this book, seemed to play such an eminently practical role in creative work that its fully unconscious quality might be doubted, at least from the viewpoint of

classical ego psychology. The link between creative dedifferentiation and poemagogic and psychotic fantasy, however, no longer
allows us to assume that we are merely dealing with superficial
'preconscious' levels of image making. Hence comes the eminent
theoretical significance of poemagogic imagery and its close link
with deeply unconscious ego processes. However wrong I may
have gone in the conceptualization of its details, all that matters
for my preliminary survey of poemagogic images is to have made
out that their dedifferentiation is the result of deeply unconscious
processes. Creative work is somehow capable of tapping these
deep levels by short-circuiting the top and bottom levels of the
creative imagination. It can thus make use of deeply unconscious
near-oceanic fantasies for solving very real, eminently practical
tasks in engineering, doing highly abstract mathematics or
painting a good picture that possesses a lively pictorial space. I
have spoken of the near-psychotic oceanic quality of the 'enveloping' pictorial space in modern art. After the provisional
survey of poemagogic imagery we might not hesitate to seek the
origin of this truly oceanic pictorial space (such as is found in
Jackson Pollock's work) in profoundly unconscious fantasies on
the oceanic-manic level. We have seen how these paintings draw
the spectator inside, obliterating the distance between him and
the work. The spectator is put to work to articulate, by secondary
revision, the oscillating surface, so that he can extricate himself
once again from its all too close embrace. It is important to
realize the very direct linkage between the structural analysis of
poemagogic fantasy and the aesthetic analysis of art's substructure, with which the first half of this book was concerned.

Poemagogic imagery poses another problem. Psycho-analytic
writing today takes it for granted that oral material is the most
primitive of all because it arises earliest in the child's history. It
tends to neglect anal material as being superimposed on the
earlier, supposedly more fundamental, oral material. Poemagogic
imagery shows a situation which is quite the opposite, a conclusion which flows directly from our greater attention to the
structure of fantasy. Oral material is structurally more differentiated than anal material and for this reason alone is more accessible
to conscious understanding. Undifferentiated imagery, whatever
its content may be, is *per se* withdrawn from consciousness. Any
increase in undifferentiation, such as is characteristic of anal

fantasy, will block conscious access more effectively. D. Winnicott, addressing the International Psycho-analytical Congress in Paris in 1957, warned against the prevalent facile assumption that what is earlier in life must necessarily be more deeply unconscious. Ernest Jones, speaking after Winnicott, found this important enough to sharpen Winnicott's point by saying that early material need not necessarily be less accessible. If, as I have suggested, structural dedifferentiation is the ego's instrument for 'repressing' mental material, any increase in structural dedifferentiation must increase both the material's inaccessibility and the depth of its 'unconscious' quality. It seems that in the ego's cyclical decomposition and rearticulation more primitive anal fantasy is often revised in terms of more accessible oral fantasy.

In the child's development the extreme undifferentiation of anal fantasies is followed by the orally tinged fantasies of the phallic stage. It is in the later phallic stage that the child indulges in compulsive voyeuristic curiosity and boastful exhibitionism, that recall the oral-schizoid Prometheus fantasies. It may well be that what appears to be early oral material in a patient's fantasy is really a comparatively late oral-schizoid elaboration of an originally anal fantasy. By concentrating on oral material, as clinical work is inclined to do, the more primitive anal foundation of creative fantasy may well be neglected. I will try to show in the next chapter that the whole of infancy could be conceived as a great cycle of advancing and receding self-destructive fantasies. The initial advance of Thanatos is reflected in the increasing dedifferentiation of the fantasies. The climax (maximum of sadism) is reached at the end of the first anal stage. This climax is followed by redifferentiation with the help of creative work under the guidance of Eros and a pacified superego. The genital Oedipus stage would mark the highwater mark of this ascending phase. The onset of latency would mark another cycle leading down to maximum dedifferentiation around the critical age of about eight at the height of latency, which marks the full awakening of the child's abstract-analytic faculties. We know by now how inimical these new faculties can become to creative imagination.

Altogether, the structural analysis of creative work promises to be a research tool of astonishing penetrating power. So far, it is mostly writers outside the psycho-analytic movement who have made any use of it. In his ambitious book *The Act of Creation* [17], Arthur Koestler sees the function of the creative imagination as the cooperation between several mental levels in much the same way as I have suggested it. The creative thinker links previously disconnected matrices. These matrices – and this the main point – function according to their different codes. Koestler assumes, however, that the code of unconscious matrices is invariant and rigid, a residue of earlier primitive modes of thought, perhaps practised in infancy, that have gradually become automatic and to this extent unconscious. The creative feat is to link the pre-existing modes of functioning with current modes. Koestler enumerates other characteristics of matrices and their unconscious codes, that bear striking similarity to the psychoanalytic concept of the primary process. Such characteristics are the substitution of vague images for precise words, symbolization, concretion, confusion of similar sound with similar meaning, displacement of emphasis, merging of opposites, etc.

Koestler has taken over a lot from psycho-analysis, but has only absorbed the psycho-analytic theory as it was developed over half a century ago. He ignores the fact that the concept of the primary process as the archaic, wholly irrational function of the deep unconscious, is now undergoing drastic revision. This revision, in Marion Milner's words, is due partly to the need for accommodating the facts of art. These facts suggest forcibly that the undifferentiated matrix is technically far superior to the narrowly focused conscious processes, if only because of its wider focus that can comprehend serial structures irrespective of their order in time and space. There is little that is primitive or infantile about Schoenberg's mastery in handling a theme without regard to its sequence in time. I have suggested that unconscious scanning of such serial structures requires the active dedifferentiation of modes of thinking that have no correlates whatsoever in the child's primitive mind. It is useless to describe such a dedifferentiation of time as a 'regression' to pre-existing infantile or primitive percepts and concepts; it is better described as the creation of an entirely new matrix, the undifferentiated structure of which is made to fit precisely a particular task. The mathematician creates an entirely new matrix for scanning the disjunctive serial structure of his problem in hand. What he finds ready-made in the low-level ego functions is their porous permeable structure that is utterly mobile and ready to absorb new serial structures in its wide amoeba-like embrace.

This constructive role of the unconscious is difficult to accept. Koestler's formulation is only a cautious extension of classical ego psychology, which considered the unconscious merely as the inert unchangeable survival of an earlier more primitive mind. It seems, however, that unconscious fantasy is innate in the human mind from its inception and grows and develops throughout our adult life. The young baby carries in itself inborn fantasies of psychotic virulence that run counter to its rational conscious experience. Conscious thought and unconscious fantasy are thus developing side by side in counterpoint, fed by the same stimuli impinging from the outside world and from inside the growing body. Creative work simply injects new and controlled stimulation into an utterly flexible unconscious fantasy. Koestler also comes close to a recent and still influential development in psycho-analytic ego psychology initiated by E. Kris. Kris thought that creative work implies a 'controlled' regression of the surface faculties towards the primary process. Koestler's conjunction of surface thought with more primitive rigid matrices in the unconscious would be such a 'controlled' regression. What is missing in Kris's concept, however, is the insight that creativity does not merely control the regression towards the primary process, but also the work of the primary process itself. It turns its potentially disruptive effect into a constructive and highly efficient instrument for making new links and shaping new, more comprehensive concepts and images. The conscious and unconscious matrices are not merely linked. Surface thought is wholly immersed in the matrix of the primary process.

The process of dedifferentiation has to serve two masters, the exigencies of irrational id fantasy and the needs of the rational objective task in hand. It is an essential feature of creativity that it can easily express both in a single structure. In a single indivisible process creativity links inside and outside. By building the external creative work it also integrates the fragmented ego within. This is why dedifferentiation is determined twice over ('*over*determined') by inner and outer needs, the technical specifications of an objective task as well as the more exacting demands of id fantasy.

It has been known all along that the primary process was wholly undifferentiated. Unconscious symbolism fails to distinguish between opposites, displaces the significant to the insignificant, condenses incompatibles and ignores the rational sequence of time and space. What has not been sufficiently realized is that unconscious *per*cepts on the level of the primary process build disjunctive serial structures of so wide a sweep that they can easily accommodate these contradictory (disjunctive) *con*cepts of primary process fantasy. Far from being chaotic, the primary process precisely matches undifferentiated id content with serial structures of exactly the same degree of undifferentiation. Accepting dedifferentiation as a precise structural principle of unconscious perception and image making allows us to remove the taint of chaos that has adhered to the primary process for far too long. It is idle to ask which comes first, the dedifferentiation of id content or the dedifferentiation of ego structure. According to the new model of ego psychology, proposed by Hartmann and his associates, id and ego once evolved together from a common undifferentiated matrix. The authors would have wholly anticipated my theory of undifferentiated image making, had they fitted the most important ego function, perception, into their new model. This they did not do, perhaps in deference to the academic theory of perception put forward by the gestalt psychologists. They maintained that the differentiation of a gestalt was built into the mechanism of perception from birth. Today such a view can no longer be entertained. It has been shaken severely, particularly by case histories of people born blind who achieved vision later in life. Perception too, like any other ego function, develops by a slow process of differentiation which, as I have suggested, is closely geared to the needs of the developing id. As id drives become more precisely aimed, so do the images of the ego. Unconscious fantasy life during our whole lifetime is supplied with new imagery by the ego's cyclical rhythm of dedifferentiation, which feeds fresh material into the matrix of image making. Far from being autonomous of the id, the ego's perception is constantly at the disposal of unconscious symbolic needs. The ego is certainly not at the id's mercy. The multiple determination of structural dedifferentiation from several – external as well as internal – causes looks after that. The ego of its own accord – and to this extent 'autonomously' – decomposes itself in order to provide new serial structures for its own creative tasks in the external world as well as for the symbolization of internal id fantasy. It makes little sense to call this periodic decomposition of the surface ego a 'regression'. It is part and parcel of the ego rhythm which makes perception work.

The neglect of the undifferentiated structure of primary process fantasy has been responsible for the deadlock which has held up the progress of psycho-analytic aesthetics for over half a century. What Freud calls primary process structures are merely distortions of articulate surface imagery caused by the underlying undifferentiation of truly unconscious fantasy. The concept of condensation bears this out. There is the truly undifferentiated condensation, where images of quite incompatible appearance interpenetrate into a single vision which can accommodate them all in their entirety; from this true condensation we have to distinguish the more familiar condensation, where the object forms have become concrete and unyielding. They will then partially obliterate each other owing to the incompatibility of their appearance. A few mutilated remnants are pushed into each other to produce some nonsensical mixture. This partial obliteration no longer repels the focus of waking attention, but this is possible only at the cost of losing much of its original substance. When we speak of truly undifferentiated primary process structures we should only include the first kind of fluid, freely interpenetrating condensation which is still undifferentiated in its structure. This can reconcile in its wider frame the full ambiguity of primary process fantasy.

Freud, in his pioneer work on the aesthetics of the joke, treated only the more superficial condensations which the joke shares with the dream. In these, mutual obliteration has occurred. Freud uses as his first example Heine's neologism 'famillionaire'. This word describes the affable behaviour of a rich man towards a poor relative. Under an affected air of familiarity it expresses the arrogance of the millionaire. The poor relative boasts to have been treated in a 'famillionaire' way. He implicitly admits that the rich man had in fact treated him haughtily. True undifferentiation would have preserved both words 'familiar' and 'millionaire' intact, though we would not be able to mould their fusion into articulate sound. We begin to understand why Freud's successful analysis of the joke's structure did not lead directly to an equivalent analysis of artistic structure, where structural undifferentiation becomes of supreme importance.

The witty formulation of a poignant joke is only a border problem of aesthetics. When it yielded to Freud's new depth-psychological approach, the way into the central problem of aesthetics, the form problem of art, seemed wide open. Freud had analysed the superficial condensations, displacements, representations by the opposite, etc. by which a dream expresses its hidden meaning. He found that the joke used precisely the same techniques for symbolizing some aggressive or obscene allusion. He compiled an exhaustive catalogue of all possible formulations of a good joke and could identify them each time with an equivalent technique of the dream. The condensation 'famillionaire' could also have occurred in a dream, though, of course, without any witty effect. In drawing up this catalogue Freud succeeded brilliantly where more conventional aesthetic research had failed. Classical aesthetics as practised by men like Hogarth, assumed that certain aesthetic qualities, like the feelings of beauty, of the sublime, of gracefulness or of wittiness, could be explained by certain objective properties of the beautiful, sublime, graceful or witty object. For instance, sublimity could be connected with large-scale structures inspiring awe by their size, or wittiness with brevity. Gradually the aestheticians lost heart; there was too much uncertainty about the most important aesthetic experience, the feeling of beauty. The modern art of their time looked unaesthetic and even ugly (for reasons which we have discussed at length). The conservative aestheticians were not slow to demonstrate the lack of proper aesthetic organization in their own 'modern' art. The trouble was that the mere passing of time and the action of secondary revision turned modern ugliness into classical beauty. There was no need for disputing at length their spurious laws of beauty. The passage of time alone saw to that. With the rise of modern psychology, the aestheticians changed their aim. Instead of searching for objective properties of beauty in the external world they turned inwards to find the source of the aesthetic experiences in our own mind.

Freud did just this in his analysis of the joke; nevertheless, he solved the problem on truly classical objective lines. The primary process structure of the joke represents an objective property of a good joke, apart from explaining its subjective origin in the unconscious. Freud's achievement in compiling an exhaustive catalogue of possible jokes could have been emulated by anyone who cared to have a closer look at the manner in which a joke expresses some half-hidden allusion. By making this allusion explicit and re-formulating its content into a sober statement that lacked wittiness he could isolate the formal qualities of a really 'good' joke. It turned out that the joke condenses, displaces and twists the rational structure of everyday language in the manner of the dream's primary process. Freud argued that this proved that the joke, like the dream, was shaped on the same primary process level of the unconscious mind. The violent twists which the joke imparts to the vocabulary, syntax and grammar of language bear a family resemblance to the schizophrenic's attack on his own language function. The schizophrenic too injects primary process structures into his handling of words. His weird conglomerates resemble the condensations of the dream and of the joke. Yet they are not condensations in the psycho-analytic sense. Bion rightly speaks of them as 'bizarre' language. The schizophrenic splinters his language and equally violently pushes the fragments into hard unyielding conglomerates. But there is no unconscious depth. In Heine's joke the condensed word 'famillionaire' still carries a halo of the total inviolate words 'familiar' and 'millionaire' from which it was condensed, because, as I have suggested, these words coexist on the un-differentiated primary process level in their totality without doing each other violence. There is no fragmentation, because the neologism still symbolizes something outside itself. The link between the new symbol and its undifferentiated matrix still holds and so allows the joke to communicate its meaning to others, while the schizophrenic's bizarre and rigid conglomerates need elaborate interpretation.

In the face of Freud's brilliant analysis of the joke it was diffi-cult to understand why his success was not paralleled in other fields of aesthetics. The stage seemed set for Freud's triumphant entry into the core of aesthetics, the origin and structure of the beautiful in art. Art more than the joke could claim deep, spon-taneous roots in the unconscious. Art's conscious superstructure may be largely composed by intellectual effort, but its vast sub-structure is shaped by (unconscious) spontaneity, as indeed is any kind of creative work. Freud was pleased to find that he could transfer without much ado the entire inventory of dream interpretation to a new depth-psychological understanding of art. Myths, tragedies, novels, paintings all carried an under-current of symbolic matter. This fantasy content of art could be extracted without difficulty by decoding it according to the cata-logue of symbols derived from the interpretation of dreams. Freud found that artists more than other people had an instinc-tive understanding of the unconscious. They were on better terms, as it were, with unconscious fantasy and did not set up the defences which other uncreative people needed in their inter-course with the unconscious. In art the exigencies of unconscious fantasy are often allowed to override the demands of reason and logic. Unconscious fantasy can express itself with less disguise in art than in any other human product, including even jokes.

The content of jokes is not a deeply repressed fantasy, as is the unconscious content of art, but merely a lightly suppressed sexual or aggressive allusion. It was more than legitimate to predict that the symbolic fantasy of art, thrown up from far deeper levels of the mind, should display the stamp of its un-conscious origin with even greater emphasis and clarity. Otto Rank duly searched the forms of art for primary process forms as proof of their unconscious roots. He pointed out that the German word 'Dichter' meant condenser. Myths, folklore, and of course also art abounded in dreamlike apparitions, composite monsters condensed from animal and human form. But these occasional intrusions of dream techniques did not add up to an exhaustive catalogue of all possible art forms, even if one exclu-ded the deliberately composed patterns of art's (conscious) superstructure. Nobody has yet succeeded in compiling all possible forms of art, which would have to include all future art. It was impossible to describe the spontaneously created compo-nents of art, such as textures, in terms of dream techniques. They often lack any structure that could be analysed in terms of definite patterns. These spontaneous (unconsciously controlled) elements – artistic handwriting and textures both in the visual arts and in music – have none of the rigour and good gestalt that characterize the conscious superstructure of art. Owing to their apparent lack of organization they cannot be identified as con-densations, displacements and the like, as the forms of a joke can; rather they demonstrate the chaos and disorganization which psycho-analytic ego psychology is all too ready to associate with unconsciously produced forms. It was strange to find that Freud's analysis of the joke could not act as a pacemaker for the analysis of art. The inapplicability of his method to art should have warned us that something was amiss or even wrong in the current concepts. The missing concept, in my view, was the un-differentiated matrix below the more superficial condensations, displacements and other so-called primary process forms. These more superficial forms may be irrational in content, but are not so in their formal gestalt structure. I have suggested that their structure is a secondary revision imposed on the truly uncon-scious undifferentiated matrix below them.

For a long time Freud's success in analysing the joke's struc-ture made me pursue the path which had brought Rank up against a blind wall. But in the end it seemed useless to batter on. After half a century of failure it seemed more fruitful to cease a frontal attack and ask oneself about the possible reasons for our failure. Non-Euclidean geometry arose from a centuries-old failure to prove all Euclidean axioms. The acceptance of the failure as final led to a new conception of space, which proved fruitful in spite of the fact that it cannot possibly be visualized. I have spoken of the several incompatible space systems that keep shifting before our searching eye and defeat any attempt at steady focusing. These conflicting spaces are, of course, typical serial structures that press vision down towards an undifferenti-ated level.

My concept of an undifferentiated matrix of perception arose from the need to interpret the long-standing failure of psycho-analytic aesthetics to find the unconscious substructure of art. One could account for the failure in two ways. It was possible to discard Freud's approach to aesthetics altogether (this was what E. Kris ultimately did), or one can assume that we have failed to find art's substructure because it defies our conscious powers of visualization. This is the solution proposed here. It does, of course, expand the use of the term 'unconscious' as understood by current theory. But this is only another way of saying that the term 'primary process' needs revision. The quality of being un-conscious is not dependent on the superego's censorship directed against certain contents, but automatically follows from a change

279

in the formal structure of image making, i.e. from the ego's de-differentiation of conscious gestalt. This implies that we cannot produce the originally undifferentiated structure of the primary process for conscious inspection, but only its conscious derivates like conglomerated, bizarre condensations, illogical displacements and the like. This difficulty should not deter us. It applies to any phenomenon of the unconscious. The concept of the unconscious is not a physical fact open to direct demonstration, but an explanatory concept which allows us to explain phenomena which otherwise could not be satisfactorily explained. Neither, for that matter, can the 'facts' of nuclear physics be demonstrated directly. They too are only explanatory concepts. All that can be observed are a few flickerings or bubbles, the rest are abstract conceptualizations not available for direct inspection. Only by becoming familiar with them in a multitude of contexts do these abstract concepts acquire an illusory plastic quality and almost physical reality that makes them emotionally undistinguishable from more concrete images. Then, the demand to produce them for conscious inspection will no longer be voiced. But as soon as a really new abstract concept is proposed, which merely explains without being tangible, the old voices of protest will be heard. They will be stilled when secondary revision has done its work and assimilated the new concept among the other pseudo-concrete images of everyday thought.

The concept of structural undifferentiation has also the virtue of simplifying the current model of the id and ego. The proposition that the ego supplies undifferentiated form exactly fitted to express the undifferentiated aims of the id, immensely simplifies the model of the primary process. This neat fit should also help us to dispense for good with the tiresome doubt that has constantly been thrown my way whether the dedifferentiated imagery of creative thought is really truly 'unconscious'. This doubt is based on lazy thinking, on an unshakeable preconception that anything that 'helps' creative work must be merely preconscious and that only disruptive fantasy can be deemed truly unconscious. 'Helping' is an ambiguous term; syntonicity is more precise. Preconscious image making is syntonic with conscious thought. It is kept from consciousness because of the extreme narrowness of focused attention. Preconscious material is kept waiting in an ante-room of consciousness ready to intrude whenever a possibility offers itself. An undifferentiated image is not syntonic in this way. Whenever it forces its way into consciousness it will either disrupt it or else press consciousness down to an undifferentiated level of awareness which is better able to deal with it. Undifferentiated imagery will assist reason only if it is kept on the level of unconscious scanning, in which case surface consciousness is partly robbed of its usual energy charge. This shift in ego functioning produces that vacant stare I have mentioned so often.

There is no sharp division between the conscious, preconscious and unconscious systems, but only a smooth transition with two or three critical thresholds. The process of dedifferentiation describes a dynamic process that works gradually within certain critical limits. From the vantage point of conscious introspection – we have no other – the transition first produces experiences of 'vagueness', then a gradual dissolution of precise space and time, and in the end, when the last critical limit has been overstepped, complete blankness occurs, still replete with intense emotional experience, the much vaunted 'full' emptiness of low-level vision.

Such a series can be best studied in the transition from tachistoscopic to subliminal perception, in the variations of the dream-screen phenomenon and possibly also in the transition of mystic orisons towards a fully oceanic 'empty' contemplation. Subliminal vision allows us to study the transition under controlled laboratory conditions. A tachistoscopic exposure lasts only a few fractions of a second and cuts off the development of vision to a fully articulate gestalt. It catches an initial more dreamlike glimpse that still possesses the vague weakly differentiated structure of low-level vision. I have discussed in earlier writings [5] how Varendonck observed split-second glimpses without the help of a tachistoscope and also came to the conclusion that their relatively vague structure was due to their dreamlike quality, belonging to a deeper level of consciousness. By cutting down further the time of the split-second exposure a critical limit is reached, where the image undergoes increasing dedifferentiation. Larger parts of the figure are swallowed up by inarticulate background textures and the figure itself is not merely vague, but distorted according to the whims of id fantasies. Charles Fisher followed up experiments that Pötzl had initiated half a century earlier. He found that unseen background elements were not lost, but penetrated into subsequent dreams, while in turn the figure tended to be neglected in dreams. When the subliminal threshold is approached the entire figure is gradually sucked into the white fog of the ground, which begins to resemble an insubstantial white dream-screen that cannot be securely localized in space. (It would be a great advantage to include among the observers in the laboratory artistically sensitive persons who could report with greater precision on the plastic pictorial space of the tachistoscopic images. Most people would not appreciate questions about the elusive quality of pictorial space.) At last, dedifferentiation oversteps the limit and the screen becomes totally blank. But this is only a quantitative step. As the threshold was approached many more background elements had become blank and invisible. The crossing of the threshold simply completes a gradual transition from figure to background quality and at last to a total immersion into a white fog.

I have mentioned earlier Charles Fisher's experiments with the subliminal exposure of Rubin's famous double profiles [10]. These experiments showed that below the threshold the bisection between figure and ground has become totally suspended. Unconscious perception can hold both profiles, a typical serial structure, in a single glance. This astonishing result agrees with the interpretation now proposed of a gradual process where the ground has increasingly sucked up elements of the figure until the entire picture plane becomes one single undifferentiated ground without a figure.

Subliminal perception can serve as the prime example for the way in which the ego provides for low-level imagery, owing to an autonomous inbuilt need. The pull of id fantasy towards dedifferentiation or the aggressive scattering action of the superego are not needed. It would be misleading to say that the excessive shortness of the physiological stimulus in tachistoscopic exposure is responsible for the fact of unconsciousness. Rather does the ego gear its process of differentiation or dedifferentiation to the duration of the exposure. Varendonck [37] is probably right in saying that every single perception goes through a rapid cycle in which it develops from a split-second undifferentiated phase to a fully blown articulate gestalt. Cutting off its full development by tachistoscopy simply retains in focus the initial undifferentiated phase which is usually forgotten when the final gestalt enters our memory. There is nothing about this that could be deemed physiological rather than psychological. We go on dreaming while we are awake. We carry on our secret fantasy life in the countless glimpses during the initial phases of waking perceptions. I once compared the many levels of perception to a television screen where the elements are touched off by the transmission in discontinuous intervals. Our conscious experience however takes in only the fully completed picture. Similarly, perception may produce several parallel chains of fantasy on different levels of differentiation, which are touched off in turn as the cycle of perception passes up or down through its several levels. A chain of deep dream fantasies and reverie-like sequences may run on underneath our waking experiences carried on in the undifferentiated phases preceding every single conscious perception.

One point perhaps needs repeating. The ego, of its own accord, sets the scene for staging these unconscious fantasies, without being prodded by the id's need for symbolization. In this sense, the ego acts 'autonomously', that is to say independently of pressures from the id. Usually the term 'ego autonomy' is used to stress the ego's freedom to function without regard to the demands of the id. Perception was, for a time, considered such an autonomous sphere of ego activity that could function in complete dissociation from id fantasy. Nothing could be further from the truth. Perception, as we have seen, sets apart from the outset a large part – perhaps even much the larger part – of its function as an unconscious subliminal substructure into which id fantasy can penetrate with the greatest ease. The ease of the id's penetration is, of course, explained by the extreme undifferentiation of unconscious vision. Its wide all-embracing sweep can use almost any object form as an assembly point for an immense cluster of other images that, for conscious analytic vision at least, have nothing in common. Any objects, however different in shape or outline, can become fully equated with each other on the unconscious 'syncretistic' level. On a near-oceanic level outer perception and inner fantasy become indistinguishable. (I prefer to talk of 'image making' to describe an undifferentiated type of imagery which is outward perception and inward-directed fantasy at the same time.)

The plastic effects in perception rest on a vast unconscious substructure, which does not seem to serve any other biological purpose. Without it, conscious vision would lose all sense of plastic reality; it would go flat and dead, unable to stimulate our rational orientation and activity. Psychotic vision can go dead and irrelevant in this way because of its lack of a 'contact barrier' with a rich unconscious substructure. For the sake of a vivid plastic feeling alone perception must set aside some part of its total range for seemingly useless 'subliminal' perceptions.

Equally mysteriously, the ego engulfs by far the greater part of the visual field into a fog of highly ambiguous imagery that is usually fully withdrawn from conscious inspection. It is therefore 'unconscious' in the wider sense of the term used here. There are some physiological factors that distinguish the clear focus of the visual field from vague periphery (in our retina cone cells fill the focal centre and rod cells the periphery). But this physiological distinction is not responsible for the truly unconscious quality of peripheral vision. Our visual field does not look like a bad photograph in which everything except the centre is grossly out of focus and blurred. Vagueness and blurredness alone do not repel conscious attention in the way the peripheral visual field does. The vagueness can be partly undone if an urgent psychological need arises. In cases of hemianopia exactly one half of the visual field goes blind. The central focus too is sliced in half with only one side retaining vision. In some cases a new focus will be formed in the seeing half of the periphery. It then loses its former vagueness and gains in visual acuity. More significant, the mutilated old focus now goes duly vague and withdraws from conscious attention. It forms part of a new peripheral halo surrounding the new focus. These case histories prove, if proof is needed, that an overwhelming psychological need exists that requires us to leave the larger part of the visual field in a vague medley of images. Only if we immobilize or blind the focus (this happens during twilight for physiological reasons) can the peripheral shapes manifest themselves in all their elusive dreamlike quality. Fantastic shapes then lurk in the corners of the visual field which we cannot identify and which are easily moulded by the reckless play of our imagination. The full terror of an anxiety dream may overwhelm us while we are wide awake. It needs a definite effort in unfamiliar surroundings to keep our eye steady and allow some unknown shapes edging into view to remain steeped in their dreamlike fog. We may try to guess their true nature and will be surprised how different their 'real' shape turns out to be. Peripheral vision has been called eidetic because of its easy malleability.

The superego may well add its censorship to the forces of the ego's repression that normally keep our peripheral vision unconscious. After a lecture on recent advances in the physiology of vision I had the opportunity of asking the lecturer a leading question about the nature of peripheral distortion. I expected that the distinguished man, who had devoted his whole professional life to the study of vision, would at some time have come across some of the low-level phenomena such as I have described. He was mystified. After a pause, obviously motivated by a wish to be polite, he quickly passed a pencil across his eye and said: 'I cannot see any distortion!' I did not insist that the experiment was futile and that an already familiar object would not prove vulnerable to peripheral distortion; the existing conscious memory image would prove stronger than fantasy. I realized that the lecturer's life-long failure to notice the undifferentiated structure of peripheral vision had something to do with its truly unconscious quality, that may have become reinforced by the superego's censorship. The careful collection of factual data as such has never led to the discovery and better understanding of unconscious phenomena. A depth-psychological attitude is necessary that takes account of the defensive processes obstructing observation in order to be able to see at all. As so often, the formulation of the problem precedes the observation of concrete facts.

I have tried to show how the ego uses structural dedifferentiation for repressing some of its imagery. We should have no hesitation in calling such repressed material 'unconscious' in a technical sense. The ego uses the same process of dedifferentiation in producing its subliminal imagery, the vagueness of peripheral vision and also the vast substructure of creative work. In all these cases the unconscious quality is due to the same structural change.

The ego contains from the outset a gradient in its structural differentiation. Owing to its inherent tendency to split, certain ego nuclei will progress in their differentiation while others will lag behind. The gradient between the various degrees of differentiation is in itself an enrichment of the ego, a diminution of entropy. Yet when tension between the differently structured parts of the ego reaches a critical limit the death instinct, as the principle of entropy, will bring about the final splitting. Once the ego has learned repression the splitting will no longer lead to free ejection and permanent loss. The undifferentiated material then sinks into an unconscious matrix to mingle with other images equally undifferentiated. With them it will fuse into new symbolic equations (it will be remembered that I am using this term in a different sense from Hanna Segal). The ego, greatly strengthened on the level of the oceanic-manic rebound, will tend to reintroject the symbolic material into consciousness. As this involves a measure of secondary revision, the ego guided by the superego selects from the undifferentiated equations between several incompatible objects a single object form as the new symbol, while the other material automatically remains 're-pressed'. It is possible that the term repression should be reserved for this unavoidable selection between several possible representations. The selection is controlled by the superego. Reinforced by anal disgust it bars the re-entry of the original material and helps to transfer its meaning to the new symbol. Depressive anxiety accompanies the unavoidable incompleteness and insufficiency of the selection (secondary revision) which all symbol formation involves.

I have stressed that the psychotic is incapable of symbol for-mation and repression. He may fail in all three phases of the creative process. He is incapable in the first place of letting go and allowing the split-off material to pass by the contact barrier (Bion) or the gate of the dream (Róheim) into the womb of the unconscious. The inner world is feared as an infinite void in which he is lost or else as a trap in which he will be buried alive. B. Lewin has spoken of an oral triad of experiences that accom-pany the act of falling asleep: a fantasy of devouring, of being devoured and of sleeping; sleep is also felt as an equivalent of death. In my view there is below this oral triad an anal triad which could be described as falling into an infinite abyss or void, being trapped or buried alive, and lastly dying.* The

* There may also be a 'genital' triad of creativity: to eject (male), to be re-ceived (female), to be reborn (child). These triads correspond to the three phases of creativity: projection, integration, re-introjection.

psychotic fear of being lost in an infinite void or being trapped and buried alive corresponds to the anal triad. The fear of the inner void refers to dedifferentiation, which is feared as emptiness, the fear of being trapped to the anal-depressive aspect of repression, which is connected with the partial burial and incomplete recovery of repressed material. Some of the repressed material must remain buried alive, possibly for ever, if only because of the narrowness of the secondary revision which all symbol formation entails. For creative man the incompleteness of symbol formation may act as a challenge to repeat once again the full cycle of creativity and so create another new symbol. For the psychotic, incapable as he is of symbol formation, the fact that some material will always remain repressed cannot but produce the fear of self-destruction. The unabated anal aggressions of the superego still ravage his ego, either scattering parts of it without direction into a void or else treating them like disgusting excrements to be buried away from sight for ever. Creativity and the process of repression and symbol formation that accompany it modify the superego's crude anal aggressions sufficiently to make the only partial recovery of split-off parts of the ego tolerable. Yet the act of artistic creation bears, at least in its first oral-schizoid phase, an almost too close family resemblance to undirected ejection of parts of the artist's self. Schizoid anxiety is never far off.

Normally psycho-analytic treatment is only concerned with resolving id conflict. It leaves it to the ego to do its own work of creative sublimation. With psychotic patients this may be insufficient. If psychosis is creativity 'gone wrong', treatment might have to be concerned with setting into motion the mutilated creative process. Only in this way can the excessive aggressions of the superego be sufficiently tempered, to allow the ego to recover. It is often said that the psychotic has no unconscious in the usual sense. He has failed to erect a 'contact barrier' which bars access to the unconscious and at the same time facilitates interchange between conscious and unconscious. If my conclusions are correct, the psychotic lacks a faculty for creative dedifferentiation, which would allow repression to act in this twofold way. I have commented frequently on the severe anxieties which the slightest attempt at dedifferentiation in artistic work can evoke in psychotic or near-psychotic art students.

One wonders whether clinical psycho-analysis has paid sufficient attention to the structural level on which the interchange between analyst and patient is carried on. I have discussed elsewhere [8] the undifferentiated structure of the analyst's 'free-floating' attention. He refuses to focus on the obvious and striking features in the patient's free associations and, like Paul Klee, dissipates (scatters) his attention impartially over the entire material. Only in this way will he extract from it some inconspicuous detail that may contain the most significant symbolism. In his interpretation he will fit this detail into its proper context and allow the patient to reintroject his own fragmented projections (free associations) on a higher structural level, which needs no further revision to be understood by his conscious surface faculties. In this interchange all three phases of creativity are present: the artist's initial free projection of fragmented material; the analyst, like the work of art, serves as a receptacle to receive the projections. Through dedifferentiation (free-floating attention) he is able to re-integrate the material and make it ready for re-introjection by the patient. What seems significant to me is that the health-giving interpretation occurs on a fully articulate surface level. This may be perfectly sound in the case of a neurotic patient who still possesses the faculty of repression and therefore is in contact with his own unconscious. He himself can reintroduce the re-introjected material into his own unconscious and create new symbols and ideas. Not so the psychotic; it is well known that a psychotic reacts to interpretations as though they were forcible re-introjections that threaten to destroy him. He is right in this. Fully articulate interpretations merely add to the already existing fragmentation of his surface ego and fail to make contact with his rudimentary unconscious. If we compare the situation with the three phases of creativity we find that the psychotic mainly needs help in the second creative phase of dedifferentiation. He clings too anxiously to his over-concrete surface imagery; he can only fragment it without ever being capable of scattering it into undifferentiated low-level imagery. For this reason, highly articulate interpretations that appeal only to the rational surface level of thinking may only invite more violent fragmentation. He is not helped to let go of his surface imagery and to make contact with his unconscious. It may be that interpretations should be given on a lower structural level, that directly connects with less differentiated modes of thinking. The work of creative dedifferentiation and re-integration (the second phase of creativity) should not be carried by the analyst to its full conclusion, but ought to be stimulated directly in the patient. The patient must do active creative work and not merely serve as a passive recipient of the finished product.

Marion Milner [24] treated a talented but severely disturbed patient for a number of years without significant progress. She recognized that her own over-active interpretations may have prevented the awakening of the patient's creativity. She observed how at a critical stage of the treatment – when the first progress was under way – she had dropped a cigarette-making machine from her lap or spilled the tobacco. Dropping meant – in the counter-transference – among other things that she was working too hard for the patient. If the awakening of creativity was part of the cure, some of the passivity and self-scattering inherent in creative work had to be accepted by both patient and analyst. The analyst must allow the patient's fragmented material to sink into the containing womb of his own (the analyst's) unconscious without premature wish to re-articulate it and put it back into the patient on a fully articulate level. This would only hinder a beginning process of self-surrender in both analyst and patient in terms of the oral or anal triads. If the analyst projects half differentiated rather than fully articulate material into the patient he may help him – or even 'teach' him – how to dedifferentiate it further without ejecting or burying it. His whole ego would have to sink temporarily to an oceanic-manic level without fear of being lost for ever and being buried alive. Passivity, both on the part of the analyst and the patient, seems crucial. The fate of the dying god must be lived through without help. Man in creative work ultimately remains alone. As beginning dedifferentiation replaces inordinate splitting, a receiving womb will eventually be prepared in the unconscious. The analyst may be content to transform the patient's fragmented projections into undifferentiated material and feed it directly into the newly formed receptacle in the patient's unconscious. In this way he assists the patient in building a health-giving unconscious fantasy life, that will give him a new sense of reality in a true rebirth of his ego.

It is important to keep in mind that the development of abstract thought is never due to a passive withdrawal from the world of concrete things. It is sometimes said that the child during the period of latency (from about six to ten years of age) withdraws from concrete reality because of the weakening of his libidinous interests; he thus becomes more amenable to abstract thinking. The capacity and inclination for abstract thought also tends to increase in middle age. Again it is said that middle-aged man withdraws his interest from concrete objects; he has reared his children and has largely achieved his aims in life. Consequently his interests turn to more abstract concepts and imagery. This view is tantamount to saying that abstract thought is due to ego dissociation, the loss of contact with concrete reality and deeper levels of the personality. The malady which so often affects the capacity of abstract thought – that is to say, its easy decadence into empty generalization due to the dissociation of unconscious levels of the personality – is taken to be its source. The misunderstanding could not be more complete. It may prevent us from grappling with the dilemma of empty abstraction in modern art, and perhaps also with the sterility of child art during the height of latency around the age of eight and the problem of middle-age neurosis. In all these cases creative sterility may be due to avoidable ego dissociation caused by a split between the surface and bottom levels of the ego.

The liveliness of abstract thought derives from its rich substructure of unconscious fantasy. If it is true that in certain periods in the life of an individual or the evolution of an entire civilization the tendency towards abstraction is greatly strengthened, one could conclude that in these critical periods the deepest levels of fantasy are stirred, possibly due to biological factors which we do not yet understand clearly. The extreme undifferentiation of deep-level fantasy could be attributed to an advance of the death instinct, though I am well aware that biological speculations of this kind are out of favour today. Nevertheless a speculative concept of the kind may help us to unify the diversity of phenomena with which we are concerned. The extreme de-differentiation of low-level fantasy may be overcome by a new surge of abstract images and concepts from these deepest levels, or else the tension within the psyche may become intolerable and lead to a sterilizing dissociation between conscious thought and unconscious fantasy. The abstraction turns into empty generalization, the flow of imagination dries up. This fate has afflicted fashionable abstraction in modern art. It was the premature decadence of modern abstract art which made me first think of the equivalent crises in the development of the individual during infancy, latency and middle age. The pioneer abstract artists attributed to their work a reality that was superior to that of traditional art. We have to accept that, knowing as we do that the plastic strength of mental imagery derives from its unconscious roots. What has probably happened is that our perception of abstract art has become shallow and isolated from unconscious fantasy. With an effort we can still scatter our attention in order to re-vitalize the unconscious substructure. Before our empty gaze the scattered elements of Abstract Expressionism will draw together according to a hidden order; the severe geometric elements of Constructivism will soften into organic unity. But it is difficult to sustain the link between normal awareness and this kind of unconscious scanning; abstract art becomes split off from its unconscious matrix and turns into empty ornament.

One wonders why the modern artist should be compelled to work from such deep levels, far removed from everyday experience, in order to remain creative. There are signs that Western art has indeed drawn its inspiration from increasingly deep levels of poemagogic fantasy. It is not too far fetched to speak of an advance of the death instinct in our society from the late Middle Ages onwards. I have mentioned how the rise of the scientific spirit at that time was accompanied by poemagogic fantasy belonging to the oral Prometheus level, which was later crudely acted out in the persecution of heretics and witches. Western art had already started the steady withdrawal from a true libidinous interest in concrete reality when the Renaissance artists began to study their subjective perceptions and distorted the constant properties of objects by perspective, chiaroscuro, etc. Later, landscapes replaced human beings as subject matter. Abstract art formed the inevitable climax of this long narcissistic withdrawal from the object into the artist's own psyche. The modern artist draws his inspiration from deep levels of awareness where the simplest geometric forms can stand for the fullness of reality. An enormous tension is set up within the image-making functions of the ego, which in the end have led to the sterilizing dissociation of the ego's top and bottom levels, of which I have spoken. Worringer, who wrote at the very beginning of modern art, prophetically linked abstraction in any art – not just modern art – with deep anxieties at large in a given society. The later rise of abstraction in modern art coincided with a growing preoccupation with themes of death and decay and the anxiety of living and dying in general. I have suggested that the theme of dying reflected processes of decomposition in the ego, which attacked our conscious sensibilities and favoured extreme undifferentiation in unconscious image making. Hence the easy dissociation of the top and bottom levels of perception; hence also the deep anxieties besetting the creation of modern art and truly fertile abstract art in particular.

This link between self-destructive attacks of the ego and abstraction is also found in the development of the individual. I have referred to three critical phases in the individual's life when the power of abstract thought is often strengthened. The most spectacular phase occurs at the time when the child acquires the gift of language around the eighteenth month of life. This critical period falls between the first and second anal stages; it coincides with the phase when the child is most vulnerable and needs his mother's support most. According to Melanie Klein it marks a maximum of sadism and self-destruction in the child's fantasy life. Most significant in our context is the now largely neglected fact put forward by Freud long ago that the child's unconscious fantasy life reaches a maximum of dedifferentiation during the anal stage; it equates all body openings, all body growths and products and comes very near to the extreme oceanic limit where even the boundaries between the self and the environment fall

away. I am inclined to think that the progressive dedifferentiation of image making starts much earlier. As I see it, Winnicott's concept of 'transitional' objects describes a scattering and
dedifferentiation in the child's vision of the world at a very early
stage. The young infant scatters (dedifferentiates) his too exclusive relationship with his mother; fluffy bits of wool, the corner
of the blanket attract and diffuse his attention to a twilight world
of 'transitional' objects, where the ego's boundaries are uncertain and objects hover between the reality of waking and
dreaming. It could be that this scattering of object relationships
on a conscious level foreshadows the progressive dedifferentiation
of his unconscious fantasy life, which as I have said reaches its
maximum around the eighteenth month of life, half-way through
the anal stage. When this maximum is reached, dedifferentiation
turns into creative abstraction, probably owing to the mysterious
short-circuit which joins the top and bottom levels of the ego.
The child's acquisition of language depends on his accepting a
measure of undifferentiation in his view of the world. The child's
curiosity about the generic names of things becomes insatiable.
Proper names reserved for single individuals are of little interest
to him; they do not presuppose the gift of abstraction. Far oftener
names, even proper names, refer to whole classes of things. The
child's achievement consists in giving the same name to an unfamiliar thing he has not seen before and which may differ in its
appearance from anything he has seen. Yet he can name it, and
in doing so takes fuller possession of it and transfers to it loves
and hates formed in his relationship with other objects. While
the unconscious dedifferentiation of fantasy moves away from
concrete reality and favours narcissistic withdrawal, abstract
name-giving, paradoxically, serves the control of concrete reality;
yet it rests on unconscious dedifferentiation. The child's new
power of abstraction must not be confused with an earlier primitive weakness in the proper differentiation of things. Then, the
child may erroneously have given the same name to different
things because he failed to recognize the essential difference between them; now he may be aware of the difference, but chooses
to ignore it by an active feat of dedifferentiation. He discounts
differences in the appearances of things in favour of a common
bond (abstract relationship) between them. Abstraction means
a transfer of object relationships in the manner in which

transitional objects were formed. Giving the right name to an object not only helps to control it, but establishes ties of love and hate. I have suggested that Thanatos, the death instinct, could be made responsible for the self-destructive effect of dedifferentiation as a temporary decomposition of the (depth) ego; abstract thought can be seen as a success of Eros, the life instinct supporting the child's object relationships and control of reality. The fragile link or short-circuit which transforms unconscious undifferentiation into conscious abstraction holds together widely divergent poles of mental life. No wonder the link is vulnerable to ego dissociation. For a fuller validation of this view it would be useful to know more about a possible connexion between pathological disturbances in the child's learning of speech and a fear of unconscious dedifferentiation (ego decomposition) which may prevent his acquisition of abstract thought.

The connexion is clearer in the collapse of child art during the latency period. I have said that it is not sufficient to dismiss latency (or middle age) as a time of life when contact with the unconscious is lost. Unfortunately this loss of contact happens only too often at the height of latency around the age of eight. What is not sufficiently realized is the fact that the collapse of child art is directly due to a potential but not often fully realized advance in the child's faculties of abstraction both in the artistic and scientific field. It is usually observed that the older child loses heart in doing art; his colours become muddy and his forms flabby though they may have gained in photographic realism compared with the 'syncretistic' art of the younger infant. This superficial gain in realism obscures the fact that the new realism is made possible only by the awakening of quite new abstract faculties. On the surface the infant's syncretistic art appears already abstract and the art of the eight-year-old more concrete. Psychologically, the reverse may hold good. Let me enlarge on what I said about syncretism in the first chapter. Around the age of five comes the climax of the classical Oedipus stage. Though the child may be moved by the emotional conflict characteristic of this stage – rivalry with his father and love for his mother – the figures of the parents have become by this time highly individualized, concrete real personalities, cleansed from the near-psychotic projections of early infancy. The child's general vision of the world at large is highly individualized. We must not allow ourselves to be misled by the apparent abstraction of his syncretistic art. The same simple forms have to do service for representing very different concrete objects, his parents, relatives, playthings, houses, pets and the like. Yet his aim is not abstract, it deals with concrete objects of high individuality. With a sudden shock we may discover highly individual traits, a squint in the eye, a wart, a missing tooth, characteristic of a particular person. The child treats such minute details with the same impartial emphasis or neglect as the more important bigger shapes. He has not yet learned to analyse the total appearance of objects in terms of important and unimportant detail. Being syncretistic, the child's vision and art goes for the whole undivided shape of the object. Seen in this way the child's syncretistic art is concrete; it faithfully reflects his highly individualized object relationships during the Oedipus stage, however abstract and generalized their representation may appear to the adult.

With the coming of latency – after passing through the Oedipus stage – the child's object relationships, vision and also his art become more generalized and in a sense 'abstract'. The child detaches himself from his parents, allows himself to be schooled and transfers his object relationships to the wider, somewhat uncertain circle of teachers and schoolmates. He tries to submerge his own sense of individuality and wants to appear like everybody else, preferably like a grown-up person. One could compare his scattering of object relationships and sense of identity with the infant's formation of 'transitional' objects as described by Winnicott, which I have interpreted as a beginning of dedifferentiation in the child's conscious fantasy life. The analogous scattering and dedifferentiation of human relationships at the beginning of latency may be a similar signal for a renewed increase in unconscious dedifferentiation. What we can observe directly is the generalization and incipient abstraction of the child's vision and art. The child no longer aims at indivisible total objects; he has become aware that objects are composed and, put together, form, in themselves, meaningless abstract details. His new capacity for decomposing individual objects into abstract elements should open up a new world of aesthetic sensibilities; he could extract from different objects the same abstract geometric element, led by undifferentiated unconscious fantasy that equates those objects. Hidden affinities between unrelated objects are exposed in this way; they might arouse his curiosity and spur him on to explore the multi-evocative meaning of abstract forms. But nothing of the kind happens. The child misuses his new faculty for breaking down total objects in terms of abstract components only to help him compare his own crude representations with the more realistic art of adults or older children. He tries to imitate the work of others even if it is presented to him in degraded examples, illustrations in school books, calendar pictures, newspapers and posters. The child becomes despondent and loses courage and interest. His art becomes a mere play with unfelt forms and colours devoid of emotional content and to this extent 'abstract' in a wrong way, very much in the way in which modern abstract art has become largely empty and meaningless. The reason is the same, that is to say, the fatal dissociation of conscious sensibilities from unconscious fantasy. This collapse of child art is now accepted as an unavoidable consequence of latency.

It is reassuring that the same problem is more successfully tackled in a related sphere of education, the teaching of mathematics at primary-school level. In the same way as art (in the adult sense) is only possible by a more sophisticated awareness of abstract form, higher mathematics presupposes an understanding of abstract symbols. The child could, but hardly ever does, acquire the gift for understanding abstract symbols at about the same age of eight. It is beyond reasonable doubt that we are faced with the same fundamental, possibly biological, change in the child's perception and thought. The educational problem must be identical. It could be said meaningfully that the very young infant's concept of number was not yet abstract, but syncretistic. A number was still treated as a total indivisible object which possesses high individuality like other concrete objects in reality. When numbers are treated as abstract symbols at a later stage, they become unstable, ready to decompose and recombine into new symbols; in this way we learn to grasp the abstract relationships between them. But this abstract dynamic treatment of numbers comes later. During the Oedipus stage when child art was still vigorous and vital, numbers also possessed a plastic life of their own, each a separate individual as real and static as any other concrete object and as resistant against change. A deterioration sets in during latency which parallels the collapse of child art at the same time. Numbers tend to lose their plastic life and individuality. The child can be drilled to rattle them off as on a cash register; they become impersonal generalized counters that are memorized and handled without understanding and emotional involvement. We cannot explain this failure away by referring to the loss of contact with unconscious fantasy, allegedly inevitable. We now know that possibly irreparable damage is inflicted to the child's future ability for doing mathematics if we are content to train him in a purely mechanical handling of mathematic symbols without emotional understanding of their dynamic abstract relationships. Today we begin to appreciate that it is not at all difficult to teach children to appreciate abstract symbolism. The child spontaneously acquires a new ability for treating abstract symbols as confidently as he treated the old syncretistic entities. Indeed abstract symbols can become as real and plastic to him as the concrete objects of reality. It is by no means necessary as is sometimes done to connect abstract symbols with practical problems encountered in everyday reality. I have emphasized throughout that abstract concepts and images owe their plastic life and feeling of being real to their link with unconscious fantasy. All we have to do is to prevent the dissociation of abstract symbols from their undifferentiated matrix in the unconscious. This could be achieved in a somewhat roundabout way by connecting them with everyday problems that matter to the child emotionally; in a more direct manner it could probably be done by stressing their dynamic instability, flexibility and manifold dynamic interaction, which mirrors the instability and flux of unconscious fantasy. The problems of abstract child art and abstract mathematics have been tackled successfully by relating mathematical symbols with construction games in which abstract visual patterns are handled. The child can scan the multiple interrelationships between the single building bricks if the teacher stresses sufficiently the many mutually exclusive (serial) possibilities in combining them, so that their easy decomposition and reassembly is visualized in any single concrete constellation. This instability and fertility of patterns and concept is easily linked with the parallel play of irrational unconscious fantasy which dedifferentiates and regroups the concrete objects of reality according to the whims and fancies of the id. Abstract concepts and images are rich and flexible enough to meet with ease the demands of inner symbolization and outer logic and necessity. Mechanical generalization has been avoided in the new methods of teaching mathematics; similar ways should be found to avoid the analogous emptying out of child art.

The British physicist-philosopher, Ernest Hutten, once pointed out the connexion between Pythagorean mathematics and Pythagorean mysticism.* The old Babylonians had been adept computers, who manipulated and assembled numbers with great dexterity; but they were not yet true mathematicians in the modern sense and failed to develop abstract mathematical concepts. Pythagoras was the first to grasp the abstract relationships between numbers because of, not in spite of, the fact that he also associated these relationships with philosophical and irrational symbolism. Numbers married, separated, combined into new entities with utter flexibility, which was increased, not diminished by the metaphysical meaning of the transactions. The instability and flux of unconscious fantasies was thus manifested openly in the conscious manipulation of numbers; it deprived them of their syncretistic solidity and permanence and made their abstract relationships emotionally more significant than the numbers themselves. Seen in this way, the metaphysical symbolism of Pythagorean mathematics was not a primitive trait of a new science, but an essential ingredient for the growth of abstract thought.

What we may have to avoid in teaching mathematics is to yield to the child's (or the teacher's) fear of undifferentiation and abstraction. I remember that I was hindered, not helped, in learning algebra by the teacher's repeated reassurance that our algebraic calculations could at any time make sense in terms of handling real apples and pears. Reconverting algebraic symbols into apples and pears at a critical stage in order to check on the correctness of the algebraic transformations only increased my sense of insecurity. In spite of bad teaching I learned to fall in love with algebraic symbols and could feel their reality, which was in no way inferior to the concreteness of pieces of fruit. As I have said, once the versatility of an abstract symbol has been appreciated, its link with unconscious fantasy life is assured,

* Ernest H. Hutten, *The Origins of Science*, London, George Allen & Unwin, 1962, p. 130.

on which the feeling of plastic reality so largely depends.

The main point I want to make is that latency, far from drying up unconscious fantasy life, seems to stimulate the deepest near-oceanic levels of fantasy from which the conscious power of abstraction stems. Extreme limits of dedifferentiation in unconscious fantasy may be reached at the height of latency. It would make good sense to interpret the phenomenon of latency as another climax in the interaction of the life and death instinct. The death instinct would not only be responsible for the temporary arrest in sexual growth (which is unique to mankind), but also for the weakening of personal relationships and the decomposition of the unconscious ego which an extreme dedifferentiation of image making entails. Such speculations, however legitimate, make little difference to the very practical issues of primary-school education which the psychological reassessment proposed here implies. As in the first cycle of infancy, the rise of abstract thought signals the turn of the cycle. At the age of eight the sexual organs resume their arrested growth and conscious experiences, if nourished by a new world of abstraction, expand. With the onset of puberty, child art – if we may still call it so – absorbs the projections of the young adolescent's own body image. Highly individualized teaching becomes necessary if only to undo the damage suffered at the height of latency.

The crisis of middle age has the same double aspect which the crisis of latency presents. I have said that middle-aged man tends to lose contact with his unconscious and may fall victim to neurosis. One could argue that his loss of contact was merely due to the process of ageing, a lowering of psychic tension due to the loss in mental energy. Jung, for one, takes the opposite view. For him middle-aged man loses contact with unconscious fantasy not because his mental life dries up, but because archetypal images, the symbols of mental rebirth, are again stirring in the depth of his mind; if he fails to respond actively to their challenge, he becomes cut off from his creative unconscious and develops neurosis. From what we have learned from ego dissociation during latency, Jung's more dynamic view of the challenge of middle age could make sense in our argument. Freud interpreted the process of ageing not merely as a passive failure of the life instinct, but also as an active victory of the death instinct. If, as I would like to think, the decomposition of the unconscious ego by dedifferentiation can be taken as an aspect of the death instinct, it could well be found that the often increased power of abstraction in older age may be due to a third and last cyclical advance and eventual recession of the death instinct in our mental life; it may lead to an increased dedifferentiation in unconscious fantasy to which we must not fail to respond in order to remain totally sane. The creative re-education of the old may turn out to be of greater clinical significance than we may be ready to concede at present.

Appendix: Glossary

Many strands of this inquiry have had to be left loose; I might have preferred to wait and see how far they will make sense in the constant progress of psycho-analytical theory. Any incursion in a fairly new field cannot fail to adapt – or if you like twist, expand, distort – existing terminology and concepts to fit new facts. The new facts themselves will re-define them. Explicit re-definitions may prevent the new usage of terms from being tested against the new range of phenomena available. But leaving the new use of old terms vague in this way may be unfair to the reader who is not conversant with their old usage. Somewhat reluctantly I will try to sum up the points in which my own use of existing terms differs from current practice.

Unconscious

Ordinarily, drives and fantasies are repressed and made unconscious because of their unacceptable content. Here it is maintained that images and fantasies can become unconscious because of their (undifferentiated) structure alone. This implies an expansion of the term 'unconscious'.

Id and Ego

The *id* is the repository and source of unconscious drives. The *ego* structures and channels the, in themselves unorganized, id drives and fantasies. The ego has an integrating and synthesizing function. There is a certain contradiction between this integrating function and my view that the ego functions could be in conflict with each other. But the complex structure of art and of the creative process suggests that the ego alternates between dedifferentiation (decomposition) and re-differentiation without the prompting of the id. In a weak ego its undifferentiated bottom levels and the differentiated surface levels may become dissociated. This is particularly the case in schizophrenia.

Oral, anal, phallic, genital

The terms denote successive stages in the child's sexual development. The child first passes through an oral stage of sucking and biting, his interests centre around the nipple and his mouth; in the second year he is much concerned with his excretory function; in the 'first' anal stage he freely expels his excrements and considers them as valued gifts, in the 'second' he learns to retain them and debases their value. In the phallic stage his interests reach the genital zones without appreciating their true genital role. This role is only appreciated in the genital Oedipus stage around the fifth year of life; then the boy courts his mother and defies his father. Genital sexuality incorporates previous stages as component drives. The non-genital aims of adult perversions coincide with earlier pre-genital stages of infantile development. Freud has therefore called the child 'polymorphously' pervert.

The history of infantile sexual drives is the history of the id as it is progressively structured by the ego. In my analysis of poemagogic fantasies the varying structural differentiation of oral, anal, phallic and genital imagery became important. On the genital Oedipus level of fantasy we meet the triangular family situation of father, mother and child. On the phallic level the mother is no longer clearly differentiated from the father and is imagined as a castrated male. Nearer the anal level the mother is often not differentiated from the father and can become ambi-sexual. The same weakening of differentiation pertains to the body zones. Oral fantasy fails to differentiate between mouth and vagina or between nipple and penis, anal fantasy confuses all body openings and body outgrowths. In poemagogic fantasy we meet with the deepest manic-oceanic level where all differentiation ceases; the child has incorporated the generating powers of his parents and remains alone. This most important level of creative fantasy cannot be fitted into the history of sexual development. It is questionable whether other poemagogic fantasies on the oral, anal and genital level refer to actual fantasies or experiences in corresponding stages of infantile development; more likely they are the product of comparatively late creative activity which produces imagery that resembles infantile material in its structure.

The paranoid-schizoid and depressive positions (Melanie Klein)
Melanie Klein was much concerned with the maturation of human relationships. In early infancy the relationship between the baby and his mother is deeply coloured by near-psychotic fantasies; they relate to adult psychosis in the way in which infantile sexuality relates to adult perversions. (Melanie Klein could have called the child a 'polymorphous psychotic'.) The child's fantasies alternate between two 'positions' named after the two main types of psychosis (schizophrenia, manic depression). In the first position, called *paranoid-schizoid*, extensive 'splitting' occurs. The child splits the mother into her good and bad aspects, who are imagined to be different persons. He also tends to split off what he feels to be bad parts of himself and projects them into his mother, who is then imagined to be a persecutor. Projections lead to introjections in the opposite direction; the child may incorporate the bad persecuting mother figure. This leads to renewed tension within the child's personality and to renewed splitting and outward projection. A vicious circle operates. The situation is relieved by the coming of the *depressive* position. The child realizes that the good and bad mother figures are really one and the same person. This realization amounts to a growing power for integration both in the experience of the outside and the inner world. But the consequence of this new understanding is 'depression' over the injury which the child wanted to inflict only on the bad mother figure and which is now seen as having harmed the good mother. If all is well the child becomes ready to make 'reparation' for his guilt. The will and capacity for reparation is the foundation of all creative work, which is felt unconsciously as helping the restoration of the good mother.

In adult manic-depressive psychosis, 'depression' alternates with 'mania'. The manic patient is overconfident, over-active and denies any possible obstacle or badness. In the context of the depressive position a manic defence serves to ward off depressive anxiety. The child by manically denying the injury he has done to the good mother, or perhaps by idealizing the mother, escapes from a depressing reality and a need for making due reparation.

My own concept of creative mania or of a 'manic-oceanic' phase in creative work does not readily fit into the Kleinian concept of only two positions. The solution may well be a realization that I am referring to comparatively late stages of ego development when the child has already achieved a rich unconscious fantasy life of extreme undifferentiation.

Oceanic, manic

Freud spoke of an 'oceanic' feeling characteristic of religious experience; the mystic feels at one with the universe, his individual existence lost like a drop in the ocean. He may re-experience a primitive state of mind when the child was not yet aware of his separate individuality, but felt at one with his mother. Fantasies of returning to the womb may have this mystic oceanic quality. It is now widely realized that any – not only religious – creative experience can produce an oceanic state. In my view this state need not be due to a 'regression', to an infantile state, but could be the product of the extreme dedifferentiation in lower levels of the ego which occurs during creative work. Dedifferentiation suspends many kinds of boundaries and distinctions; at an extreme limit it may remove the boundaries of individual existence and so produce a mystic oceanic feeling that is distinctively manic in quality. Mania in the pathological sense endangers the normal rational differentiations on a conscious level and so impairs our sense of reality. By denying the distinction between good and bad, injury and health, it may serve as a defence against depressive feelings. But on deeper, usually unconscious, levels of the ego dedifferentiation does not deny, but transforms reality according to the structural principles valid on those deeper levels. The reality of the mystic may be manic-oceanic, but it is not a pathological denial of reality. The artist must not rely on the conventional distinctions between 'good' and 'bad' if he attempts truly original work. Instead he must rely on lower undifferentiated types of perception which allow him to grasp the total indivisible structure of the work of art. This grasp can have a manic quality which transcends the distinction between the good and bad details contained in the work. The scanning of the total structure enables him to revalue details that initially appeared good or bad. He may have to discard a happy detail achieved too early, which now impedes the flow of his imagination; instead he may take an apparently bad feature as his new starting point. The scanning of the total structure often occurs during a temporary absence of mind. One could say that during this gap in the stream of consciousness the ordinary distinctions between good and bad are 'manically' suspended. Oceanic dedifferentiation usually occurs only in deeply unconscious levels and so escapes attention; if made conscious, or rather, if the results of unconscious undifferentiated scanning rise into consciousness, we may experience feelings of manic ecstasy. The swing between manic and depressive states may be a direct outcome of the rhythmical alternation between differentiated and undifferentiated types of perception which all creative work entails.

Schizoid splitting and ego dissociation

Melanie Klein speaks of splitting mainly in terms of splitting off parts of an object or of the self. Because this inquiry deals with the creative working of the fully developed personality, it occasionally uses the term schizoid splitting for 'horizontal' fissures in the ego. The stratification of a fully matured ego is built up from many levels which function according to different principles. The horizontal split with which we are mainly concerned causes the dissociation of the ego's undifferentiated bottom levels from its highly differentiated top levels. To avoid unnecessary confusion with more primitive splitting processes, I have generally preferred to use the term ego dissociation. Psychologically, the two kinds of splitting are very close. I have found in my teaching of psychotic border cases that the ego dissociation underlying creative sterility represented a 'schizoid' trait common to all of them.

Death instinct (Thanatos)

Many writers reject Freud's concept of a death instinct. Melanie Klein made use of it in order to account for the self-destructive aggressiveness of early infantile fantasies. It is a concept that has many aspects. I have proposed to attribute the

305

ego's innate propensity towards dedifferentiation to the death instinct, because it fits some of these aspects. It represents a temporary decomposition of the ego, at least in its deepest levels; it tends to weaken object relationships and favours narcissistic withdrawal; most significantly, as a structural principle dedifferentiation is tautological with Freud's concept of the death instinct. Dedifferentiation (entropy) is part of life's tendency to return to the inorganic state. According to Schroedinger, organic matter is characterized by a highly differentiated and stable molecular organization resisting the entropy of inorganic matter, while inorganic molecular structure tends to be uniform and undifferentiated. The ego, in striving towards unconscious undifferentiation, aims at the uniform state of inorganic dead matter. Death is undifferentiation.

References

1 B. Bettelheim, *Symbolic Wounds: Puberty Rites and the Envious Male*, London, Thames and Hudson, 1955

2 F. R. Bienenfeld, *The Rediscovery of Justice*, London, G. Allen and Unwin, 1947

3 W. R. Bion, *Learning from Experience*, London, Heinemann, 1962

4 A. Ehrenzweig, 'The Origin of the Scientific and Heroic Urge', *Intern. J. Psychoanal.*, 30/2, 1949

5 A. Ehrenzweig, *The Psycho-analysis of Artistic Vision and Hearing*, New York, Geo. Braziller, 1965 (2nd edition)

6 A. Ehrenzweig, 'Alienation versus Self-expression', *The Listener*, LXIII, 1613, 1960

7 A. Ehrenzweig, 'Towards a Theory of Art Education', *Report on an Experimental Course for Art Teachers*, London, University of London, Goldsmiths' College, 1965

8 A. Ehrenzweig, 'The Undifferentiated Matrix of Artistic Imagination', *The Psychoanalytic Study of Society*, III, 1964

9 A. Ehrenzweig, 'Bridget Riley's Pictorial Space', *Art International*, IX/1, 1965

10 C. Fisher and I. H. Paul, 'The Effects of Subliminal Visual Stimulation, etc.', *J. Americ. Psychoanal. Assn.*, 7, 1959

11 Else Frenkel-Brunswik, 'Psychodynamics and Cognition', *Explorations in Psychoanalysis* (ed. R. Lindner), New York, Julian Press, 1953

12 E. H. Gombrich, *Art and Illusion*, London, Phaidon, 1960

13 E. H. Gombrich, *Meditations on a Hobby Horse*, London, Phaidon, 1963

14 M. Grotjahn, *Beyond Laughter*, New York, Blakiston, 1957

15 J. Hadamard, *The Psychology of Invention in the Mathematical Field*, Princeton, Princeton University Press, 1945

16 P. Klee, *The Thinking Eye*, London, Lund Humphries, 1961

17 A. Koestler, *The Act of Creation*, London, Hutchinson, 1964

18 B. D. Lewin, 'Reconsideration of the Dream Screen', *Psychoanal. Quart.*, 22, 1953

19 V. Lowenfeld, *The Nature of Creative Activity*, London, Kegan Paul, 1939

20 Ida Macalpine and R. A. Hunter, 'Observations of the Psycho-analytic Theory of Psychosis', *Brit. J. Med. Psych.*, 27, 1954

21 Marion Milner (pseudonym Joanna Field), *An Experiment in Leisure*, London, Chatto and Windus, 1937

22 Marion Milner, 'The Role of Illusion in Symbol Formation', *New Directions in Psycho-analysis*, London, Tavistock Publications, 1955

23 Marion Milner, 'Psycho-analysis and Art', *Psycho-analysis and Contemporary Thought*, London, Hogarth Press, 1958

24 Marion Milner, *The Hands of the Living God*, *A Psychoanalytic Experience*, London, Hogarth Press, 1969

25 H. Read, *Icon and Idea*, London, Faber, 1955

26 G. Róheim, *The Gates of the Dream*, New York, International University Press, 1953

27 Hanna Segal, 'Notes on Symbol Formation', *Intern. J. Psycho-anal.*, 38, 1957

28 M. von Senden, *Space and Sight*, London, Methuen, 1960

29 E. Simenauer, '"Pregnancy Envy" in Rainer Maria Rilke', *American Imago*, 11, 1954

30 A. Stokes, 'Form in art', *New Directions in Psycho-analysis*, London, Tavistock Publications, 1955

31 A. Stokes, *Michelangelo*, *A Study in the Nature of Art*, London, Tavistock Publications, 1955

32 A. Stokes, *Three Essays on the Painting of our Time*, London, Tavistock Publications, 1962

33 H. Weisinger, *Tragedy and the Paradox of the Fortunate Fall*, London, Routledge, 1953

34 D. W. Winnicott, *Collected Papers*, London, Tavistock Publications, 1958

35 L. Wittgenstein, *Philosophical Investigations*, Oxford, Blackwell, 1963

36 A. Turel, *Bachofen-Freud*, Bern, Hans Huber, 1939

37 J. Varendonck, *The Evolution of the Conscious Faculties*, London, G. Allen and Unwin, 1923

Index

triple goddess (White Goddess),
193, 195, 200, 227
in literature, 212, 217–18, 261,
262
Turandot (Puccini), 249

unconscious, concept modified,
34, 280, 301
role in creativity, 19–21, 273
fantasy, 72, 240–1, 263, 269–70,
278
abstract thought and, 290–1,
298–300
dreams and, 27
scanning, 20, 24–5, 32, 44,
46–59
undifferentiation, definition, 21,
34
Uranus, 228, 242

vagina symbols, 254–5
vampirism, 244
Van Gogh, Vincent, 173–4
Varendonck, J., 281, 282
vase painting, Greek, 153, *7*
vibrato, 43–4

viewing frame, 148
vision, 181, 284–5
visualization, precise, 58–9, 159
voyeurism, 244–5, 254, 256, 271

Wagner, Richard, 69–70, 87,
104–5, 218
waltz rhythm, 129
water-colour, 76
Weisinger, H., 188
White Goddess, *see* Triple goddess
Wieland, 257
Winnicott, D., 271, 293, 295
witches, 244–5, 246, 252, 291
Witches' Hammer, 244
Wittgenstein, L., 53–5, 126
woodcarving, 72
Wordsworth, William, 151
womb fantasies, 186–7, 199,
230–1, 234–5, 304
symbols, 144, 214, 225–6, *29*
Wotruba, Fritz, *26*

Zeus, 242

The Sociology of Art

Jean Duvignaud
With an Introduction by John Fletcher

'The better our understanding of the fact that there is a permanent relationship, varying according to the social setting, between all the forces at work within the framework of collective life, the deeper our awareness of the existential reality of the work of art.' – *Jean Duvignaud*

This radical reappraisal of the nature of sociology and art distinguishes Jean Duvignaud from such critics as Benjamin, Lukács and Sartre, with whom he is usually discussed. Regarding cinema and television, the 'happening' and the collage as representative forms of contemporary culture, Duvignaud refuses to be bound by any absolute concept of art or society.

In *The Sociology of Art* he brilliantly analyses the limitations of traditional aesthetics and Marxist dialectic, and presents his own account of the artistic process and its social significance. With a wide range of examples, Duvignaud traces the changing aesthetic attitudes held throughout history from the primitives to the moderns, and describes the functions exercised by the various arts in different cultures.

As John Fletcher remarks in his introduction, what is attempted in *The Sociology of Art* is 'nothing less than a sketch or prolegomenon to a sociology of the *imaginative function itself*'. As highly praised in France as Lévi-Strauss, Edgar Morin and Roland Barthes, this is the first of Duvignaud's major works to appear in English.